Alan Roger

Italy
2004

Quality Camping and Caravanning Sites

Compiled by: Alan Rogers Guides Ltd

Cover design: Paul Effenberg, Vine Cottage

Maps created by Customised Mapping (01769 560101)
contain background data provided by GisDATA Ltd

Maps are © Alan Rogers Guides and Gis DATA Ltd 2003

© Alan Rogers Guides Ltd 2003

Published by: Alan Rogers Guides Ltd, Burton Bradstock, Bridport, Dorset DT6 4QA

British Library Cataloguing-in-Publication Data:
A catalogue record for this book is available from the British Library.

ISBN: 0 901586 98 6

Printed in Great Britain by The Friary Press

Contents

the Alan Rogers approach

IT IS 36 YEARS SINCE ALAN ROGERS PUBLISHED THE FIRST CAMPSITE GUIDE THAT BORE HIS NAME. SINCE THEN THE RANGE OF TITLES HAS EXPANDED, WITH NEW GUIDES TO ITALY AND SPAIN & PORTUGAL BEING PUBLISHED FOR 2004. WHAT'S MORE THE ALAN ROGERS GUIDES ARE FAST BECOMING A FORCE TO BE RECKONED WITH IN THE NETHERLANDS TOO: IN 2004 ALL SIX TITLES WILL BE AVAILABLE FOR THE FIRST TIME, STOCKED BY WELL OVER 90% OF ALL DUTCH BOOKSHOPS.

There are several thousands of campsites in Italy of varying quality: this guide contains impartially written reports on no less than 170 of the very finest, each being individually inspected and selected. Plus it incorporates a new section on our popular Travel Service (page 8), as well as all the usual maps and indexes, designed to help you find the choice of campsite that's right for you. We hope you enjoy some happy and safe travels – and some pleasurable 'armchair touring' in the meantime!

INDEPENDENT AND HONEST

Whilst the content and scope of the guides have expanded considerably since the early editions, our selection of campsites still employs exactly the same philosophy and criteria as defined by Alan Rogers 36 years ago.

'warts and all'

Firstly, and most importantly, our selection is based entirely on our own rigorous and independent inspection and selection process. Campsites cannot buy their way into our guides – indeed the extensive Site Report which is written by us, not by the site owner, is provided free of charge so we are free to say what we think and to provide an honest, 'warts and all' description. This is written in plain English and without the use of confusing icons or symbols.

> " ...the campsites included in this book have been chosen entirely on merit, and no payment of any sort is made by them for their inclusion."
> Alan Rogers, 1968

INSPECTED SINCE 1968 & SELECTED

A question of quality

The criteria which we use when inspecting and selecting sites are numerous, but the most important by far is the question of good quality. People want different things from their choice of campsite so we try to include a range of campsite 'styles' to cater for a wide variety of preferences: from those seeking a small peaceful campsite in the heart of the countryside, to visitors looking for an 'all singing, all dancing' site in a popular seaside resort. Those with more specific needs, such as sports facilities, cultural or historical attractions, are also catered for.

The size of the site, whether it's part of a campsite chain or privately owned, makes no difference in terms of it being required to meet our exacting standards regarding its quality and it being 'fit for purpose'. In other words, irrespective of the size of the site, or the number of facilities offered, the essentials (the welcome, the pitches, the sanitary facilities, the cleanliness and the general maintenance) must all be of a high standard.

Expert opinions

We rely on our dedicated team of Site Assessors, all of whom are experienced campers, caravanners or motorcaravanners, to visit and recommend sites. Each year they travel some 100,000 miles around Europe inspecting new sites and re-inspecting old ones. Our thanks are due to them for their enthusiastic efforts, their diligence and integrity and their commitment to the philosophy of the Alan Rogers Guides.

We also appreciate the feedback we receive from many of our readers, and we always make a point of following up complaints, suggestions or recommendations for possible new sites. Of course we get a few grumbles too – but it really is a few, and those we do receive usually arrive at the end of the high season and relate mainly to overcrowding or to poor maintenance during the peak school holiday period.

Please bear in mind that although we are interested to hear about any complaints we have no contractual relationship with the sites featured in our guides and are therefore not in a position to intervene in any dispute between a reader and a campsite. If you have a complaint about a campsite featured in our guides the first step should be to take the matter up with the site owner or manager.

Widely regarded as the 'Bible' by site owners and readers alike, there is no better guide when it comes to forming an independent view of a campsite's quality. When you need to be confident in your choice of campsite, you need the Alan Rogers Guide.

☑ Sites only included on merit

☑ Sites cannot pay to be included

☑ Independently inspected, rigorously assessed

☑ Impartial reviews

☑ 36 years of expertise

USING THE ALAN ROGERS GUIDES

Written in plain English, our guides are exceptionally easy to use, but a few words of explanation regarding the layout and content may be helpful. For this brand new guide, we have based our 18 regions on the official regions defined by the Italian Tourist Board, combining some and creating our own new 'holiday' region of Lake Garda. We provide a full page introduction to each region highlighting its main areas of interest, places to visit and details of the local cuisine.

Indexes

Our three indexes allow you to find sites by site number and name, by region and site name or by the town or village where the site is situated.

Campsite Maps

The maps will help you to identify the approximate position of each campsite within its region.

The Site Reports – *Example of an entry*

Number Site Name

Postal Address (including region)

A description of the site in which we try to give an idea its general features – its size, its situation, its strengths and its weaknesses. This column should provide a picture of the site itself with reference to the facilities that are provided and if they impact on its appearance or character. We include details on pitch numbers, electricity (with amperage), hardstandings etc. in this section as pitch design, planning and terracing affects the site's overall appearance. Similarly we continue to include reference to pitches used for caravan holiday homes, chalets, and the like. Importantly at the end of this column we indicate if there are any restrictions, e.g. no tents, dogs.

Facilities	Directions
Lists more specific information on the site's facilities, as well as certain off site activities.	Separated from the main text in order that they may be read and assimilated more easily by a navigator en-route. Bear in mind that road improvement schemes can result in some road numbers being altered. Websites like **www.mappy.com** and others give detailed route plans.

At a glance

Welcome & Ambience ✓✓✓✓✓	Location ✓✓✓✓✓
Quality of Pitches ✓✓✓✓✓	Range of Facilities ✓✓✓✓✓

Charges 2004

Reservations including contact details

Open

Facilities

Toilet blocks: We assume that toilet blocks will be equipped with at least some British style WCs, washbasins with hot and cold water and hot showers with dividers or curtains, and will have all necessary shelves, hooks, plugs and mirrors. We also assume that there will be an identified chemical toilet disposal point, and that the campsite will provide water and waste water points and bin areas. If not the case, we comment. We continue to mention certain features that some readers find important: washbasins in cubicles, facilities for babies, facilities for those with disabilities and motorcaravan service points. Readers with disabilities are advised to contact the site of their choice to ensure that facilities are appropriate to their needs.

Shop: Basic or fully supplied, and opening dates.

Bars, restaurants, takeaway facilities and entertainment: We try hard to supply opening and closing dates (if other than the campsite opening dates) and to identify if there are discos or other noisy entertainment.

Children's play areas: Fenced and with safety surface (e.g. sand, bark or pea-gravel).

Swimming pools: If particularly special, we cover in detail in the first column but reference is always included in the second column. Opening dates, charges and levels of supervision are provided where we have been notified.

Leisure facilities: For example, playing fields, bicycle hire, organised activities and entertainment.

Dogs: If dogs are not accepted or restrictions apply, we state it here. Check the quick reference list on page 194.

Off site: This briefly covers leisure facilities, tourist attractions, restaurants etc nearby. Geographical tourist information is more likely to be in the first column.

At A Glance: All Alan Rogers sites have been inspected and selected – they must meet stringent quality criteria. A campsite may have all the boxes ticked when it comes to listing facilities but if it's not inherently a 'good site' then it will not be in the guide.

These 'at a glance' ratings are a unique indication of certain key criteria that may be important when making your decision. Quite deliberately they are subjective and, modesty aside, are based on our inspectors' own expert opinions at the time of their inspection.

Charges: These are the latest provided by the sites. In those few cases where 2003 or 2004 prices are not given, we try to give a general guide.

Telephone numbers: All numbers assume that you are phoning from within Italy. To phone Italy from outside that country, prefix the number shown with the relevant International Code: 00 39. Do NOT drop the first 0 of the area code (as is required in many other European countries).

Opening dates: Are those advised to us during the early autumn of the previous year – sites can, and sometimes do, alter these dates before the start of the following season, often for good reasons. If you intend to visit shortly after a published opening date, or shortly before the closing date, it is wise to check that it will actually be open at the time required. Similarly some sites operate a restricted service during the low season, only opening some of their facilities (e.g. swimming pools) during the main season; where we know about this, and have the relevant dates, we indicate it – again if you are at all doubtful it is wise to check.

Reservations: Necessary for high season (roughly mid-July to mid-August) in popular holiday areas (ie beach areas). You can reserve via our own Alan Rogers Travel Service or through tour operators. Or be wholly independent and contact the campsite(s) of your choice direct, using the phone, fax or e-mail numbers shown in the site reports, but please bear in mind that many sites are closed all winter.

Points to bear in mind

Some site owners are rather laid back when it comes to opening and closing dates. They may not be fully ready by their opening date – grass and hedges may not all be cut or perhaps only limited sanitary facilities open. At the end of the season they also tend to close down some facilities and generally wind down prior to the closing date. Bear this in mind if you are travelling early or late in the season – it is worth phoning ahead.

The Camping Cheque low season touring system goes some way to addressing this in that participating campsites are advised to have all facilities open and running by the opening date and to remain fully operational until the closing date.

Whether you're an 'old hand' in terms of camping and caravanning or are contemplating your first trip, a regular reader of our Guides or a new 'convert', we wish you well in your travels and hope we have been able to help in some way. We are, of course, also out and about ourselves, visiting sites, talking to owners and readers, and generally checking on standards and new developments.

The Alan Rogers Team

modern
campsites

Ask a non-camper about campsite life and you're likely to hear about muddy fields, chilly ablutions blocks and soulless or non-existent facilities. For many non-campers their view of camping is based on distant childhood memories of trips with the scouts or brownies. Either that or hopelessly optimistic weekend jaunts with Dad, grappling with a tent dragged from the loft.

But the true picture of today's family-friendly continental campsites is rather different. Beauty is in the eye of the beholder so you'll come across a range of 'styles' from large to small; lively and commercial to sleepy and low key.

Take eating, which features prominently in most visits to continental campsites. You may find a large cafeteria-style eaterie with plenty of choice (but perhaps a bit impersonal), or a simple on site restaurant which serves nothing but the dish of the day (a dish made in heaven, using home-grown produce).

What about pool-based activities? Gone are the days of the hole-in-the-ground pool. Whilst there are honourable exceptions, most modern campsites recognize the importance of a decent pool. Mostly with safe children's pools for toddlers and increasingly some of the most exhilarating waterslides, flumes and 'chutes to be seen anywhere in Europe.

Whatever the 'style' of an individual campsite there is no right or wrong, as far as the Alan Rogers Guides are concerned. What matters is that they achieve what they set out to offer and are good examples of the best of modern campsites.

A HOLIDAY IS USUALLY A ONCE-A-YEAR TREAT WHEN YOU DON'T WANT TO COMPROMISE ON QUALITY. YOU WANT TO KNOW YOU'VE CHOSEN A QUALITY CAMPSITE THAT MEETS YOUR CRITERIA. THAT'S WHY OUR INSPECTORS TRAVEL AROUND 100, 000 MILES EACH YEAR, AND THAT'S WHY WE'VE SELECTED SOME OF THE FINEST ALAN ROGERS INSPECTED AND SELECTED SITES, IN THE MOST ATTRACTIVE HOLIDAY DESTINATIONS. CHECK OUT THE ALAN ROGERS GUIDES FOR THE FULL REPORT.

quality control

Campsites have come a long way. Whether purpose-built or converted from old farms and orchards, the best examples have up to date facilities that would put a quality hotel to shame.

the Alan Rogers story

By the late sixties, numbers of campsites had proliferated hugely. Then, as now, holidaymakers wanted to cut through the brochure-speak and make an informed choice based on the impartial opinion of an expert who had visited the campsite.

Today there are well over 25,000 campsites in Europe to choose from – for most people their holiday is an important matter and they want to book with confidence. The chief aim of the first Alan Rogers Guide was to provide an honest, factual description of a selection of Europe's best campsites, providing the reader with first-hand advice. The very first Alan Rogers Guide of 1968 included 50 campsites while today six different titles cover 2,000 inspected and selected campsites across 21 countries in Europe.

life in
the easy lane

HOLIDAYING IN A MOBILE HOME IS ALL ABOUT RELAXING AND GOING AT YOUR OWN PACE. YOU'LL QUICKLY ESTABLISH YOUR OWN DAILY RHYTHMS AND IT'S GOOD TO KNOW THERE ARE NO HOTEL RESTRICTIONS, NO FORMALITIES AND NO SET MEAL TIMES TO CONFORM TO.

Campsites have their own 'style' but one thing is constant: it's all about people doing what they want, when they want. Take a midday wander around a campsite and you'll find children splashing in the pool and toddlers enjoying the swings in the play area before lunch. Some excited jabbering in the distance suggests the arrival of the Children's Club, trooping by on their treasure hunt. Over in the corner, under a shady tree, a couple sit in companionable silence, quietly getting stuck into their holiday paperbacks, glass of wine to hand.

In true continental style, several plumes of smoke lazily indicate barbecue plans for lunchtime, while others are busying with ciabatta, cheeses and cold cuts and deliberating over red or white. Over at the terrace restaurant, under the Campari parasols, several groups are settling down to order the day's special.

For some it's not long since they were breakfasting in pyjamas. For others it's not long before they'll be enjoying that afternoon nap. But this is camping: they don't care, each to their own.

The afternoon heralds activity for some: a trip to the beach, a cultural visit, a canoe trip, some wine tasting (educational, of course!), a game of tennis, a cruise out to the islands, a pony ride, a family bike ride, a visit to the market, a stroll along the headland, an ice cream treat…

Decisions, decisions.

For others, there's a chance for a little R&R. Maybe beside the pool while the kids let off steam. Maybe away from the action back 'at home'.

Either way, there are choices to be made for everyone and it really doesn't matter, there's no fixed itinerary – everyone can please themselves on a camping holiday.

take time out

Take time out as a family: you'll notice the difference. Eat outside as a family; sit down to a long, lazy family lunch together; take a trip to the supermarket together – even the apparently mundane chore can be more interesting on holiday. Let the younger ones stay up a little later than usual while you take the time to enjoy a coffee and finish off that rather nice bottle of red.

Campsite self catering is a great option, and so easy. Most sites have their own restaurant, in many cases of sufficient quality to be frequented by locals – always a good sign. Most also provide a handy takeaway service, which might serve anything from simple, family favourites to really good quality dishes typical of the region. And of course collecting a big bowl of chips and bringing them back to complement your own barbecue is one of camping's simpler pleasures.

camping
for fun

Quite simply, children love camping, and campsites love children.
Children are welcomed in bars and restaurants and so much of campsite life is geared towards them, making life more relaxing for all. It's a cliché but if the kids are happy, then Mum and Dad are too!

And if they want action, there's nowhere better to find it than on a campsite. All Alan Rogers inspected and selected campsites offer a range of excellent facilities, starting with great pools, most with waterslides. Some are elaborate waterparks with multiple pools, lagoons, bridges, wave machines and huge waterchutes. Others are smaller scale, a bit more tranquil perhaps and better suited to toddlers, especially in high season.

Sporting activities, for which there is usually a small charge, might include windsurfing, riding, tennis, golf, cycling, archery, fishing and more.
The choice is huge – see the details listed alongside each site.

Above all a campsite holiday is so child-friendly. Whatever their age, children thrive on campsite life: they enjoy the fun and novelty of living outdoors, perhaps sleeping 'under the stars' in a little tent next to the mobile home. There's always entertainment on the doorstep, activities galore, new friends to make (strange how language is no barrier for children) and new experiences to savour.

A typical campsite is a safe environment too. Children of a certain age can wander relatively freely, or jump on their bikes, all in a controlled environment and all in the healthy, fresh air. And how pleasant to spend two weeks away with no mention of TV!

entertainment laid on

Most, if not all, campsites organise activities for children. Mostly in high season, these might range from sports tournaments to fancy dress competitions or treasure hunts, depending on the campsite and the ages of the children. Many sites also lay on high season family entertainment like themed evening meals in the restaurant, magic shows, music and family discos. In addition, many campsites also provide a regular Children's Club, usually high season only.

the magic of camping

KIDS LOVE CAMPING: THE OPEN AIR FREEDOM, THE EASY GOING ROUTINES, LOADS OF NEW FRIENDS, THE NOVELTY OF SLEEPING UNDER THE STARS....

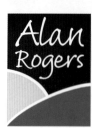

THE AIMS OF THE TRAVEL SERVICE ARE SIMPLE.

- To provide convenience - when booking a campsite yourself can be anything but convenient.
- To provide peace of mind - when you need it most.
- To provide a friendly, knowledgeable, efficient service - when this can be hard to find.
- To provide a low cost means of organising your holiday – when prices can be so complicated.

HOW IT WORKS

1 Choose your campsite(s)

2 Choose your dates

3 Choose your ferry crossing

Then just call us for an instant quote

0870 405 4055

or visit

www.alanrogersdirect.com

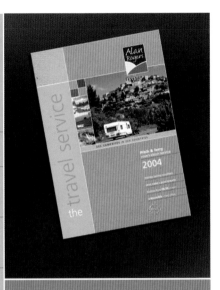

For full details see our 2004 brochure

FREE

0870 405 4055

Ask about our incredible Ferry Deals

☑ **Caravans GO FREE**

☑ **Motorhomes Priced as Cars**

Let us book your pitch and ferry for you

don't miss out
book early

Because so many of our best campsites are booked well in advance by those in the know, we do advise early action. We make it as simple as possible, and it's risk-free. A £100 deposit is all it takes to confirm those important campsite dates and secure the vital ferry crossing. The balance is not due until 10 weeks before departure, leaving you plenty of time to relax knowing that next year's holiday is 'in the bag'. Each year we unfortunately have to disappoint a number of would-be travellers who have left it just too late for the high summer dates (and ferry crossings) – please don't allow yourself to be one of them.

extra nights
FREE

Booking with The Alan Rogers Travel Service always means great value and real peace of mind. Now we've negotiated new special offers for 2004 – all designed to save you more money.

These are generally extra nights **FREE** of charge, subject to certain conditions and availability. Examples might be 7 nights for 6 or 12 nights for 10. Qualifying dates are usually in the off-peak period.

Ask for details or see our 2004 brochure (above).

WE ACT AS AGENTS FOR ALL THE CAMPSITES AND FERRY OPERATORS FEATURED IN THE TRAVEL SERVICE. AS SUCH, WE CAN BOOK ALL YOUR TRAVEL ARRANGEMENTS WITH THE MINIMUM OF FUSS AND AT THE BEST POSSIBLE PRICES. THE BASE PRICES BELOW INCLUDE 12 NIGHTS PITCH FEES AND RETURN FERRY CROSSING.

First night on site	Base Price 2 adults + car 12 nights	extra adult	child (0-13)	extra/fewer nights
Before 18 May	£294	£25	FREE	£12
18 May – 18 June	£314	£25	FREE	£12
19 June - 2 July	£345	£25	FREE	£12
3 July – 13 August	£415	£25	FREE	£12
14 August – 23 August	£375	£25	FREE	£12
From 24 August	£314	£25	FREE	£12

The base price of your holiday includes 12 nights pitch fees and a mid-week return ferry crossing from Dover to Calais with P&O Ferries for a car and five passengers (outward sailing times must be between 14:01 and 06:59. Inward sailing times must be between 20:01 and 14:59). Additional supplements are payable for caravans, trailers and motorhomes at all times and for cars at weekends and times outside those given above. There will also usually be a campsite supplement payable (see opposite). Call us on **0870 405 4055** for details and a quote.

If your holiday is longer or shorter than 12 nights, simply add or subtract £12 per night. Holidays must be for a minimum of 3 nights, with ferry (many sites have a minimum stay requirement). For holidays longer than 21 nights please call for a quotation. You may stay on as many sites as you wish, subject to individual site requirements, with a one-off £10 multi-site fee.

LOW £100 DEPOSIT
A special low deposit of just £100 secures your holiday
(full payment is required at the time of booking for travel within 10 weeks)

12 nights pitch fees + ferry for car and passengers	from **£294** DOVER - CALAIS
12 nights pitch fees + ferry for motorhome and passengers	from **£310** PORTSMOUTH - LE HAVRE/ CHERBOURG
12 nights pitch fees + ferry for car and caravan and passengers	from **£294** DOVER - CALAIS

* ***Special Offers***: *Look for our famous money-saving deals: Caravans Go Free, Motorhomes Priced as Car. Ask us for details.*

Site Supplements

All sites operate their own independent pricing structure, and in order to reflect the differences in cost from one site to another, we will add a nightly 'site supplement' to the Base Prices indicated above. Although some sites in our brochure have very low supplements (eg 80060 Val de Trie: 2 adults and car/ caravan/motorhome carries no supplement all season), others may carry much higher supplements (eg 83020 Esterel Caravaning: 2 adults and car/caravan/motorhome = £28 supplement per night in high season).

Additional supplements can often apply for electricity, water and drainage or special pitches.

The simplest next step is to just call us for an immediate price quotation for your chosen site and all the available options, as well as any other important information, such as any minimum stay requirements.

CALL US NOW **0870 405 4055** FOR AN INSTANT QUOTE

OR VISIT **www.alanrogersdirect.com**

Leave The Hassle To Us

- All site fees paid in advance – you won't need to take extra currency with you.
- Your pitch is reserved for you – travel with peace of mind.
- No endless overseas phone calls or correspondence with foreign site owners.
- No need to pay foreign currency deposits and booking fees.
- Take advantage of our expert advice and experience of camping in Europe.

Already Booked Your Ferry?

We're confident that our ferry inclusive booking service offers unbeatable value. However, if you have already booked your ferry then we can still make a pitch-only reservation for you. Your booking must be for a minimum of 10 nights, and since our prices are based on our ferry inclusive service, you need to be aware that a non-ferry booking will always result in somewhat higher prices than if you were to book direct with the site.

You still benefit from:

- Hassle-free booking with no booking fees and foreign currency deposits.
- Comprehensive Travel Pack.
- Peace of mind: site fees paid in advance, with your pitch reserved for you.

FULL DETAILS IN OUR 64 PAGE 2004 COLOUR BROCHURE CALL

0870 405 4055

book
on-line
and save money

NEW for 2004 www.alanrogersdirect.com is a brand new website designed to give you everything you need to know when it comes to booking your Alan Rogers inspected and selected campsite, and your low cost ferry.

Our glossy brochure gives you all the info you need but it is only printed once a year. And our friendly, expert reservations team is always happy to help on **0870 405 4055** – but they do go home sometimes!

Visit www.alanrogersdirect.com and you'll find constantly updated information, latest ferry deals, special offers from campsites and much more. And you can visit it at any time of day or night!

alanrogersdirect.com
book on-line and save

Campsite Information

☑ Details of all Travel Service campsites - **instantly**
☑ Find latest special offers on campsites - **instantly**
☑ Check campsite availability - **instantly**

Ferry Information

☑ Check ferry availability - **instantly**
☑ Find latest ferry deals - **instantly**
☑ Book your ferry online - **instantly**
☑ Save money - **instantly**

Save Money!
BOOK YOUR CAMPSITE AND FERRY - INSTANTLY

NEW Perfect Match
Find the campsite that's right for you

With so many sites to choose from it can be difficult to find a short-list. With the unique Alan Rogers Perfect Match system you can quickly find a campsite that meets your requirements. This powerful and searchable database of top campsites, all Alan Rogers inspected and selected, means you can quickly find an ideal site, book it on-line and relax in the knowledge that your holiday is safely reserved.

Ferry Deals On-line

FOR 2004 WE HAVE ARRANGED SOME EXCEPTIONAL OFFERS ON KEY CROSS-CHANNEL ROUTES. THESE ARE CERTAIN TO MAKE YOU WANT TO THINK ABOUT YOUR HOLIDAY NOW AND NOT RISK MISSING OUT.

Caravans Go **FREE**
Trailers Go **FREE**
Motorhomes Priced as Cars

Dover – Calais
Portsmouth – Cherbourg
Portsmouth – Le Havre

Portsmouth – Caen
Poole – Cherbourg

Conditions apply – ask for details or see page 26.

Don't delay – this offer is strictly subject to availability and will be first come, first served.

IN ESTABLISHING OUR PROGRAMME, WE HAVE ENSURED A SELECTION OF SITES IN EVERY CORNER OF FRANCE AND, AS WELL AS OFFERING SITES IN WELL KNOWN AREAS AND WELL ESTABLISHED RESORTS, WE HAVE ALSO SOUGHT TO INCLUDE SOME SMALLER SITES IN LITTLE KNOWN AREAS, BUT WHICH ARE WELL WORTH A VISIT. THIS IS A SELECTION OF THE SITES WE CAN BOOK FOR YOU, WITH FERRY, IN 2004.

(M) Mobile   (P) Pitch   (T) Ready erected tents

Italy

IT6022 (M) (P)
Portofelice
Cabrelle Maurita

A well organised site offering plenty of activities for children of all ages

IT6240 (P)
Valle Romantica
Cannobio

Attractive, floral site with good facilities in scenic situation.

IT6245 (P)
Riviera
Cannobio

Good lakeside site near northern end of Lake Maggiore, with access for watersports.

(P)

IT6280 (T) (M) (P)
Camping Weekend
Cisano

Modern, well equipped site with friendly ambience and superb views over Lake Garda.

IT6275 (T) (M) (P)
Fornella
San Felice

Good site with pools, good restaurant with direct access to Lake Garda.

IT6000 (P)
Mare Pineta
Sistiana

Site west of Trieste with good pool and sea views over the Sistiana Bay.

FREE BROCHURE
INCLUDING 155 EUROPEAN SITES
0870 405 4055

Crossing the Channel

One of the great advantages of booking with the Alan Rogers Travel Service is the tremendous value we offer. A package of 12 nights on site and return ferry costs from just £294 – check current public ferry fares and you'll see what incredible value this represents. As agents for all the cross-Channel operators we can book all your travel arrangements with the minimum of fuss and at the best possible rates.

Just call us for an instant quote

0870 405 4055

or visit

www.alanrogersdirect.com
Book on-line AND SAVE

Short Sea Routes

Hop across the Channel in the shortest possible time and you can be on your way. We offer all main routes at great prices (when you book a pitch + ferry 'package' through us). And why not take advantage of our Ferry Deals? Caravans and trailers can go **FREE** on Dover – Calais with P&O Ferries.

Caravans can even go **FREE** with **Eurotunnel** - ask for details.

SEAFRANCE
DOVER-CALAIS FERRIES

P&O Ferries
Dover - Calais

hoverspeed
Dover – Calais
Newhaven - Dieppe

EURO TUNNEL
Folkestone – Calais

Stena Line
Harwich – Hook of Holland

THIS FORM WILL
save you money

TO QUALIFY FOR SOME MONEY SAVING OFFERS, AND USE-
FUL INFORMATION, SIMPLY RETURN THE COUPON.
NO STAMP REQUIRED.

Register me for savings - today

Ferry savings
Please keep me posted with the latest ferry savings,
special offers and up to date news

Discounts on Alan Rogers Guides
Please offer me discounts on future editions of the
Alan Rogers' Guides plus other camping and caravan-
ning publications

www. alanrogers .com

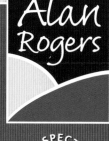

INSPECTED
CAMPSITES
& SELECTED

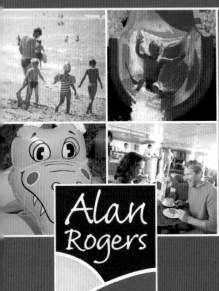

Save over 50% on your holiday

Camping Cheque ©

- 400 sites – all just £9.95 per night
- Maximum flexibility - go as you please
- Fantastic Ferry Deals

After 5 years Camping Cheque is still the fastest growing programme of its type. For choice, value and unbeatable Ferry Deals there is simply no alternative. Last year 120,000 people used nearly 1 million Camping Cheques and enjoyed half-price holidays around Europe. Make sure you don't miss out this year.

Huge off peak savings

400 quality campsites in 18 European countries, including the UK, all at just £9.95 per night for pitch + 2 adults, including electricity. That's a saving of up to 55% off normal site tariffs. And with special free night deals (14 nights for 11 Cheques, 60 nights for 30 Cheques etc) the price can reduce to under a fiver a night!

ferry savings

Ask about our famous special offers

- ☑ Caravans/trailers Go FREE
- ☑ Motorhomes Priced As Cars

Conditions apply – ask for details

CALL NOW
for full details
of how to
save 50%

For full information visit the all-new website
www.campingcheque.co.uk
Buy Cheques, check ferry availability, book everything on-line AND SAVE!

0870 405 4057

Italy

Whether you want to explore historical cities, stroll around medieval hill towns, relax on sandy beaches or simply indulge in opera, good food and wine, Italy has it all. Roman ruins, Renaissance art and beautiful churches abound. For the more active, the Italian Alps are a haven for winter sports enthusiasts and also offer good hiking trails.

Italy only became a unified state in 1861, hence the regional nature of the country today. With 20 distinct regions each one has retained its own individualism which is evident in the cuisine and local dialects.

In the north, the vibrant city of Milan is great for shopping and home to the famous opera house, La Scala, as well as Leonardo's Last Supper fresco. It is also a good jumping-off point for the Alps; the Italian Lake District, incorporating Lake Garda, Lake Como and Lake Maggiore; the canals of Venice and the lovely town of Verona. Central Italy probably represents the most commonly perceived image of the country and Tuscany, with its classic rolling countryside and the historical towns of Florence, Siena, San Gimignano and Pisa, is one of the most visited areas. Further south is the historical capital of Rome and the city of Naples. Close to some of Italy's ancient sites such as Pompei, Naples is within easy distance of Sorrento and the Amalfi coast.

Population: 57.8 million

Capital: Rome (Roma).

Language: Italian. There are several dialect forms and some German is spoken near the Austrian border.

Climate: The south enjoys extremely hot summers and mild, dry winters, whilst the mountainous regions of the north are cooler with heavy snowfalls in winter.

Currency: The euro (€).

Telephone: The country code is 0039.

Banks: Mon-Fri 08.30-13.00 and 15.00-16.00.

Shops: Mon-Sat 08.30/09.00-13.00 and 15.30/16.00-19.30/20.00, with some variations in larger cities.

Public Holidays: New Year; Easter Monday; Liberation Day 25 April; Labour Day; Assumption 15 August; All Saints 1 November; Immaculate Conception 8 December; Christmas 25, 26 December; plus numerous special local feast days.

Tourist Information:

Italian State Tourist Board, 1, Princes Street, London W1B 2AY

Tel: 020 7408 1254 or 09065 508925 (brochures)   Fax: 020 7399 3567

E-mail: italy@italiantouristboard.co.uk   Internet: www.enit.it

Regions of Italy

Fringed by the French and Swiss Alps in the far north of the country, home to several ski resorts, with vineyard clad-hills in the south, Piedmont and Valle d'Aosta is renowned for its fine wines and local cuisine.

The region is made up of the following provinces:
Alessandria, Aosta, Asti, Biella, Cuneo, Ivrea, Novara, Verbania and Vercelli

In the heart of Piedmont is Turin, home to the most famous holy relics of all time, the Turin Shroud, and the Fiat car company. It also boasts a superb Egyptian Museum, Renaissance cathedral, elegant piazzas plus designer shops and good restaurants. In the east set in a vast plain of paddy fields along the River Po – which stretches right across northern Italy – is Vercelli, the rice capital of Europe. Further south are the wine-producing towns of Alba, renowned for its white truffles and red wines; and Asti, the capital of Italy's sparkling wine industry, where the famous 'spumante' is produced. There are numerous wine museums, vineyards and cantinas in the area, from where you can purchase wine, including those at Barolo, Annuziata and Costigliole d'Asti.

Studded with picturesque castles, the Valle d'Aosta offers great walking and skiing country with its dramatic mountains, beautiful valleys and lush meadows, most notably in the Gran Paradise National Park. This huge park is also home to over 3,000 ibex, a relative of the deer family, 6,000 chamois plus golden eagles and rare butterflies.

Cuisine of the region

Bagna cauda: local variation on fondue, vegetables dipped into a sauce of oil, anchovies, garlic, cream and butter

Fontina: a semi-hard cheese made in the Valle d'Aosta

Manzo al Barolo: lean beef marinated in red wine and garlic and stewed gently

Soupe á la cogneintze: soup with rice

Spumone piemontese: a mousse of mascarpone cheese with rum

Tora di Nocciole: nut tart including hazelnuts, eggs and butter.

Zabaglione: dessert made with a mixture of egg yolk, sugar and Marsala

Places of interest

Aosta: attractive mountain town with Roman architecture and ruins

Avigliana: small town perched beside two lakes surrounded by mountains, medieval houses

Biella: renowned for its wool industry

Domodossola: mountain town of Roman origin, arcaded medieval centre, starting point of a scenic train ride across to Switzerland

Lake Orta: set among the foothills of the Alps, in the middle of the lake rises the Island of San Guilo, with a basilica

Saluzzo: medieval town, Gothic church, castle

Susa: medieval town, 11th century castle and church

tip

THE VALLE D'AOSTA IS BILINGUAL WITH FRENCH COMMONLY SPOKEN, AND FRENCH DIALECTS CAN BE HEARD IN THE REMOTE VALLEYS OF PIEDMONT.

IT6219 Camping International Touring

11010 Sarre (Aosta)

The Aosta Valley is surrounded by some of the best known Alpine peaks, Mont Blanc, Monte Rosa, Matterhorn, to name but three. The region also offers the contrast between its warm, Mediterranean temperatures and beautiful mountain villages. Camping International lies around five kilometres from Aosta, close to the little village of Sarre. This site offers an attractive, flat camping area with shaded pitches of a reasonable size, most with electrical connections. There is a small range of leisure amenities, notably a small swimming pool, tennis court and table tennis (all free). The good restaurant/ pizzeria specialises in local cuisine. Road noise from the nearby A5 autostrada and S26 is audible in all parts of the site.

Facilities
Three sanitary blocks are well equipped and kept clean. Washing machine. Small bar and shop, and a good restaurant/pizzeria. Play area. Regular bus service to Aosta. Off site: Canoeing on the Dora Baltea, fishing, all mountain sports 1 km. Gran Paradiso National Park 20 km.

At a glance
Welcome & Ambience	✓✓✓✓	Location	✓✓✓✓
Quality of Pitches	✓✓✓	Range of Facilities	✓✓✓

Directions
Site is 38 km. south of the Mont Blanc tunnel. Take the Sarre exit from the A5 to join the S26 and then clear local directions.

Charges 2003
Per person	€ 5.30
child (7-10 yrs)	€ 3.70
pitch incl. electricity	€ 8.00
small pitch	€ 4.80
electricity 6A	€ 2.50

Reductions in low season.

Reservations
Contact site. Tel: 0165 257061.
Email: campingtouring@libero.it

Open
15 May - 15 September.

ITIT6220 Camping Mombarone

Settimo Vittone Reg, 10010 Torre Daniele (Piedmont)

This is a small rustic all year site alongside the SS26 road, suitable as an en-route stop or for exciting climbing. It has 120 pitches, 80 of which are given over to permanent units, but there will always be a space for tourers. The Peretto family take pride in looking after their guests and English is spoken. The site is thoughtfully laid out with attractive plants and shrubs and trees for shade. It is surrounded by very attractive mountains and wooded hills, with vines bedecking the eastern slopes. This is an ideal base for climbers as the mountains in this area are extremely popular. The many famous valleys including Valle di Champorcher and Valle di Gressony are within easy driving distance, as is the Parco Nazionale del Gran Paradiso. There is a small wooden bar on site but shops and good restaurants are close by in the village of Quincinetto. There is a small framed and supported pool for children or they can paddle in the shallow river and catch tiddlers on the northern boundary. If you are here in October help the family pick their own grapes, make the wine (in the Nebbiolo style) and share the fun; the wine is sold at the bar.

Facilities
The sanitary facilities are spotless with both British and Turkish WCs and a washing machine. When you leave tell them how many showers taken and settle up accordingly! Bar. Toddlers' pool. Volleyball, table tennis, table football. Fishing. Off site: Riding 5 km. Shops and restaurants in the town.

At a glance
Welcome & Ambience	✓✓✓✓✓	Location	✓✓✓
Quality of Pitches	✓✓✓	Range of Facilities	✓✓✓

Directions
Take the SS26 north from Ivrea. Site between 45 and 46 km. markers just before entering the town of Torre Daniele. From motorway take Quiuinetto A5 exit (Milan-Aosta).

Charges 2003
Per person	€ 3.00
child (under 10 yrs)	€ 2.50
caravan	€ 3.00
car	€ 1.50
motorcaravan	€ 4.50
electricity	€ 1.50

No credit cards.

Reservations
Write to site. Tel: 0125 757907.
Email: camping-mombarone@libero.it

Open
All year.

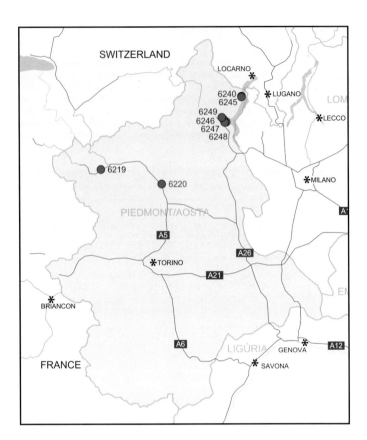

IT6240 Camping Valle Romantica

Via Valle Cannobina, 28822 Cannobio (Piedmont)

The pretty little town of Cannobio is situated between Verbania and Locarno on the western shore of Lake Maggiore. It could make a base for exploring the Lake and its islands, although progress along the winding lakeside road, hemmed in by mountains, is slow. Serious mountain walkers are well catered for, and the Swiss resort of Locarno is not far. In a scenic situation, this lovely site was established about 40 years ago by the present owner's father, who planted some 20,000 plants, trees and shrubs, and there is much to interest botanists in this tree-clad mountain valley. The site's swimming pool is in a sunny position and there is a pool in the river, where, except after heavy rain, children can play. The 188 numbered pitches for touring units are on flat grass among the trees, which provide good shade and serve to separate the pitches (but mean some narrow site roads). Electricity is available on most pitches, although long cables are necessary in some parts. Used by tour operators (30 pitches). The owner takes a keen and active personal interest in the site, and English is spoken.

Facilities

The three sanitary blocks provide good facilities with free showers of a reasonable size, with hooks, screen and a small dressing space, controlled by taps. Washing machines. Gas supplies. Motorcaravan services. Small, well stocked supermarket. Pleasant bar/restaurant with waiter service and takeaway. Pizzeria. Swimming pool (1/5-15/9). Fishing (licence required). Sailing and windsurfing schools. Fridge boxes for hire. Off site: Bicycle hire 500 m. Boat launching 1.5 km.

At a glance

Welcome & Ambience	✓✓✓✓	Location	✓✓✓
Quality of Pitches	✓✓✓	Range of Facilities	✓✓✓

Directions

After crossing the border from Switzerland, continue for 4 km. to outskirts of Cannobio. Turn right to Valle Cannobina and continue for 1 km. (do not turn right for Traffiume).

Charges 2003

Per person	€ 5.50 - € 6.50
child (1-12 yrs)	€ 3.50 - € 4.00
pitch	€ 9.00 - € 11.50
dog	€ 3.50
electricity (4A)	€ 3.00

No credit cards.

Reservations

Contact site. Tel: 0323 71249.
Email: valleromantica@riviea-valleromantica.com

Open

27 March - 30 September.

IT6247 Camping Tranquilla

Via Cave 2, 28831 Baveno (Piedmont)

Tranquilla is a family run site on the western slopes above Baveno, close to Lake Maggiore. Reception is housed in an attractive old railway carriage from where the Luca family will make you welcome to the site with excellent English spoken. The site is in two terraced sections, both with electricity connections. The pitches, both permanent (55) and touring (56) are of average size and are randomly mixed, with trees offering some shade. Although on the small side, the site's two swimming pools are very welcome in the height of summer as the 1.5 km. walk to the lake, where swimming can be difficult, is down a steep slope, and would prove difficult for older or disabled visitors. The site has an unusually large restaurant with two terraces, a large menu at reasonable prices and live entertainment in season. The terrace has a fountain, some views and is very popular. Tourist information is available and reception will book any of the local activities and facilities including watersports. The site is an ideal base to explore the local area which is most attractive but your own transport is necessary as there is no bus service.

Facilities

The southern site has a recently built ladies' sanitary block, which is spotless and includes facilities for disabled campers, whilst the male side is more mature, but very clean. The northern side (with all the support facilities) has several older sanitary blocks that have recently been modernised and have an improved hot water supply and are again kept clean. British and Turkish style WCs. Freezer and refrigerator service. Laundry. Motorcaravan services. Bar. Restaurant, pizzeria and takeaway. Swimming pools (10/5-30/9). Play area. Table tennis. Table football. Electronic games. Excursions arranged. Off site: Fishing 800 m. Bus service 800 m. Golf and riding 3 km. Camping items in store next to site, shops nearby.

At a glance

Welcome & Ambience	✓✓✓✓✓	Location	✓✓✓✓
Quality of Pitches	✓✓✓✓	Range of Facilities	✓✓✓

Directions

From Avora follow SS33 road north to Baveno, site is signed to the left in the northern part of the town. Site is approx. 1.5 km. uphill and well signed.

Charges 2003

Per person	€ 4.00 - € 5.00
child (1-3 yrs)	€ 2.50 - € 3.50
child (4-12 yrs)	€ 3.00 - € 4.20
pitch	€ 6.00 - € 9.00
dog	€ 2.00
electricity (4/5A)	€ 2.00

Low season offers. No credit cards, but travellers cheques and British currency accepted.

Reservations

Write to site. Tel: 0323 923452.
Email: info@tranquilla.com

Open

1 March - 31 October.

IT6245 Camping Riviera

Via Casali Darbedo 2, 28822 Cannobio (Piedmont)

With scenic views across the water and surrounding mountains, this 22,000 sq.m. site is directly beside Lake Maggiore. Under the same active ownership as Valle Romantica, the whole site has a well cared for appearance and it is certainly one of the best lakeside sites in the area. Over 250 numbered pitches are on flat grass, either side of hard surfaced access roads and divided by trees and shrubs. There are 220 with electricity (long cables may be needed). There is a small jetty and easy access to the lake for boats, swimming and other watersports. Sailing and windsurfing regattas are organised. The site could make a suitable base for exploring the area, although progress on the busy winding road may be slow.

Facilities

The five sanitary blocks, one new and two with facilities for disabled visitors, are of good quality. Washing machines. Fridge boxes for hire. Gas supplies. Motorcaravan services. Well stocked site shop. Pleasant bar/restaurant with covered terrace, providing waiter service and takeaway. Pizzeria. Swimming pool (1/5-15/9). Fishing (licence required). Boat slipway. Sailing and windsurfing schools. Off site: The town is only a short distance. Bicycle hire 500 m.

At a glance

Welcome & Ambience	✓✓✓✓	Location	✓✓✓✓✓
Quality of Pitches	✓✓✓	Range of Facilities	✓✓✓

Directions

After the border crossing from Switzerland, continue for 4 km. to the entrance of the town of Cannobio. There are several sites nearby – Riviera is the last site before the bridge, at the lakeside (on the left).

Charges 2003

Per person	€ 5.50 - € 6.50
child (1-12 yrs)	€ 3.50 - € 4.00
pitch	€ 9.00 - € 11.50
dog	€ 3.50
electricity (4A)	€ 3.00

No credit cards.

Reservations

Made for min. 14 nights with deposit (€ 60) and fee (€ 40). Tel: 0323 71360.
Email: riviera@riviera-valleromantica.com

Open

27 March - 31 October.

IT6246 Camping Village Isolino

Via per Feriolo 25, 28924 Verbania Fondotoce (Piedmont)

Lake Maggiore is one of the most attractive Italian lakes and Isolino Camping Village is one of the largest sites in the region. The long entrance road to the site – rolled gravel and fairly uneven – is rather off-putting but then the stunning location and attractive swimming pool with its lovely views across the lake to the fir-clad mountains beyond is breathtaking and worth finding. Most of the 710 tourist pitches have shade from a variety of trees and are of a good size in regular back-to-back rows. All have electrical connections. There is a small sandy beach and a wide range of watersports (no jet-skis) can be enjoyed on the lake. The social life of the campsite is centred around the large bar which has a stage for musical entertainment, pool-side terrace and takeaway with a restaurant on the floor above sharing the magnificent views across the lake. The site is owned by the friendly Manoni family who also own Camping Continental Lido at nearby Lake Mergozzo and good English is spoken.

Facilities

Six well-built toilet blocks, most refurbished, have free hot water. Washing machines and dryers. Fridge boxes for hire. Motorcaravan service point. Large well stocked supermarket. Most attractive swimming pool with children's pool at one end and sunbathing area. Football pitch. Tennis courts. Fishing. Watersports. Bicycle hire and guided mountain bike tours. Beach volleyball and organised activities for children and adults and weekly disco in July/Aug. Raised barbecues are permitted. Off site: Golf 3 km. Riding 12 km.

At a glance

Welcome & Ambience	✓✓✓✓	Location	✓✓✓✓
Quality of Pitches	✓✓✓✓	Range of Facilities	✓✓✓✓

Directions

Leave A26 motorway at exit for Stresa/Baveno, turn left towards Fondotoce and follow signs to site on right.

Latest charges

Per unit incl. 2 persons and electricity (6A)	€ 16.85 - € 26.00
extra person	€ 3.90 - € 6.25
child 3-5 yrs	free - € 5.10
child 6-11 yrs	€ 2.95 - € 5.10
dog	€ 2.95 - € 5.10

Credit cards accepted with 1.4% commission.

Reservations

Contact site. Tel: 0323 496 080.
Email: info@isolino.com

Open

2 April - 19 September.

Lago Maggiore

CHILDREN GRATIS
0-2 all the season long
3-5 till 10.07. and
from 21.08.

ISOLINO
camping village

Via Per Feriolo, 25
I-28924 Fondotoce di Verbania
Tel. 0039 / 0323496080
Fax 0039 / 0323496414
E-mail: info@isolino.com
Http: www.isolino.it

The lightly leaning sandy beach is ideal for children - the campsite lies in a very quiet position with wonderful view. Bar, restaurant, supermarket, free hot showers, children's playground, basketball and volleyball facilities, table tennis, windsurfing school. We rent bicycles, pedalò, canoes, boats and surfboards. Bungalows, mobile homes, and apartments for rent. Internet-point.

Special Offer

From 5 nights: from 02.04. to 20.05. and from 04.09. to 19.09

From 7 nights: from 20.05. to 03.07. and from 28.08. to 04.09.

1000 mq swimming pool and Animation program from 15.05. to 14.09.04

IT6249 Camping Continental Lido

Via 42 Martiri, 156, 28924 Fondotoce di Verbania (Piedmont)

Continental Lido is situated on the shore of the small Lake Mergozzo, about one kilometer from the better known Lake Maggiore. The 500 small to normal sized tourist pitches are back-to-back in regular rows on grass. All have electricity (6A) and there is shade from a variety of trees in some parts. There is no swimming pool but a small sandy beach slopes gently into the lake where swimming and watersports can also be enjoyed (no powered craft may be used). Fir-clad mountains provide a scenic background. An unusual feature is the nine hole golf course. Under the same ownership as Isolino Camping Village, this site is managed by son Giano Paolo who speaks good English.

Facilities

Five refurbished toilet blocks have free hot water, facilities for disabled visitors and washing machines and dryers. Well stocked shop. Bar/restaurant with terrace and takeaway. TV. Tennis courts. Volleyball, basketball and 9-hole golf course. Playground. Watersports canoes, kayaks. Games room. Bicycle hire. Entertainment and activities (mid-June to mid-September). Off site: Site is within easy range of botanical gardens and the Swiss Ticano canton.

At a glance

Welcome & Ambience	✓✓✓✓	Location	✓✓✓✓
Quality of Pitches	✓✓✓✓	Range of Facilities	✓✓✓✓

Directions

Site is on the SS34 road between Fondotoce and Gravellona.

Charges 2003

Per person	€ 3.95 - € 4.55
child (3-11 yrs)	free - € 4.25
pitch	€ 16.20 - € 18.70

Reservations

Contact site. Tel: 0323 496300.
Email: info@campingcontinental.com

Open

23 March - 22 September.

IT6248 Camping Parisi

Via Piave 50, 28831 Baveno (Piedmont)

Camping Parisi is a quiet, family run site on the western shore of Lake Maggiore within the town of Baveno. The small and compact site has just 61 pitches, all for tourers. The pitches are shaded by mature trees and there are stunning views over the lake which is this site's real strength. An early reservation would be necessary if you wish to occupy one of the lakeside pitches (extra charge). Whilst there is no swimming pool, it is possible to paddle and swim from the lake shore which is also good for sunbathing (but care must be taken with children). The site has a restaurant and bar, reached through a gate on the northern boundary. The public also have the use of these facilities through a separate access which is secured by night. This shared community complex also has limited fixed entertainment such as five-a-side soccer on sand, satellite TV in the bar, volleyball, table tennis, a small children's play area and a large beach area with sun-beds. Live entertainment is offered next to the restaurant at weekends during high season.

Facilities

Central sanitary facilities are clean with free hot showers and British style WCs but, as yet, no facilities for disabled campers. These facilities are supplemented by day in the 'community area' where a modern complex offers coin slot showers, British toilets and sinks. Washing machine and dryer. The site has no shop as the town is 100 m. distant. Freezer service. Community complex with bar, TV. Restaurant (from 1/5). Volleyball. Five-a-side soccer. Play area. Table tennis. Reception will make bookings for local activities. Off site: Shops nearby.

At a glance

Welcome & Ambience	✓✓✓	Location	✓✓✓✓
Quality of Pitches	✓✓✓✓	Range of Facilities	✓✓✓

Directions

From A26 Genoa - Gravellona take Baveno exit and turn right on main road to site. From Simplon or Gothard the first site sign is in Feriolo. From Arona follow SS33 road north to Baveno. Site is signed to the right in the centre of the town on the right but a sharp eye is needed to pick out the small sign high on the wall at a narrow part of the street.

Charges 2003

Per person	€ 5.20 - € 6.00
baby (1-3 yrs)	€ 2.10 - € 2.30
child (4-12 yrs)	€ 4.20 - € 5.10
pitch	€ 7.80 - € 9.20
electricity	€ 2.20
dog	€ 1.60 - € 2.10

Reservations

Write to site. Tel: 0323 923156.
Email: campingparisi@tiscali.it

Open

20 March - 10 October.

The region of Lombardy stretches from the Alps, on the border with Switzerland, down past the romantic lakes of Como and Maggiore to the broad, flat plain of the River Po.

The region is made up of the provinces: Bergamo, Brescia, Como, Cremona, Lecco, Lodi, Mantova, Milano, Pavia, Sondrio and Varese.

Lake Garda has a separate section

Lombardy is one of the most developed resorts in Italy, its major draw being the beautiful scenic lakes. Surrounded by abundant vegetation Lake Como is set in an idyllic landscape of mountains; tall peaks that seem to rise directly from the water's edge. With a number of places to visit along the shores, including the prosperous towns of Como and Lecco, the area is also great for walking and in most places the lake is clean enough for swimming. Lake Maggiore has a mediterranean atmosphere, with citrus trees and palms lining the shores, and offers a more sedate pace. There are good walks in the surrounding hills. Lying in the centre of the lake near Stresa are the Borromean Islands, of which Isola Bella is the most popular. It is home to the 17th century Palazzo Borromeo and its splendid garden of landscaped terraces, fountains, peacocks and statues. A lesser known lake, Lake Iseo, is the fifth largest in northern Italy. Situated in wine-producing country, surrounded by mountains and waterfalls, it is popular for its watersports and boasts the largest lake-island in Italy, Monte Isola. All three lakes are well served by ferries which zigzag from shore to shore, and within easy reach of the vibrant city of Milan.

Cuisine of the region

Food varies considerably from town to town. Risotto is popular, the short grain rice is grown in the paddy fields of the Ticino Valley, as is green pasta and polenta. Lombardy is one of the largest cheese making regions in the country – Gorgonzola and Mascarpone is produced here.

Biscotti: biscuits flavoured with nuts, vanilla and lemon

Costolette alla Milanese: veal escalope

La Casoêula: pork stew

Ossobuco: shin of veal

Panettone: light yeast cake with candied fruit

Pizzoccheri: buckwheat noodles

Risotto alla Milanse: rice cooked in meat stock with white wine, onion, saffron and grated parmesan

Places of interest

Bellagio: beautiful town by Lake Como, hilly old centre with steep cobbled streets

Bergamo: hill-top town, medieval and Renaissance buildings

Brescia: Roman ruins, 12th century church

Certosa di Pavia: magnificent Rennaissance Charterhouse

Cremona: where the violin was developed, home of famous violin maker Stradivarius

Lodi: charming medieval town of pastel-coloured houses with pretty courtyards

Milan: fashion capital, great for shopping, art museums, home of famous opera house La Scala and Leonardo Da Vinci's *Last Supper* fresco

tip

VISTI THE NATIONAL PARK AT CAPO DI PONTE IN THE VAL COMONICA, WHICH CONTAINS A SERIES OF PREHISTORIC ROCK CARVINGS SPANNING 8,000 YEARS.

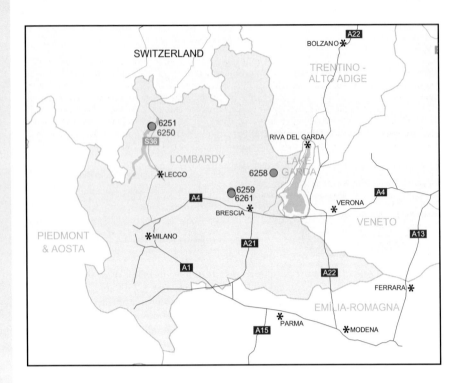

IT6250 Camping Au Lac de Como

Via Cesare Battisti 18, 22010 Sorico (Lombardy)

Au Lac du Como is situated in a most pleasant location at the head of Lake Como in the centre of the village of Sorico facing south down the water and surrounded by wooded mountains. There is direct access to the lake for swimming, boating, windsurfing and other watersports. Static units predominate but the camping area is directly by the lake where there is said to be room for 74 touring units, with 3A electricity connections. However, as pitches are not marked out, pitching can be a little haphazard and the area may become crowded at times, particularly in high season when advanced booking is advised. Cars are parked just away from tents and caravans and there is further parking outside the entrance. The owner speaks good English and insists on respect for other residents so ball games, barbecues and loud music are not allowed. The site is well situated for exploring the area, with Switzerland nearby via the Splugen Pass. There are also marked paths and trails for walking and biking in the mountains with an interesting nature park close by. The majority of guests are German and Dutch but British visitors are also very welcome.

Facilities

There is one good sanitary block in the centre of the static part and two smaller basic ones, all with mainly British style WCs. Hot water in the larger block is on payment but free in the other two except for washing up and laundry. Washing machine and dryer. Motorcaravan services. Supermarket. Hotel bar and restaurant open all day, offering excellent buffet breakfast service and evening meals. Heated swimming pool (21 x 7 m). Sauna and solarium. Fishing. Range of watersports possible. Canoe and bicycle hire.

At a glance

Welcome & Ambience	✓✓✓✓✓	Location	✓✓✓✓✓
Quality of Pitches	✓✓✓	Range of Facilities	✓✓✓

Directions

Easiest route is north on SS36 from Lecco to Nuovo Olonio and west on SS402 (signed Gravelona) to Sorico; site is then on the left in centre of village. Can be approached on SS340 from Como on lake-side road which is quite narrow in places but an interesting drive (not advised for larger units).

Latest charges

Per person	€ 6.50
child	€ 4.50
pitch	€ 11.00
dog	€ 6.00
extra car	€ 6.00

Less 10-50% for over 1 night outside July/August.

Reservations

Advised for high season; write to site. Tel: 0344 84035. Email: infoaulac@aulacdecomo.com

Open

All year.

IT6251 Camping La Riva

Via Poncione, 3, 22010 Sorico (Lombardy)

La Riva was opened in 2000 and lies at the northern end of Lake Como, close to the nature reserve of Pian di Spagna and within walking distance of Sorico, a pretty town with a range of bars and restaurants. This is a small, quiet site which enjoys direct lake access and is well located for trekking in the surrounding mountains, or for mountain biking. It's also ideally located for exploring the beautiful Lake Como area. Pitches are generally level and of a reasonable size (typically 80 sq.m). They are marked by trees and many have attractive views across the river to the mountains. Most have electrical connections. Close by, the campsite reception houses a small bar, which incorporates a snack bar and takeaway, and a small shop. There is a small childrens' pool and play area.

Facilities

The centrally located sanitary building contains modern showers (tokens needed), toilets and washbasins and is kept very clean. Facilities for disabled people. Washing machine. Small supported pool for children. Bicycle hire. Fishing, water skiing. Canoe and dinghy hire. Off site: Guided walks. Riding. Golf. Local market.

At a glance

Welcome & Ambience	✓✓✓✓	Location	✓✓✓✓✓
Quality of Pitches	✓✓✓✓	Range of Facilities	✓✓✓

Directions

Site is located on the River Mera as it joins Lake Como at Sorico. Approaching on S340 from Menaggio you pass site shortly before reaching Sorico.

Charges 2003

Per person	€ 5.50
child (0-7 yrs)	€ 4.50
pitch incl. electricity	€ 11.00

Discounts in low season.

Reservations

Contact site. Tel: 0344 94571.

Open

1 April - 3 November.

the travel service
TO BOOK
THIS SITE
0870 405 4055
Expert Advice &
Special Offers

37

IT6258 Azur Camping Idro Rio Vantone

Via Vantome, 45, 25074 Idro (BS) (Lombardy)

The German company Azur have some 20 sites in the home country and just two in Italy, of which this is one. Lake Idro, one of the smaller of the northern Italian lakes, is tucked away in the mountains to the west of the better known Lake Garda. Rio Vantone is situated on the southeast shore of the lake with marvellous views across the water to the small villages on the opposite bank and surrounding mountains. The ground slopes gently down to the water's edge with most of the 240 tourist pitches in level rows divided by hedges and a wire fence, with others between tall trees. All have electricity (6/10A) and there are ten with water and drainage as well. The ones nearest the lake attract a higher charge. Being away from the main highways the site is more suitable for longer stays than one night stops but it is a peaceful spot in which to relax and from which to explore the countryside and nearby small towns. The lake is ideal for windsurfing and the surrounding countryside for walking and climbing. There are 30 tour operator tents but these are not intrusive.

Facilities

The main, heated sanitary block occupies the ground floor of a large building and is of excellent quality with all the usual facilities, including en-suite cabins (WC, washbasin and shower) and special ones for children. A smaller block is also open in high season. Facilities for disabled people. Washing machines and dryer. Motorcaravan services. Gas supplies. Cooking rings. Well stocked shop (all season). Excellent restaurant just outside the entrance (1/6-10/9). Daily programme for children in high season. Windsurf school. Boat and mountain bike hire. Volleyball and badminton. Paddling pool and playground (supervision is needed as the entry is near a boat slip-way down to the lake). Torches useful in some areas. Off site: Fishing 1.5 km.

At a glance

| Welcome & Ambience | ✓✓✓✓ | Location | ✓✓✓✓ |
| Quality of Pitches | ✓✓✓✓ | Range of Facilities | ✓✓✓✓ |

Directions

From A4 Milan - Venice motorway, take 'Brescia Est' exit. Go north on SS 45bis towards Salo then SS237 via Vobarno and Barge to Lemprato. Rio Vantone is at the southeast corner of the lake after camps Belvedere and Pineta. From Brescia, follow signs 'Lago d'Idro'.

Charges 2003

Per person	€ 4.50 - € 6.50
child (2-12 yrs)	€ 3.50 - € 5.00
pitch (acc. to position, facilities and season)	€ 5.00 - € 26.00
electricity	€ 2.20
dog	€ 2.20

Camping Cheques accepted.

Reservations

Write to site. Tel: 036 583125. Email: idro@azur-camping.de.

Open

15 April - 15 November.

IT6259 Camping Punta d'Oro

Via Antonioli 51-53, 25049 Iseo (Lombardy)

Camping Punta d'Oro, at the town of Iseo in the southeast corner of the lake, is a small, delightful campsite, which has been run by the professional Brescianini-Zatti family for the last 30 years. It slopes gently down to the lake from the railway line (they say, an infrequent local service) and there could be some road noise. The very pretty site, adorned with trees and plants, has 64 grass pitches (with just 15 static caravans) on either side of decorative brick roads. Electrical connections are available and trees at the corners define the places. There is a lakeside area on the northeast boundary but pitches at the water's edge are more expensive. There are excellent views across the lake to wooded mountains on the opposite shore where small villages shelter down by the water and further mountains rise behind the site. It is a good centre for exploring around the lake. With no enter-tainment programme, this could well suit those who are looking for a very pleasant base without the activity of a larger site.

Facilities

The two small sanitary blocks have been refurbished to a high standard with a mix of British and Turkish style WCs and hot water in washbasins, showers, dishwashing and laundry sinks. All these services were immaculate when seen. Washing machine. Motorcaravan services. Shop. Small bar/restaurant with a terrace. Games room. TV in bar. Access to lake for swimming, fishing with two narrow slipways for boat launching. Off site: Bicycle hire 500 m. Riding 1.5 km. Golf 5 km.

At a glance

| Welcome & Ambience | ✓✓✓✓✓ | Location | ✓✓✓✓ |
| Quality of Pitches | ✓✓✓✓ | Range of Facilities | ✓✓✓ |

Directions

Leave A4 (Milan-Venice) autostrada at Ospitaletto exit, go north to Rodengo and then take SS510 to Iseo. Punta d'Oro is at northern end of town - cross the railway line and turn right at corner where site is signed. Care should be taken on entry as this is tight for large units.

Charges 2003

Per person	€ 4.20 - € 6.20
child (1-9 yrs)	€ 3.40 - € 4.80
pitch acc. to size and season	€ 8.50 - € 15.50
dog	€ 1.70 - € 2.80

Electricity (5A) included.

Reservations

Write to site. Tel: 030 980084. Email: info@puntadoro.com

Open

1 April - 31 October.

IT6261 Camping Del Sole

Via per Rovato, 26, 25049 Iseo (BS) (Lombardy)

Del Sole lies on the southern edge of Lake Iseo, just outside the pretty lakeside town of Iseo, and enjoys direct access to the lake. In total the site has 360 pitches, some taken up with chalets and mobile homes, and many with fine views of the surrounding mountains. Pitches are generally flat and of a reasonable size, most with electrical connections. The site has a good range of leisure amenities, notably a large swimming pool and smaller childrens' pool. A good supermarket is open for most of the season, and there is a bar/restaurant with pizzeria, and a snack bar by the beach. A lively entertainment programme and excursions around the lake are organised, notably to Lake Iseo's three islands and the wine cellars of Franciacorta.

Facilities

Sanitary facilities are modern and well maintained, including special facilities for disabled visitors. Washing machines and dryers. Bar, restaurant, pizzeria and snack bar. Supermarket. Motorcaravan service point. Bicycle and pedal boat hire. Tennis. Volleyball. Off site: Golf 5 km. Riding 6 km.

At a glance

Welcome & Ambience	✓✓✓	Location	✓✓✓✓✓
Quality of Pitches	✓✓✓	Range of Facilities	✓✓✓✓

Directions

Exit Milan - Venice A4 autostrada at Rovato exit. Head towards Lago d'Iseo for 12 km. and the site is well signed.

Charges 2003

Per person	€ 7.50
child	€ 7.00
pitch incl. electricity	€ 16.00
small pitch	€ 13.00

Reductions in low season.
Camping Cheques accepted.

Reservations

Contact site. Tel: 030 980288.
Email: info@campingdelsole.it

Open

1 April - 21 September.

Trentino-Alt0 Adige is a mixed German-Italian region, much of which has only been part of Italy since 1919. The landscape is dominated by the majestic Dolomites, snow-clad in winter and carpeted with Alpine plants in summer.

There are two provinces in the region: Bolanzo and Trento

Before 1919 Alto Adige was known as the South Tyrol and formed part of Austria. However, at the end of the First World War Austria ceded it to the Italians. As a result there are marked cultural differences between the provinces as reflected in the cuisine, architecture and language (both German and Italian are spoken).

The landscape of Trentino-Alto Adige is dramatic and amongst the most beautiful in the country. With only a couple of snow-free months a year, the region is a skiing and winter sports haven, and there is also a good network of well established trails, which vary in length from a day's walk to a two-week trek or longer. Covering the whole Ortles range and topped by one of Europe's largest glaciers is the Stelvio National Park. One of Italy's major parks, it is popular with skiers, walkers and cyclists; the annual Giro d'Italia passes through here, Italy's answer to the Tour de France. It also boasts an abundant wildlife, with red deer, elk, chamois, golden eagles and ibex. There are several other parks in the region including the Panevéggio National park, a predominantly forested area with numerous nature trials, a lake and a visitors' centre.

Cuisine of the region

The food is a mix of Germanic and Italian influences. Traditional dishes include game and rabbit with polenta, sauerkraut, and sausages with horseradish sauce (*salsa al cren*). Desserts are often based on apples, pears or plums readily available from the local orchards. The region also produces a variety of wines including the famous Pinot Grigios and Chardonnays.

Apfel strudel: apple pastry

Canederli: bread dumplings flavoured with smoked ham

Soffiato alla Trentino: meringue trifle

Strangolapreti: bread and spinach gnocchi

Places of interest

Bolzano: 15th century church, archaeology museum with a 5,300 year old preserved mummy

Canazei: mountainside town, good place for exploring the Dolomites

Cembra: wine-producing town

Merano: attractive spa town

Ortisei: major centre for wood carving

Roverto: 15th century castle converted into a war museum

Trento: attractive town with 13th-15th century church, Romanesque cathedral, impressive city square

tip

FOLLOW THE WINE ROAD IN TRENTINO, STOPPING OFF TO SAMPLE THE HOME-MADE FOOD AND WINE, SERVED BY THE LCOAL FARMERS AND VINEYARD OWNERS.

IT6200 Camping Olympia

39034 Toblach (Trentino-Alto Adige)

In the Dolomite mountains, Camping Olympia, always good, has been given a face-lift, including the the redesigning of the camping area and the refurbishment of the already excellent sanitary accommodation. Tall trees at each end of the site have been left, but most of those in the centre have been removed and the pitches re-laid in a regular pattern. They include 12 fully serviced ones with electricity, water, waste, gas and TV and telephone points. The static caravans are grouped together at one end leaving the centre for tourists and with a grass area at the other end for tents. An attractive centre piece has fountain surrounded by flowers. On the far side of the site, where campers can walk amidst the woods, is a little children's play area and a few animals.

Facilities

The excellent sanitary provision, on two floor levels, is housed in the main building. There are also seven cabins with WC, washbasin and shower to rent. Two small blocks at each end of the site provide further WCs and showers. Shop. Attractive restaurant is open all day, All year. Snack bar (not April/May or Oct/Nov). Tennis. Swimming pool (open when weather permits). Sauna, solarium, steam bath and whirl pools. Field for games. Table tennis. Minigolf. Fishing (on payment). Bicycle hire. Play area. Animation programme in high season for children and adults.

At a glance

Welcome & Ambience	✓✓✓✓	Location	✓✓✓
Quality of Pitches	✓✓✓✓	Range of Facilities	✓✓✓✓

Directions

Site is between Villabassa and Toblach/Dobbiaco. From A22 Innsbruck-Bolzano autostrada, take Bressanone/Brixen exit and travel east on SS49 for about 60 km. From Cortina take SS48 and SS51 northwards then west on SS49.

Charges 2003

Per person	€ 6.20 - € 7.23
child (3-12 yrs)	€ 3.62 - € 5.17
pitch	€ 8.26 - € 11.36
small tent pitch	€ 5.16 - € 8.26
dog	€ 4.13

Reservations

Write to site. Tel: 0474 972147.
Email: intercamp@dnet.it

Open

All year.

IT6201 Camping Antholz

39030 Antholz (Trentino-Alto Adige)

Appearances can be deceptive and this is the case with Camping Antholz, an all year campsite in the heart of the Dolomites. At first sight the 130 pitches, numbered but only roughly marked out, make this a very ordinary looking campsite. Just inside the entrance is a pleasant looking building with reception and a smart restaurant. It is when one investigates the sanitary accommodation that one realises that this is no ordinary site, as the provision is quite superb. High up in the Anterselva valley, the site has splendid views of near and distant peaks. There are few trees on the site but many provide a nice background. The pitches have electrical connections. This is good skiing country in winter (ski bus, ski school, ski lifts) and, with a new National Park near, provides good walking in summer.

Facilities

The toilet block with under-floor heating, in addition to the normal facilities, also provides a hair salon, cosmetics room and a baby room. Washing machine and dryer. Motor-caravan services. Restaurant (all year). Shop for basics. Playground. TV room. Table tennis. Bicycle hire. Limited entertainment programme for children in high season. Off site: Tennis near. Winter sports, summer walking.

At a glance

Welcome & Ambience	✓✓✓	Location	✓✓✓✓
Quality of Pitches	✓✓✓	Range of Facilities	✓✓✓

Directions

From Bressanone exit on A22, go east on SS49 through Brunico and turn north (signed Antholz) for about 12 km. Pass Antholz village and site is on right.

Latest charges

Per unit incl. 2 persons and electricity (4A)	€ 18.07 - € 22.21
extra person	€ 4.39 - € 5.68
child (2-12 yrs)	€ 3.09 - € 3.87
dog	€ 2.32 - € 2.58

Reservations

Write to site. Tel: 0474 492204.
Email: info@camping-antholz.com

Open

All year.

41

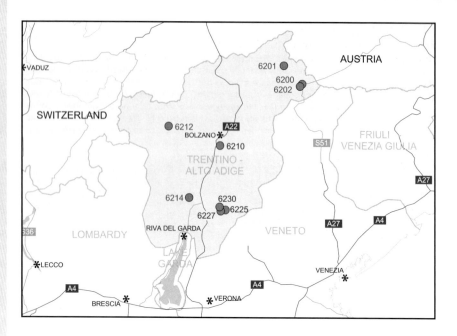

IT6202 Camping Toblacher See

Toblacher See 3, 39034 Toblach-Dobbiaco (Trentino-Alto Adige)

Camping Toblachersee is situated between the busy SS51 and a small, quiet lake surrounded by mountains. The 190 pitches, except for a small grass area for tents, are all on hardstandings of sharp, white gravel and, as these slope, levellers are required. All have electricity and 20 have water and drainage. The bar, restaurant and takeaway with terrace is pleasantly situated by the lakeside with scenic views across the water to the mountains beyond. Undoubtedly the crowning glory of this site is its splendid toilet block where all facilities are in private cabins. Unless you wish to linger by the lake or are a bird watcher, this is more a site from which to explore the area, go climbing, walking or mountain biking or skiing in winter than stay on all day although there is some entertainment during August.

Facilities

A single toilet block (mentioned above) also includes a washing machine and dryer and facilities for disabled visitors. Family bathrooms for hire. Shop with basic supplies. Bar/restaurant and takeaway (closed Mondays). Pizzeria. Bicycle hire. Fishing. Cross country ski slopes. Guided walks. Barbecues are not permitted. Off site: Riding 20 km. Golf 30 km.

At a glance

Welcome & Ambience	✓✓✓✓	Location	✓✓✓✓✓
Quality of Pitches	✓✓✓	Range of Facilities	✓✓✓

Directions

Leave the A22 [Brenner-Bolzano] motorway at Bressanone. Go east on SS49 to Toblach/Dobbiaco and south on SS51 towards Cortina for 2.5 km; site on right.

Charges 2003

Per person	€ 5.90 - € 8.90
child (10-16 yrs)	€ 4.90 - € 7.90
child (2-9 yrs)	€ 3.90 - € 6.90
pitch for caravan or motorcaravan	€ 8.50 - € 11.50
pitch for tent	€ 5.50 - € 7.50
electricity per kw. hour	€ 0.60
local tax	€ 0.60

Package deal available for 3, 4 or 6 days including half-board, an excursion and guided mountain bike tour. Camping Cheques accepted.

Reservations

Contact site. Tel: 0474 972294. Email: camping@toblachersee.com

Open

All year.

42

IT6210 Camping Steiner

Kennedy Straße 32, 39055 Laives (Bolzano) (Trentino-Alto Adige)

Being on the main S12 which now has a motorway alternative, Camping Steiner is very central for touring with the whole of the Dolomite region within easy reach. It has its share of overnight trade but, with much on site activity, one could spend an enjoyable holiday. It is a smallish site with part taken up by bungalows. The individual tourist pitches, mostly with good shade and hardstanding, are in rows on either side of access roads. There are electricity connections. The site becomes full in season. It is run personally by the proprietor's family who provide a friendly reception, with good English spoken.

Facilities

The two sanitary blocks, one new, can be heated in cool weather. Excellent small restaurant and takeaway service, with good choice. Cellar bar with taped music, dancing at times. Shop. Two free swimming pools on the site – an open air one, 20 x 10 m. (open May-Sept. and heated in spring), and a 12 x 6 m. enclosed, heated pool (open all season, except July/Aug). Playground and paddling pool. Table tennis. Off site: 18 hole golf course is 30 minutes away.

At a glance

Welcome & Ambience	✓✓✓✓	Location	✓✓✓✓
Quality of Pitches	✓✓✓	Range of Facilities	✓✓✓

Directions

Site is on S12 in northern part of Leifers, 8 km. south of Bolzano. From motorway if approaching from north, take Bolzano-Süd exit and follow Trento signs for 7 km; from south take Ora exit and proceed for 14 km. towards Bolzano.

Latest charges

Per person	€ 5.00 - € 6.00
child (0-9 yrs)	€ 3.00 - € 4.00
pitch incl. car and 6A electricity	€ 10.00 - € 12.00
dog	€ 5.00

Less in low season. Less 5-10% after 2 weeks stay.

Reservations

Made for min. one week with reasonable deposit. Tel: 0471 950105. Email: steiner@dnet.it

Open

28 March - 7 November.

IT6212 Camping Latsch an der Etsch

Reichstraße 4, 39021 Laces-Latsch (Trentino-Alto Adige)

An enthusiastic reader's report on this site prompted a visit and we found, as suggested, a delightful little campsite. Latsch (or Laces) is situated in the Venosta Valley and Gasthof Camping Latsch is 640 m. above sea level between the SS38 road and the river, with splendid views across to the surrounding mountains. About 20 of the 120 tourist pitches are on a terrace by reception with the remainder on a lower terrace alongside the river. They are in regular rows which are separated by hedges with thin grass on gravel. All have electricity connections (and 47 also have water, drainage, sewage and TV points. Trees provide shade to some parts. A unique feature of the site is the large underground car park which protects vehicles from winter snow and summer sun and, if used, gives a reduction in pitch charges. Another interesting feature is a water wheel which provides three kw of power and this is supplemented by solar heating. Although right by a main road, the Gasthof and terracing screen out most of the road noise. The friendly, English speaking owner has created a very pleasant ambience and appeared very popular with those staying there. Mountain walkers will be in their element and several chair-lifts give access to higher slopes. Interesting drives can be made over nearby passes with Merano, Bolzano, the Dolomites and the duty-free town of Livigno within range.

Facilities

The modern sanitary block is on two floors (to serve each section) has all the usual facilities and is heated in cool weather. Twenty excellent private bathrooms (basin, shower, toilet) are for hire. Motorcaravan service point. Washing machine and dryer. Bar and pleasant restaurant (all season). Shop. Small heated indoor pool, plus sauna, solarium and fitness room. Larger, irregularly shaped outdoor pool with marble surrounds, small waterfall and sunbathing area. Playground. Off site: Bowling, fishing (licence), tennis, golf and riding near.

At a glance

Welcome & Ambience	✓✓✓✓	Location	✓✓✓✓
Quality of Pitches	✓✓✓	Range of Facilities	✓✓✓

Directions

Latsch/Laces is 28 km. east of Merano on SS38 Bolzano-Silandro road. Site entrance on the right of the Gasthof (keep on main road, don't turn off to village).

Charges 2003

Per person	€ 5.20 - € 6.20
child (2-12 yrs)	€ 4.20 - € 5.70
electricity (6A)	€ 2.10
dog	€ 4.40 - € 5.20

Reservations

Contact site. Tel: 0473 623 217. Email: camping.latsch@dnet.it

Open

All year except 8 Nov - 15 Dec.

IT6214 Camping Spiaggia Lago di Molveno

Via Lungolago 25, 38018 Molveno (Trentino-Alto Adige)

This site was recommended to us by a reader and when we visited it we could see why. Camping Spiaggia is on the edge of the pretty little village of Molveno on the lake of the same name and is run by a company set up and controlled by the local authority to promote tourism in the area. It occupies a most scenic location at the foot of the Brenta mountains with views across the lake. It is an attractive site, adorned with plants and trees and has 132 tourist pitches, with about the same number of static caravans, on level grass, marked and separated with each having an electrical connection (4A). Right next to the site is a sports complex with free access for campers to the tennis courts and heated swimming pool (15/6-8/9). In June and September and week-ends during May and October a free return ticket is given for the funicular to Pradel in the Brenta Parco Naturali. Being open all year it is an ideal location from which to ski in winter or to go walking and climbing in summer.

Facilities

Three modern, heated toilet blocks have free hot water. Facilities for disabled visitors. Well stocked shop (open all year). Attractive bar/restaurant with takeaway (closed October, November and weekends in winter. Playground. In June, August and September entertainment is organised in the village for children and adults. Off site: Just outside the site is a football field, bowls, volleyball, basketball, minigolf and pedalos and boats for hire.

At a glance

| Welcome & Ambience | ✓✓✓✓✓ | Location | ✓✓✓✓ |
| Quality of Pitches | ✓✓✓✓ | Range of Facilities | ✓✓✓✓ |

Directions

From A22 (Brenner - Modena) motorway leave at exit for S. Michele north of Trento and head northwest on SS43 - signed Val di Non - and then SP64 following signs to Moveno and site.

Latest charges

Per person	€ 4.50 - € 8.00
child (3-12 yrs)	€ 3.00 - € 5.50
pitch	€ 5.50 - € 12.00
dog	€ 1.00 - € 2.50

Reservations

Contact site. Tel: 0461 586 978.
Email: camping@molveno.it

Open

All year.

IT6225 Camping Due Laghi

Localita Costa 3, 38056 Levico Terme (Trentino-Alto Adige)

This good, modern site is close to the main road but is quiet, with mountain views and only five minutes walk from the Levico lake where it has a small private beach where one can put boats. A most attractive site with a variety of trees and flowers, there are 426 numbered pitches on flat grass, in rows marked by slabs and all with electricity (3/6A). Most are said to be around 80 sq.m. but there are 60 larger pitches (90 sq.m) with electricity, water, TV and phone connections. The site has a good swimming pool, so it may be suitable for a stay as well as overnight. It is said to become full from 15 July - 5 August, but there is always a chance of finding space. The site supplies a comprehensive descriptive guide to the attractions of the region. English is spoken.

Facilities

The central toilet block is both of good quality and very large, with British and Turkish type WCs, some washbasins in cubicles and a unit for disabled people. The hot water supply can be variable. Some private WCs may be hired. Laundry. Gas supplies. Motorcaravan services. Shop. Restaurant, pizzeria and café/bar with takeaway. Music weekly in high season. Swimming pool (over 300 sq.m) and children's pool. Sauna. Playground. Tennis. Bicycle hire. Off site: Walks from site. Fishing 500 m. Riding 2 km. Golf 5 km.

At a glance

| Welcome & Ambience | ✓✓✓ | Location | ✓✓✓ |
| Quality of Pitches | ✓✓✓✓ | Range of Facilities | ✓✓✓✓ |

Directions

Site is 20 km. southeast of Trento just off S47 road towards Padova (camp sign at turning).

Charges 2003

Per person	€ 6.00 - € 8.50
child (2-8 yrs)	€ 4.00 - € 4.50
child (9-16 yrs)	€ 5.00 - € 6.00
pitch	€ 7.00 - € 15.00
dog	€ 2.00 - € 3.00

Club card for entertainment, activities, etc. obligatory in July/Aug. Discounts for longer stays in low season. Camping Cheques accepted.

Reservations

Made for at least 1 week in peak season, with substantial deposit and fee. Tel: 0461 706290. Email: cduelaghi@tin.it

Open

18 May - 15 September.

IT6227 Camping Al Pescatore

Via dei Pescatori 1, 38050 Calceranica al Lago (Trentino-Alto Adige)

The small lake of Calceranica lies just to the east of Trento in the foothills of the Dolomites amidst splendid scenery. Camping Al Pescatore is a very pretty, small campsite about 50 metres from the lake where swimming and watersports can be enjoyed. There are 173 tourist pitches on grass under tall trees some of which are in an over-flow section immediately opposite the entrance and all have electricity connections (4A). The lakeside is very popular at weekends and during our visit on a Sunday in mid-June, a many people were enjoying the scenery and the two large restaurants opposite the beach were both very busy, although it was peaceful on the site. In July and August a small bar and shop are open. A friendly site, English is spoken at reception.

Facilities

The two toilet blocks on the main site provide the usual facilities and there is a single unisex block in the overflow section. Facilities for disabled visitors. Washing machines. Shop and bar July/Aug. Playground. In July and August there are organised activities for children and music and dancing for adults.

At a glance

Welcome & Ambience	✓✓✓✓	Location	✓✓✓✓
Quality of Pitches	✓✓✓	Range of Facilities	✓✓✓

Directions

Leave A22 (Brenner - Modena) motorway at Trento Nord, follow SS47 in the direction of Padova to S. Cristoforo and follow signs to Calceranica and site.

Charges 2003

Per adult	€ 6.00
child (under 12 yrs)	€ 5.50
pitch	free - € 8.30
dog	€ 2.60

Reservations

Contact site. Tel: 0461 723062.
Email: trentino@campingpescatore.it

Open

16 May - 16 September.

IT6230 Camping San Cristoforo

Via dei Pescatori, 38057 Pergine Valsugana (Trentino-Alto Adige)

Lake Caldonazzo is one of the smaller lakes, but is excellent for watersports, with lifeguards on duty in the season. Camping San Cristoforo is a relatively new site on the edge of the small town of the same name and is separated from the lake by a minor road, but with easy access. Owned by the friendly Oss family whose policy is to get to know their guests and build a family atmosphere, the site has 160 pitches. On flat grass on either side of hard access roads and separated by trees, the pitches are of a good size, numbered in front and with 3A electricity. The lake is very close offering watersports and fishing. This quiet mountain site has a well cared for air and English is spoken. Used by a tour operator.

Facilities

The modern sanitary block provides some washbasins in cabins. Dishwashing and laundry sinks. Facilities for disabled people. Washing machine and dryer. Small well stocked shop. Attractive bar/restaurant (all year) by the pool with terrace, serving reasonably priced food and takeaway. Swimming pool (20 x 20 m.) with sunbathing area and small children's pool. Bicycle hire. Minigolf. Off site: Village shops close. Fishing and boating 200 m. Golf 2 km. Riding 5 km.

At a glance

Welcome & Ambience	✓✓✓	Location	✓✓✓✓
Quality of Pitches	✓✓✓✓	Range of Facilities	✓✓✓✓

Directions

Site is southeast of Trento, just off the SS47 road; well signed from the village of San Cristoforo.

Charges 2004

Per person	€ 6.00 - € 8.00
child (2-5 yrs)	€ 4.00 - € 5.00
child (6-11 yrs)	€ 5.00 - € 6.00
pitch	€ 10.00 - € 12.80
dog	€ 2.00 - € 3.00

Discounts for longer stays in low season.

Reservations

Not accepted. Tel: 0461 512707.
Email: info@campingclub.it

Open

29 May - 5 September.

IT6232 Camping Al Sole

38060 Molina di Ledro (Trentino-Alto Adige)

Lake Ledro is only nine kilometres from Lake Garda, its sparkling waters and breathtaking scenery offering a low key alternative for those who enjoy a natural setting. The drive from Lake Garda is a real pleasure and prepares you for the treat ahead. This site has been owned by the same friendly family for over 30 years and their experience shows in the layout of the site with its mature trees and the array of facilities provided. Situated on the lake with its own pretty grass and sand beach, the facilities are constantly upgraded and include a new pool and a children's play area. It came as no surprise to hear that many people choose to return to Camping Al Sole year after year. The local community welcomes tourists and offers free hiking programmes beginning with a Monday evening information night so that you can choose the most appropriate guided walks. A very nice peaceful site for extended stays or sightseeing.

Facilities

The new sanitary block has plenty of hot water and good facilities for disabled campers. Washing machines. Freezer. Small supermarket. Pleasant restaurant and pizzeria with outdoor terrace. Bar serving snacks and takeaway. Large screen TV. New swimming pool with sunbeds and shower. Play area. Table tennis. Lake for swimming, boating, windsurfing, fishing and canoeing. Live music and dancing twice weekly in July/Aug. Torches needed in some areas. Bicycle hire. Off site: Pedaloes for hire nearby. The area is also ideal for hiking, mountain biking, climbing and canyoning. Riding 2 km. Golf 20 km.

At a glance

Welcome & Ambience	✓✓✓✓	Location	✓✓✓✓
Quality of Pitches	✓✓✓✓	Range of Facilities	✓✓✓✓

Directions

From autostrada A22 exit for Lake Garda North to Riba del Garda. In Riva follow sign for Ledro valley. Site is well signed as you approach Lago di Ledra.

Charges 2003

Per person	€ 5.00 - € 6.50
child (3-12 yrs)	€ 4.00 - € 5.00
Per pitch	€ 6.50 - € 8.50
dog	€ 3.50 - € 4.50

Electricity included.

Reservations

Advised for high season. Tel: 0464 508496.
Email: info@campingalsole.it

Open

20 April - 30 September.

The largest and cleanest of the Italian lakes, Lake Garda is also the most popular. The low-lying countryside of the southern stretches give way to the dramatic, craggy mountains of the north, while the western shore is fringed with olive groves, vines and citrus trees.

In this popular tourist region we have included the lakeside areas of the regions of Veneto, Lombardy and Trentino-Alto Adige

The lake's largest town, Desenzano del Garda, lies on the southern shore. Bars and restaurants line the lakefront and a walk to the town's castle affords spectacular views. Nearby, Sirmione is popular with those seeking cures in its sulphurous springs. It has the remains of a Roman spa plus a 13th century fairy-tale castle, which is almost entirely surrounded by water. Along the sheltered stretch of the western shore, otherwise known as the Riviera Bresciana, are the lush groves and fruit trees; Saló is a good place to stock up on the local produce. Gardone is best known for its exotic botanical garden and Il Vittoriale, the home of the notorious writer Gabriel D'Annunzio, which is filled with curiosities. Up in the mountains behind Gardone is the little alpine village of San Michele, and there are good walks to the springs and waterfalls in the surrounding hills. At the northwest tip of the lake, Riva del Garda is one of the best known resorts and a favourite with windsurfers, as is Torbole, where sailing and mountain biking are popular too. On the eastern shore, Malcesine boasts a 13th century turreted castle and a funicular, which climbs to the summit of Monte Baldo, offering panoramic views. And near the lively resort of Garda, are white shingle beaches and small coves.

Cuisine of the region

Fish is popular; there are 40 different species in the lake including carp, trout, eels and pike. Regional dishes include trout filled with oranges and lemons, risotto with tench, and *sisam,* a traditional way of preparing lake minnows. The fruits grown on the western shore are used to make olive oil, citrus syrups and Bardolino, Soave and Valpolicella wines.

Places of interest

Bardolino: home of the light, red Bardolino wine, Festival of the Grape is held between Sept-Oct

Gargano: olive factory, 13th century church, good place for sailing

Peschiera: attractive enclosed harbour and fortress

Puegnago del Garda: home of Comincioli vineyard that has been producing wine since the 16th century

Torri del Benaco: considered to be the prettiest lakeside town, with old centre, cobbled streets and castle

tip

VISIT GARDALAND, ITALY'S MOST POPULAR AMUSEMENT PARK AT CASTELNUOVO DEL GARDA, WHICH ATTRACTS TWO MILLION VISITORS A YEAR.

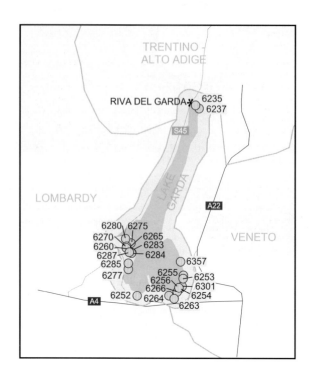

IT6235 Camping Monte Brione

Via Brione 32, 38066 Riva del Garda (Trentino-Alto Adige)

The small resort of Riva lies at the head of Lake Garda. Although it lacks the sophistication of the southern end of the lake, it is a picturesque tourist resort, popular with windsurfers. Thus, this end of the lake tends to have a younger clientele and there is a late night vibrancy. A municipal site, Camping Monte Brione is situated on the edge of town at the foot of an olive covered hill, about 500 m. from the town centre and lake side. There are 131 pitches on flat, well mown grass, marked by trees and posts in groups of four around a water and electricity (6A) service point. Unmarked terraces on the hillside take 21 tents. Good tarmac roads dissect the site which has a neat, well tended air. Although near residential developments, there are good views of the mountains.

Facilities

Two sanitary blocks, which will be due for refurbishment soon, are at either end of the site and have mixed Turkish and British style WCs, washbasins in cabins, and facilities for disabled people. Motorcaravan services. Shop for basic supplies. Snack bar, bar and covered terrace. Good sized swimming pool with a sunbathing area (1/6-30/9). Minigolf. Table tennis. Bowls. TV/video. Bicycle hire. Two play areas. Off site: The town has many shops and restaurants and is popular with the young windsurfers. Fishing 1 km. Riding 3 km. Sailing, boating and tennis near.

At a glance

Welcome & Ambience	√√√	Location	√√√√
Quality of Pitches	√√√√	Range of Facilities	√√√

Directions

Leave A22 at Garda-Nord exit for Torbole and Riva. Just before Riva, through short tunnel, then turn right at camp signs.

Latest charges

Per person	€ 6.70
child (4-12 yrs)	€ 4.40
pitch	€ 8.80 - € 10.35
dog	€ 3.30
Less 15% in low season.	

Reservations

Write to site with 20% deposit (refundable) of anticipated bill. Tel: 0464 520885.
Email: campingbrione@rivadelgarda.com

Open

Easter/1 April - early October.

IT6237 Camping Al Porto

38069 Torbole (Trentino-Alto Adige)

This is a small unassuming site built on what was the owner's family farm fifty years ago. It is peaceful, set back from the main road, and close to the water. Lake access is about 80 metres along a road to the rear of the site and here there is a slow shelving beach ideal for launching windsurfers (the area is a mecca for windsurfing). Near the modern reception there is a small bar and terrace area where coffee and basic snacks are served. Although the services on site are limited there is a choice of places to eat in Torbole. The grass pitches are level with mature trees providing shade. Hedges separate the two camping areas, one with numbered pitches with electricity for tourers. The other area, less formal area is primarily for tents (no electricity) has a secure hut for windsurfing equipment to one side. A no frills site which is good for stop-overs and excellent for windsurfers.

Facilities
The clean, modern sanitary block has British and Turkish style WCs and hot water throughout. Facilities for disabled campers. Washing machines. Motorcaravan services. Bar with snacks incl. light breakfasts. Play area. Off site: Swimming, windsurfing and sailing in the lake. Mountain biking, hiking, climbing, canoeing, canyoning and fishing nearby. Shops and cafés a short walk.

At a glance
Welcome & Ambience	✓✓✓✓	Location	✓✓✓✓
Quality of Pitches	✓✓✓✓	Range of Facilities	✓✓✓

Directions
Site is on the northeast tip of Lake Garda. Take Roverto south exit for Lake Garda north, then A240 for Nago. From Nago to Torbole and leave Torbole in direction of Riva del Garda. Site is immediately on left before the town exit bridge.

Charges 2004
Per pitch	€ 9.00
adult	€ 6.50
child (1-12 yrs)	€ 5.00
dog	€ 2.00
electricity	€ 0.50
sailing boat	€ 3.00

Discounts in low season. No credit cards.

Reservations
Not taken. Tel: 0464 505891.
Email: alporto@torbole.com

Open
1 April - 6 November.

IT6252 Camping San Francesco

Strada Vicinale, 25015 Rivoltella (Lombardy)

This large, well organised site is situated to the west of the Simione peninsula on the southwest shores of Lake Garda. This position allows wonderful views of the lake. The Facchini family used to grow grapes for Lagana wine on this land, their aim is now to ensure you enjoy your stay. This impressive site has 308 marked pitches which are generally on flat gravel and sand, enjoying natural shade from mature trees. The pitches are generally of average size, a new system in part of the site offering three types of pitch from 'lakeside large', through superior to standard. All have electricity (6A) and easy access. A private wooded beach area of about 400 m. on the lake can be used for sunbathing, windsurfing, canoeing, sailing and power-boating; it also has a jetty for boating. The management maintain rescue boats for water activities on the lake, despite the fact that there is no legal requirement for this. The site's well equipped sports centre, accessed via a tunnel under the road, includes three large, supervised pools, a larger one with an impressive island, one for children, plus a separate area for organised water activities. Near the pool complex is an equally impressive entertainment area. There may be some noise disturbance from an adjoining holiday complex in high season (but not after 11 pm).

Facilities
Sanitary facilities are in two large, identical, centrally located buildings. Very clean when seen, they offer every facility a camper could want with hot water at all points. Excellent facilities for disabled campers. Shop. Restaurant. Bar. Pizzeria and snacks. Takeaway. Swimming pools (15/4-20/9) and jacuzzi. Sports centre, football stadium, tennis. Playground. Entertainment programme, organised activities and excursions. Big screen satellite TV. RC chapel in high season. Torches required in some areas. The large, busy reception will advise and organise any of the myriad of activities, tours and ferry trips. Bicycle hire. Off site: Riding 5 km. Golf 10 km.

At a glance
Welcome & Ambience	✓✓✓✓✓	Location	✓✓✓✓✓
Quality of Pitches	✓✓✓✓	Range of Facilities	✓✓✓✓✓

Directions
From autostrada A4, between Brescia and Verona, exit towards Sirmione and take S11 to Rivoltella. Site well signed.

Charges 2003
Per person	€ 5.40 - € 8.80
child (under 6 yrs)	free - € 7.70
pitch incl. electricity	€ 11.30 - € 19.10
superior pitch	€ 13.30 - € 22.70

Camping Cheques accepted.

Reservations
Contact site. Tel: 0309 110245.
Email: info@campingsanfrancesco.it

Open
1 April - 30 September.

IT6254 Camping Lido

Via Peschiera 2, 37017 Pacengo (Veneto)

Camping Lido is one of the largest and best of the 120 campsites around Lake Garda and is situated in the southeast corner of the lake. There is quite a slope from the entrance down to the lake so many of the 700 grass touring are on terraces which give lovely views across the lake. The pitches are of varying size, separated by hedges and all have electrical connections (5A). This is a most attractive site with tall, neatly trimmed trees standing like sentinels on either side of the broad avenue which runs from the entrance right down to the lake. A wide variety of trees provide shade on some pitches and flowers add to the overall appearance. Near the top of the site is a large, well designed pool and a fitness centre. The site has its own beach with a landing stage that marks off a large area for swimming on one side and on the other an area where boats can be moored. Every night in high season there is a free bus service for teenagers to a local disco returning at 2 am. One could happily spend all the holiday here without leaving the site but with so many attractions nearby this would be a pity.

Facilities

Seven modern toilet blocks have the usual facilities including provision for disabled visitors and three family rooms with baths. Washing machines and dryer. Fridge rental. Restaurant, bars, pizzeria, takeaway and well stocked supermarket. Swimming pool and children's pool. Fitness centre with fully equipped gym, sauna and Turkish bath. Playground. Football field. Tennis. Bicycle hire. Watersports. Fishing (permit required). Volleyball. High season organised activities for children and adults. Shingle beach with private landing stage for boats. Dogs are not accepted in high season (6/7-15/8). Off site: Gardaland Theme Park, Verona.

At a glance

Welcome & Ambience	✓✓✓✓✓	Location	✓✓✓✓
Quality of Pitches	✓✓✓✓	Range of Facilities	✓✓✓✓

Directions

Leave A4 Milan - Venice motorway at exit for Peschiera. Head north on east side of lake on SS249. Site entrance on left after Gardaland Theme Park.

Charges 2003

Per person	€ 4.10 - € 5.90
child (3-5 yrs)	free - € 3.60
pitch incl. services	€ 8.00 - € 14.20

Reservations

Contact site. Tel: 045 759 0030.
Email: info@campinglido.it

Open

1 April - 18 October.

IT6253 Camping Piani di Clodia

Localita Bagatta, 37017 Lazise (Veneto)

Piani di Clodia is one of the best large sites at Lake Garda giving a positive impression of space and cleanliness. It is located on a slope between Lazise and Peschiera in the southeast corner of the lake, with lovely views across the water to Sirmione's peninsula and the opposite shore. You are greeted at the gate by English speaking attendants who are keen to please, as are reception staff. The site is very close to Gardaland, one of the biggest theme parks in Europe and the huge Caneva aqua park. The rectangular site slopes down to the water's edge and has over 1,000 pitches, all with electricity (5A), terraced where necessary and back to back from hard access roads. There is some shade from mature and young trees. The pool complex is truly wonderful with three pools, the whole area being fenced and supervised, with a pleasant sunbathing area and bar. At the centre of the site is a quality rooftop restaurant, huge lower self service restaurant plus pizzeria and table service for drinks. From most of this area you will be able to enjoy the free entertainment on the large stage. The enthusiastic animation team provide an ambitious variety of entertainment. There is a fence between the site and the lake with access points to a private beach and opportunities for a variety of watersports.

Facilities

Seven modern, immaculate sanitary blocks are well spaced around the site with a mix of British and Turkish style WCs and hot water in washbasins, sinks and showers. All have facilities for disabled visitors and one has a baby room. Washing machines, dryers and laundry service. Motor-caravan services. Shopping complex with supermarket, general shops for clothes, etc. Two bars. Self-service restaurant with takeaway and pizzeria and gelaterie. Swimming pools - one for straightforward swimming which can be heated, another with a variety of slides and hydro-massage and the third for children. Tennis. Table tennis. Gymnastics. Bicycle hire. Large grass space for volleyball and other ball games. Large children's playground. Outdoor theatre with animation programme. Off site: Riding near. Golf 12 km. Caneva aqua park, Gardaland theme park close by.

At a glance

Welcome & Ambience	✓✓✓✓✓	Location	✓✓✓✓
Quality of Pitches	✓✓✓	Range of Facilities	✓✓✓✓

Directions

Site is south of Lazise on road SS249 before Peschiera.

Latest charges

Per person	€ 3.39 - € 7.75
child (1-9 yrs)	€ 2.58 - € 5.16
pitch with electricity	€ 8.78 - € 18.08
pitch with electricity and water	€ 9.81 - € 19.63

Reservations

Write to site. Tel: 045 7590456.
Email: info@pianidiclodia.it

Open

20 March - 5 October.

IT6287 Camping San Biagio

Via Cavalle, 19, 25080 Manerba del Garda (Lombardy)

Recommended by our Italian Agent, this site will be inspected in 2004. San Biagio is on a peninsula at Lake Garda with direct access for swimming and boating. There are 165 individual pitches with electrical connections (3A) and a shop and bar/pizzeria.

Directions

From A4 autostrada take Desenzano exit towards Manerba where the site is signed

Charges 2003

Per person	€ 4.47
child (3-12 yrs)	€ 3.40 - € 5.50
pitch with electricity	€ 11.00 - € 15.00
pitch near the lake	€ 11.00 - € 18.50
dog	€ 2.00 - € 4.00

Reservations

Contact site, discount for 2 week stays out of high season. Contact site. Tel: 0365 551549.
Email: sanbiagiogardalake.it

Open

27 March - 30 September.

Camping San Biagio is the peninsula San Biagio with a small island. It is situated in a particular area with a beautiful panorama covered by Mediterranean vegetation, with direct access to the lake in whole camping site. Here you can find quietness and relax. Small supermarket, children's playground and buoies. Restaurant-Pizzeria in an ancient house near a small harbour. Modern sanitary facilities, also for disabled persons. In a hotel at 200 mt. bedrooms and apartments. The little island San Biagio is reachable by foot for the camping guests. There you find snacks and drinks. Booking is possible starting from February. You are welcome!

**I-25080 Manerba (BS) • Tel. in Summer 0039/0365551549
Fax 0039/0365551046 • Fax in Winter 0039/0365551046
E-mail: sanbiagio@gardalake.it
Http: www.gardalake.it/sanbiagio**

IT6301 Eurocamping Pacengo

Via del Porto 13, 37010 Pacengo di Lazise (Veneto)

Eurocamping is a large site at the south eastern corner of Lake Garda, with direct lake access, and with a pleasant private beach. It's possible to launch boats here and there is a little harbour nearby. Although not the most manicured of sites, Eurocamping is a friendly, typically Italian site and is equipped to a high standard. Expanded recently, it now includes a mobile home area. Most pitches however, although generally quite small, are attractive with reasonable shade and all have electrical connections (3A). The new swimming pool is large and popular and incorporates a jacuzzi. There is a separate children's pool with a number of water features.

Facilities

The sanitary blocks are quite old but kept clean. Bar/restaurant/pizzeria. Second bar at the poolside. Boat launching facility. Well-stocked supermarket. Large childrens' play area. Tennis court. Animation in July and August. Off site: Gardaland theme park 5km.

At a glance

Welcome & Ambience	√√√	Location	√√√√
Quality of Pitches	√√√	Range of Facilities	√√√√

Directions

Pacengo is located between Peschiera and Lazise. The site is clearly signposted from the village.

Charges 2003

Per person	€ 2.90 - € 4.00
child (2 - 8 yrs)	€ 1.75 - € 3.10
pitch	€ 6.90 - € 11.30

Reservations

Not accepted for peak season but site operates an overflow area which offers space until it is available in the main part of the site. Tel/Fax: 045 759 0012
E-mail: eurocamping.pacengo@camping.i

Open

5 April - 22 September.

the travel service
TO BOOK THIS SITE
0870 405 4055
Expert Advice & Special Offers

IT6255 Camping La Quercia

37017 Lazise sul Garda (Veneto)

A spacious, popular site on a slight slope leading down to Lake Garda, La Quercia can accommodate around 1,000 units and is decorated by palm trees and elegantly trimmed hedges. There is a strict security regime in high season with passes required at all times including the beach security points. Pitches are in regular double rows between access roads, all with electricity (4/6A). Most are shaded by mature trees, although those furthest from the lake are more open to the sun. Although siting is not always easy, staff do help in high season. La Quercia has a fine sandy beach on the lake, with diving jetties and a roped-off section for launching boats or windsurfing (high season). Much of the site a ctivity centres around the Olympic-size pool and terrace bar, restaurant and pizzeria which overlook the animation stage. A second self service restaurant is nearer the beach, part of which is dominated by a large screen TV (can have high volume settings) plus an ice-cream bar. The evening entertainment is a little daunting at first, with the young team working hard to involve everyone. The site is a short distance from the exquisite lakeside towns of Lazise and Peschiera, which have a wide choice of restaurants. La Quercia has always been a popular site and, although its prices have been quite high, it does offer a great deal for your money, including a wide choice of organised activities and amenities, most free. Many of the courses require enrolment on a Sunday. A reader reports that on Saturday nights in high season there may be some late night noise from a disco outside the site. English is spoken. Used by tour operators.

Facilities
The six toilet blocks are perfectly sufficient and are of a very high standard. Laundry. Supermarket. General shop. Bar, restaurant, self-service restaurant and pizzeria. Swimming pool, children's pool and a large, landscaped spa pool (small charge). Tennis court. Table tennis. Riding stables. Football. Aerobics and yoga. Facilities for boats on the lake. Scuba club. Playground with water play. Organised events (sports competitions, games, etc.) and free courses in swimming, surfboard. canoeing, Roller blading. tennis, archery, climbing, judo, with multi-gym, volleyball and tennis courts also available. Minigolf. Evening entertainment or dancing. Baby sitting service. Internet. ATM. Free weekly excursion. Medical service. Off site: Supermarkets en-route to Verona. 'Guardaland' supposedly the largest theme park in Italy and the enormous Caneva Aqua Park nearby.

At a glance

Welcome & Ambience	✓✓✓	Location	✓✓✓✓✓
Quality of Pitches	✓✓✓✓	Range of Facilities	✓✓✓✓✓

Directions
Site is on south side of Lazise. From north on Trento - Verona A22 autostrada take Affi exit then follow signs for Lazise and site. From south take Peschiera exit and site is 7 km. towards Garda and Lazise.

Latest charges

Per person	€ 4.80 - € 8.01
child (under 5 yrs)	€ 2.79 - € 5.37
pitch	€ 9.55 - € 18.33
reserved pitch	€ 10.59 - € 21.95

No credit cards. Low season discount for pensioners.

Reservations
Are made Sat - Sat for certain pitches.
Tel: 045 6470557.

Open
10 days before Easter - 30 September.

IT6256 Camping del Garda

Via Marzan 6, 37019 Peschiera del Garda (Veneto)

Although Camping del Garda is not directly on the lake (a cul-de-sac leading to a watersports centre runs between camp and water) it has access via a large gate to the beach and for launching boats. This is one of the largest campsites around Lake Garda and more a self contained holiday village. There are many trees, some providing shade on the 800 level grass tourist pitches which are back-to-back in 59 numbered rows. With access from hard roads and trees marking corners, all have electricity. Several days of heavy rain immediately before our visit had prevented the mowing of some pitches but other-wise it was a neat, tidy site with flower beds adding to its attraction. It is within easy walking distance of the picturesque little town of Peschiera and the busy waterfront from where boat trips can be made. There are two large swimming pools with lifeguards. A wide variety of sports is available, entertainment programmes for children and adults are provided and there is provision for boat enthusiasts to launch boats.

Facilities
Eleven good quality toilet blocks have the usual facilities with free hot water in sinks, washbasins and showers. Facilities for disabled visitors in two blocks. Washing machines and dryers. Bars, restaurant and takeaway. Supermarket. Swimming pools (from 1 June). Tennis courts and tennis school. Minigolf. Watersports including windsurf school. Fishing. Playground. Full programme of organised activities in high season. Table tennis. Bowls. Dogs or motorcycles are not accepted. Off site: Gardaland, Zoo Safari, Verona.

At a glance

Welcome & Ambience	✓✓✓✓	Location	✓✓✓✓
Quality of Pitches	✓✓✓✓	Range of Facilities	✓✓✓✓

Directions
Leave the A4 [Milan-Venice] motorway at exit for Peschiera, head towards town and follow signs from roundabout.

Latest charges

Per person	€ 4.00 - € 7.00
child (under 5 yrs)	free - € 4.50
pitch incl. electricity (4A)	€ 9.00 - € 15.00

Reservations
Contact site. Tel: 045 755 0540.
Email: campingdelgarda@icmnet.net

Open
1 April - 30 September.

IT6357 Campings Cisano & San Vito

Via Peschiera 48, 37010 Cisano di Bardolino (Veneto)

This is a combination of two sites and some of the 700 pitches have superb locations along the shaded lakeside contained in Cisano. Some are on sloping ground and most are shaded but the San Vito pitches have no lake views. Both sites have a family orientation and considerable effort has been taken in the landscaping to provide maximum comfort even for the largest units. The support facilities are constantly upgraded, although visitors with disabilities should select their pitch carefully to ensure an area appropriate to all their needs (there are some slopes in Cisano). A pleasant family style restaurant (some road noise) also sells takeaway food and is accessed through a tunnel under the road. Excellent pools and play equipment, along with a children's club and animation in high season are all here. The friendly efficient staff speak English at both sites. San Vito is the smaller and more peaceful location with no lakeside pitches and shares many of the facilities of Cisano which is a short walk across the road. Each site has its own reception and Cisano's three pools with spa are great.

Facilities

Plentiful, good quality sanitary facilities are provided in both sites (9 blocks at Cisano and 2 at San Vito) including facilities for disabled visitors. Shop, bar, restaurant (open all season). TV in restaurant. Pleasant swimming pool. Play area. Fishing and sailing from site. Free windsurfing and canoeing. Boat launching and storage. No ball games allowed on beach. Dogs are not accepted (cats are). Motorcycles not allowed on site (parking provided). Off site: Indoor pool 2 km. Bicycle hire and tennis 2 km. Riding 15 km. Golf 20 km.

At a glance

Welcome & Ambience	✓✓✓✓✓	Location	✓✓✓✓✓
Quality of Pitches	✓✓✓	Range of Facilities	✓✓✓

Directions

Leave A4 autoroute at Pescheria exit and head north towards Garda on lakeside road. Pass Lazise and site is signed (small sign) on left halfway to Bardolina. Site is 12 km. beyond the Gardaland theme park.

Charges 2003

Pitch	€ 8.00 - € 15.50
adult	€ 3.00 - € 8.00
child	free - € 4.00

Camping Cheques accepted.

Reservations

Accepted in high season only with deposit (Sat-Sat. only). Tel: 045 72 10 067.
Email: cisano@camping-cisano.it

Open

29 March - 6 October.

IT6263 Camping Bella Italia

Via Bella Italia 2, 37019 Peschiera del Garda (Veneto)

Peschiera is a picturesque village on the southern shore of Lake Garda and Camping Bella Italia is a large, well organised site, just one kilometre west from the centre of the village. In the grounds of a former farm, the site slopes gently down to the lake; ideal for swimming and boating. Although about one third of the total area is taken by the site's own accommodation (apartments and bungalows) and tour operators, there are some 850 tourist pitches, most towards the lakeside and reasonably level on grass under trees. All have electricity (3A), are separated by shrubs and numbered on the campsite plan but not on the ground. They are grouped in regular rows on either side of hard access roads which are named after composers (east side) and artists (west side) of the wide central road which leads to the shops, pleasant restaurants and terrace and entrance to lakeside path. There are fine views across the lake from many parts. A feature of the site is the group of pools of varying shape and size with an entertainment area at the road end of the site. A range of supervised activities is organised. Strict regulations (a long list is given on arrival) are in place to ensure a peaceful site particularly during the afternoon siesta and during the hours of darkness. English is spoken by the friendly management.

Facilities

Seven good sanitary blocks, including two new ones, have British style toilets, free hot water in washbasins (some in cabins), showers and sinks, facilities for disabled visitors, and good provision for washing up and laundry. Washing machines. Motorcaravan services. Shops. Bars. Waiter service restaurant and terrace with splendid views across to the opposite shore and new restaurant in the old farm building. Swimming pools. Tennis. Football. Volleyball. Basketball. Playgrounds (small). Games and TV room. Watersports. Bicycle hire. Organised activities. Dogs are not accepted. Off site: Fishing 1 km. Gardaland is about 2 km. east of Peschiera.

At a glance

Welcome & Ambience	✓✓✓	Location	✓✓✓✓✓
Quality of Pitches	✓✓✓	Range of Facilities	✓✓✓✓✓

Directions

From Peschiera exit on A4 (Milan - Venice) autostrada, turn left and drive through town to site 1 km. from centre, on the right.

Charges 2003

Per person	€ 4.00 - 8.50
child (under 5 yrs)	free - € 5.00
pitch	€ 9.00 - € 17.00

Four charging seasons. No credit cards.
Camping Cheques accepted.

Reservations

Advised for high season; contact site. Tel: 045 640 0688. Email: bellaitalia@camping-bellaitalia.it

Open

1 April - 7 October.

IT6260 Camping Europa Silvella

Via Silvella 10, 25010 San Felice del Benaco (Lombardy)

This large, modern, lakeside site was formed from the merger of two different sites with the result that the 323 pitches (about 295 for tourists) are spread among a number of different sections of varying type. The chief difference between them is that the marked pitches alongside the lake are in smaller groups and closer together so that one has less space. However, in the larger, very slightly sloping or terraced grassy meadows further back one can have 80 sq.m. or more instead of just 50. There is reasonable shade in many parts and all pitches have 4A electricity, 45 with water and drainage. Some areas also contain bungalows, mobile homes and log cabins. The site has frontage to the lake in two places (with some other property in between), with a beach, jetty and moorings. The private beach is very pleasant, with all manner of watersports available. There is a windsurfing school in season, along with an organised animation programme with live entertainment. A new, large modern swimming pool complex has a jacuzzi and a children's pool.

Facilities

Toilet blocks include washbasins in cabins, facilities for disabled visitors and a superb children's room with small showers. Laundry. Supermarket. Bazaar. Restaurant/bar. Swimming pools (hats required). Tennis courts. Volleyball courts and five-a-side soccer pitch. Table tennis. New children's playground. Bowling alley. Surf boards, canoes and bicycles for hire. Animation and entertainment (every night in season). Disco. Tournaments, swimming, windsurfing and tennis lessons. First aid room.

At a glance

Welcome & Ambience	✓✓✓	Location	✓✓✓✓
Quality of Pitches	✓✓✓✓	Range of Facilities	✓✓✓✓

Directions

From Desenzano at southerly end of Lake Garda follow S572 north towards Salo. Following signs for San Felice turn off towards lake. Then follow yellow tourist signs bearing campsite name.

Charges 2003

Per person	€ 3.87 - € 6.35
child (2-9 yrs)	€ 3.36 - € 5.32
pitch with electricity, water and drainage	€ 11.10 - € 16.53
pitch with electricity only	€ 9.55 - € 13.94
dog	€ 5.16

Reservations

Not usually necessary for caravans and tents, but will be made for min. 7 days with 30% deposit and € 20,66 fee. Tel: 0365 651095.

Open

23 April - 27 September.

IT6264 Camping San Benedetto

Via Bergamini 14, 37010 San Benedetto (Veneto)

Overlooking Lake Garda and in a position central to local historic attractions and theme parks, San Benedetto has 100 reasonably sized pitches on grassy areas with trees. There are twice as many mobile homes as pitches on the site. Much work was in progress when we visited and a large area near the entrance was being used for storing building materials and boats (supervision of children recommended). Once past this the campsite was attractively presented. The restaurant and bar is basic with a large covered terrace area for eating and drinking. Beyond the camp fence the beach area is stony and reedy. A marina and new boat launching area is outside the rear site gates and the sub-aqua club is in the same area where there is an attractive walkway along the lake edge in the public area. This is an uncomplicated site suitable for visiting local attractions.

Facilities

Three good toilet blocks provide mainly British toilets but have no facilities for disabled campers. Washing machines and dryers. Motorcaravan service point. Shop selling basics. Restaurant and snack bar. Two swimming pools. Aerobics. Play areas. Beach volleyball. Small boat launching. Canoe, motorcycle and bicycle hire. Mini-club and animation. Off site: Sailing 1.5 km. Fishing. Golf and riding 5 km.

At a glance

Welcome & Ambience	✓✓✓	Location	✓✓✓
Quality of Pitches	✓✓✓	Range of Facilities	✓✓✓

Directions

Leave autostrada A4 at Pescheria de Garda exit and take lakeside road to Desenzano. At San Benedetto site is well signed on the right.

Charges 2003

Per person	€ 3.50 - € 7.00
senior (over 60 yrs)	€ 3.00 - € 6.00
child (under 10 yrs)	free - € 4.50
pitch	€ 5.50 - € 13.50

Reservations

Made for min. 7 days with deposit. Tel: 0457 550544. Email: sanbenedetto@gardalake.it

Open

31 March - 10 October.

IT6265 Camping Ideal Molino

Via Gardiola 1, 25010 San Felice del Benaco (Lombardy)

Molino is a small, garden-like site with charm and character, which may appeal to those who do not like the larger and more ordered sites. A friendly family atmosphere is being maintained at the site by the daughter of the original owners. Ingeborg is delightful and speaks perfect English. The family house, of which the charming restaurant is part, has a huge water wheel constantly turning which was used to crush the olives from the local area. This explains the name of the campsite and the old mill equipment can still be seen under the house, although it is now disconnected. The site is mainly on fairly level ground beside Lake Garda with a hill rising quite sharply behind. It is in two main parts divided by the site buildings, and pitches vary in character, some by the lake, some for tents on terraces, and many in rows with pergolas and flowering shrubs. All pitches are well shaded, have electricity, water and drainage, and can be reserved (in high season most advisable). The excellent restaurant has superb lake views and the huge lakeside barbecue operates twice weekly. Whilst all facilities are of a good standard, they are being continually updated. There is a pleasant stony beach at one end; elsewhere one steps straight down into shallow water. Boats can be launched and there is a floating pontoon for sunbathing, diving or boat landing. The management does not like loud radios or TVs, or any noise after 11pm. A shallow stream runs along the boundary and there is pond behind reception.

Facilities

All three small sanitary blocks have been rebuilt to a very high standard, with automatic lighting and facilities for disabled visitors. They have British style WCs, individual washbasins with hot water and adjustable hot showers. Laundry (attended). Motorcaravan services. Shop. Restaurant/bar. Bicycle hire. Table tennis. Fishing. Water ski-ing. Free organised entertainment in season. Boat excursions to markets in lakeside towns. Dogs are not accepted.

At a glance

| Welcome & Ambience | ✓✓✓✓ | Location | ✓✓✓✓✓ |
| Quality of Pitches | ✓✓✓ | Range of Facilities | ✓✓✓ |

Directions

From Desenzano at southerly end of lake Garda follow S572 north towards Salô. Turn off towards lake, following signs for San Felice. Then follow yellow signs bearing camp name. Watch for sudden stop sign on final descent to site! Site is about 4 km. outside Salô.

Charges 2003

Per unit incl. electricity (4A)	€ 9.30 - € 15.50
adult	€ 4.50 - € 7.50
child (2-9 yrs)	€ 3.90 - € 6.00

No credit cards.

Reservations

Made for min 7 days from January onwards with fee and deposit. Tel: 0365 62023. Email: info@campingmolino.it

Open

16 March - 30 September.

IT6266 Camping Gasparina

Via Gasparina 13, 37010 Cavalcaselle (Veneto)

Camping Gasparina is of average size for this area and of reasonable quality, but a little away from the towns around the lake in a peaceful location giving the appearance of being in the countryside. As the site slopes towards the lake, levellers are needed in some parts. There are 430 grass tourist pitches in back-to-back rows separated by gravel roads. Many trees and flowers adorn the site, with shade in most parts. Near reception are the supermarket, bar/restaurant and swimming pool (30 x 10 m) which is enclosed by a neat well clipped hedge and has a comprehensive set of rules for safety and enjoyment of guests. There is a small beach and boats can be launched here.

Facilities

Two refurbished and one new toilet block have the usual facilities with warm water in two blocks. Facilities for disabled visitors. Washing machines and dryer Shop. Bar/restaurant with terrace. Swimming pool. Playground. Tennis courts. Watersports. Animation in high season. Off site: Bicycle hire 2 km. Riding 3 km.

At a glance

| Welcome & Ambience | ✓✓✓✓ | Location | ✓✓✓✓ |
| Quality of Pitches | ✓✓✓ | Range of Facilities | ✓✓✓ |

Directions

Leave A4 [Milan-Venice] motorway at exit for Peschiera, go north on east side of lake on SS249 towards Lazise for entrance road on your left.

Charges 2003

Per person	€ 3.00 - € 7.00
child (up to 10 yrs)	€ 2.00 - € 3.50
pitch	€ 5.50 - € 10.00
boat trailer	€ 13.00 - € 18.00

Reservations

Contact site. Tel: 045 7550775. Email: info@gasparina.com

Open

25 March - 28 September.

IT6277 Camping Fontanelle

Via del Magone 13, 25080 Moniga del Garda (Lombardy)

Camping Fontanelle is a sister site to Fornella (no. IT6275), situated near the historic village of Moniga and enjoying excellent views across the lake. The site sits on the south-western slopes of Lake Garda and has 200 pitches on flat and terraced ground. Approximately 25% of these are given over to tour operators but there is little impingement. All are marked and have electrical connections and there are some very pleasant lakeside pitches (extra cost). Some for tents and tourers are very secluded but are distant from the campsite facilities, although small blocks with toilets are close by. The swimming pools are superb, one for adults with the children's pool alongside (closed 13.00-15.00 hrs). The lakeside pitches have access to the beach through gates in the safety fence. The lake is a public area and there is no lifeguard, although the local equivalent to the RNLI is active on the lake. We are told there is no problem with security here although the public gain access to the beach along fenced paths through the site. Good English is spoken.

Facilities
The two main toilet blocks are modern and clean, with hot water throughout. Facilities for disabled campers in these blocks. Washing machines and dryers. Motorcaravan services. Large mini-market with prices to compete with local supermarkets. Restaurant/bar. Takeaway. Shop. Swimming pools (from 15/5, supervised). Table tennis. Tennis. TV room. Electronic games. Animation and live entertainment in season. Off site: Bicycle hire 1 km. Golf 5 km. Riding 20 km.

At a glance
Welcome & Ambience	✓✓✓✓	Location	✓✓✓✓
Quality of Pitches	✓✓✓✓	Range of Facilities	✓✓✓

Directions
From A4 or E70 Milano - Verona road travel north on the west side of the lake to Moniga; site is well signed.

Charges 2003
Per adult	€ 4.60 - € 8.50
child (3-7 yrs)	€ 3.60 - € 6.80
pitch incl. electricity (6A)	€ 9.30 - € 16.00
boat	€ 6.00 - € 11.50
dog	€ 4.20 - € 5.20

Reservations
Made for min 7 days from November onwards with fee and deposit; write to site. Tel: 0365 502079. Email: info@campingfontanelle.it

Open
1 May - 19 September.

IT6270 Villaggio Turistico La Gardiola

Via Gardiola, 36, 25010 San Felice del Benaco (Lombardy)

This small, modern site is set directly beside the lake in a very popular area. The 40 pitches (25 for tourers) are on flat, shaded terraces and all pitches have electricity and water. The site is separated from the shingle beach by a small private service road. The views from the site are stunning across the lake and the family atmosphere, and friendly owners give the site a very homely feel. English is spoken. If you enjoy small sites with an uncomplicated atmosphere, then this could be for you. Reservations are accepted.

Facilities
An innovative sanitary block just below ground level has a lift system for disabled visitors. The facilities are quite adequate and there is free hot water throughout. Laundry. Small kiosk with terrace for coffee and snacks. Small playground. Table tennis. Fishing. Off site: Restaurants, shops, pizzerias nearby.

At a glance
Welcome & Ambience	✓✓✓✓	Location	✓✓✓✓
Quality of Pitches	✓✓✓✓	Range of Facilities	✓✓✓

Directions
Near San Felice on SS572 Salo - San Felice road, site is well signed at San Felice. Take care from the town as the road is very narrow.

Charges 2003
Per unit incl. electricity	€ 9.30 - € 18.00
adult	€ 3.90 - € 6.80
child (1- yrs) and over 60s	€ 3.00 - € 5.30
dog	€ 2.00 - € 4.00

Reservations
Contact site. Tel: 0365 559240. Email: info@lagardiola.com

Open
10 April - 30 September.

IT6275 Fornella Camping

Via Fornella 1, 25010 San Felice del Benaco (Lombardy)

Fornella Camping is another of the good sites in this region where one is spoilt for choice. It is the sister site of Fontanelle (no. IT6277) and of similar high standards. An open site, it is surrounded by olive and other trees with a backdrop of mountains and good views. Although there is access to the lake, this cannot be seen from all parts of the site as a tree covered hill intervenes. There are 230 marked and numbered pitches for tourers, separated by access roads on flat grass and terraced where necessary, all with electricity. Many pitches are shaded by young trees. Mobile homes and bungalows edge the touring pitches but do not intrude. The well appointed bar/restaurant and the shop are by the lakeside with a terrace giving splendid views over the lake. A new swimming pool is a super addition for the 2003 season. The lakeside area and private pebble beach is pleasant and there are two separate lake accesses for boats and windsurfers. Being well away from the main road, this is a quiet, peaceful site. The friendly management speak excellent English. Used by tour operators (30%).

Facilities

Three very clean, modern sanitary blocks, well dispersed around the site, have mainly British type WCs and hot water in washbasins (some in cabins), showers and sinks. Facilities for disabled people. Washing machines, dryer and irons. Motorcaravan services. Bar/restaurant. Pizzeria and takeaway at certain times. Shop. Supervised swimming pool and children's pool (15/5-15/9). Tennis. Table tennis. Volleyball. Two playgrounds and animation for children in season. Beach. Fishing. Off site: Bicycle hire 4 km. Golf 8 km. Riding 10 km.

At a glance

Welcome & Ambience	✓✓✓✓	Location	✓✓✓✓✓
Quality of Pitches	✓✓✓✓	Range of Facilities	✓✓✓✓

Directions

From main SS572 Desenzano-Salo road on the west side of the lake, head for San Felice and follow signs.

Charges 2003

Per person	€ 4.60 - € 8.80
child (3-7 yrs)	€ 3.60 - € 6.80
pitch incl. electricity (6A)	€ 9.30 - € 16.50
boat	€ 6.00 - € 11.50
dog	free - € 5.90

Charges acc. to season and pitch location. Various low season discounts.

Reservations

Made with deposit and fee; contact site.
Tel: 0365 62294. Email: fornella@fornella.it

Open

1 May - 21 September.

IT6285 Camping Zocco

Via del Zocco 43, 25080 Manerba del Garda (Lombardy)

Lake Garda is a very popular holiday area with a good number of sites well placed to explore the many attractions nearby. Camping Zocco is an excellent site in a quiet, scenic location sloping gently down to the lake where there is a jetty and a long pleasant shingle beach. There are 200 pitches for tourists, all with electricity, and are sized from 60-80 sq.m., the pitches are either on slightly sloping ground from gravel roads, on terraces or around the perimeters of two open meadows. A variety of trees, including olives which provide oil for the owners and may be bought in attractive personalised bottles as a memento, give shade in some parts. The site has a very well cared for appearance. Watersports can be enjoyed on the lake and boats may be launched from the site. The Fratelli family who run this site give British visitors a warm welcome and English is spoken. When we visited the final touches were being put to a superb new pool complex and an administrative block. These additions make Zocco a most attractive option if you prefer a smaller site with excellent facilities. Used by tour operators (20 pitches).

Facilities

Three tiled sanitary blocks, amongst the cleanest we have seen, are well spaced around the site. Mainly British style WCs, hot water in the washbasins, sinks and showers. Facilities for disabled people. Washing machines. Motorcaravan services. Good restaurant/pizzeria with terrace and bar. New coffee shop. Well stocked shop (1/5-15/9). Bar on beach (reduced hours in low season). New swimming pool complex with jacuzzi (free to campers). Watersports. Fishing. Tennis. Football. Play area. Entertainment for children during July/Aug. Off site: Bicycle hire 1.5 km. Riding and golf 4 km.

At a glance

Welcome & Ambience	✓✓✓✓	Location	✓✓✓✓✓
Quality of Pitches	✓✓✓✓	Range of Facilities	✓✓✓✓

Directions

From Desenzano head north on road 572 towards Salo and take minor road to Manerba from where Zocco is signed.

Charges 2004

Per person	€ 4.30 - € 6.80
child (3-11 yrs)	€ 3.50 - € 5.80
pitch incl. electricity (4A)	€ 8.90 - € 13.40
dog	€ 2.10 - € 3.90

Reservations

Made for min. 7 days with deposit (€ 78) deducted from final bill. Tel: 0365 551605. Email: info@campingzocco.it

Open

3 April - 26 September.

IT6283 Camping La Rocca

Via Cavalle 22, 25080 Manerba (Lombardy)

Set high on a peninsula, there are delightful views from this very friendly, family-orientated campsite. With 200 attractive touring pitches enjoying shade from the tree canopy which also protects the campers from the summer heat, this is a 'real' campsite (20 pitches have lake views). The director Livio is charming and very engaging with his pleasant, halting English. Located in the idyllic Gulf of Manerba on Lake Garda, near the La Rocca natural park, it has the choice of two pretty, pebble lakeside beaches which can be accessed from the site, and a very nice pool complex. Close to traditional Italian villages and modern theme parks there is something for eveyone here. The site has a friendly family feel with all modern amenities without losing its distinctive Italian ambience. Nothing is too much trouble for the management.

Facilities

Two sanitary blocks with smart new units for disabled campers and baby changing areas which are kept in pristine condition at all times. Washing machines. Restaurant for basic meals with a pleasant terrace shared with the bar. Small shop for basics (town close). Swimming pools. Tennis courts. Play area. Volleyball. Table tennis. Bicycle loan. Fishing (with permit). Small boat launching. Music in the evenings. Mini-club in high season. Torches required on beach steps and tunnel. Off site: Theme parks. Fishing. Golf 2 km. Riding 3 km. Sailing.

At a glance

Welcome & Ambience	√√√√	Location	√√√√√
Quality of Pitches	√√√√	Range of Facilities	√√√√

Directions

From A4 autostrada take Desenzano exit and follow SS572 to Manerba. Site is well signed off this road.

Charges 2003

Per pitch	€ 7.00 - € 12.00
adult	€ 3.80 - € 6.50
child	€ 3.00 - € 5.00

Reservations

Advised for July/Aug. (min. 1 week) with deposit. Tel: 0365 551 738. Email: info@laroccacamp.it

Open

27 March - 26 September.

Camping LA ROCCA ✳✳✳✳
Via Cavalle, 22 • I-25080 MANERBA
LAGO DI GARDA (BS)

Tel. 0039/0365/551738
Fax 0039/0365/552045
Http: www.laroccacamp.it
E-mail: info@laroccacamp.it

Opening: from 27.03. to 26.09.04

The camping site is situated between the peninsula S. Biagio and Rocca Manerba. It provides two swimming pools and tennis court. The beach is right by the lake. At disposal bar, mini market, post service and telephone box, playground and table tennis. The camping site is open from 27.03.04 till 26.09.04. Reservations possible.

IT6280 Camping Week-End

Via Vallone della Selva 2, 25010 San Felice del Benaco (Lombardy)

Created among the olive groves and terraced vineyards of the Chateau Villa Louisa, which overlooks it, this modern well equipped site enjoys some superb views over the small bay which forms this part of Lake Garda. On reaching the site you will pass through a most impressive pair of gates. Although the site is 400 m from the lake for many campers the views resulting from its situation on higher ground will be ample compensation for it not being an actual lakeside site. Being set in quiet countryside, it provides an unusually tranquil environment, although even here it can become very busy in the high season. The site has a good sized supervised pool which make up for its not actually having frontage onto the lake, and some visitors, particularly families with children, will doubtless prefer this. There are some 220 pitches, all with electricity (from 3A), of which about 30% are taken by tour operators and statics. The touring pitches are in several different areas, and many enjoy views. Some pitches for larger units are set in the upper terraces on steep slopes and manoeuvring can be challenging, and low olive branches may cause problems for high units. The large, attractive restaurant has a thoughtfully laid out terrace and lawn with marble statues from which there are more wonderful views

Facilities

The three sanitary blocks, one below the restaurant/shop, are modern, well maintained and include hot water for showers, basins and washing-up areas. Mainly British style WCs, a few washbasins in cabins and facilities for disabled people. We have had reports of congestion in the facilities at peak periods. Washing machines and dryer. Motorcaravan services. Bar/restaurant (waiter service). Takeaway. Shop. Supervised swimming pool and children's pool. Volleyball. Barbecues. Entertainment programme in season. Two playgrounds. First aid room. English spoken. Off site: Fishing 2 km. Golf 6 km. Riding 8 km. Windsurfing, water skiing and tennis near.

At a glance

Welcome & Ambience	✓✓✓✓	Location	✓✓✓✓
Quality of Pitches	✓✓✓✓	Range of Facilities	✓✓✓✓

Directions

Approach from Saló (easier when towing) and follow site signs. From Milano - Venezia autostrada take Desenzano exit towards Saló and Localita Cisano - S. Felice.

Charges 2004

Per unit incl. electricity	€ 10.00 - € 13.50
adult	€ 5.00 - € 7.50
child (3-10 yrs)	€ 3.90 - € 5.70
dog	€ 3.90 - € 6.00

Camping Cheques accepted.

Reservations

Contact site. Tel: 0365 43712. Email: info@weekend.it

Open

24 April - 26 September.

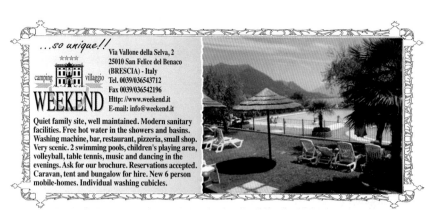

IT6284 Camping Belvedere

Via Cavalle, 5, 25080 Manerba (Lombardy)

Situated along a promontory reaching into Lake Garda, this campsite has been landscaped with terracing to give many of the 84 pitches a good vantage point to enjoy the wonderful views. There is plentiful access to the long pebbly beach for a relaxing swim and a dedicated area for boat launching. The delightful restaurant and bar with pretty flowers is under shady trees at the water's edge. The site has lots of grassy areas and alternated with attractive olive trees are others to give a cool canopy for campers. There are no facilities for disabled campers and really young children would require supervision as the terracing is unguarded in places and there are steep slopes which may hinder the infirm. The landscaping and atmosphere are delightfully Mediterranean with charming Italian vistas. This is a good site from which to explore all the exciting sights the area has to offer.

Facilities

Five decent sanitary blocks are very much to the sites credit, however, with no facilities for disabled visitors. Shop selling basics. Restaurant, bar and takeaway. Play area. Full size tennis court. Music in bar. TV. Torches useful. Off site: Fishing. Golf and bicycle hire 2 km. Riding 4 km. Bars and restaurant (limited menu). Watersports. Theme parks.

At a glance

| Welcome & Ambience | ✓✓✓ | Location | ✓✓✓✓✓ |
| Quality of Pitches | ✓✓✓✓✓ | Range of Facilities | ✓✓✓✓ |

Directions

Leave autostrada at Desenzano exit and take SS572 to Manerba. Site is well signed off this road.

Charges 2003

Per adult	€ 3.75 - € 6.00
child	€ 3.00 - € 4.80
pitch with electricity	€ 7.80 - € 14.00
dog	€ 2.00 - € 3.00

Reservations

Accepted with a deposit. Tel: 03 65 55 11 75. Email: info@camping-belvedere.it

Open

24 March - 6 October.

Home to the unique city of Venice, the historic towns of Verona, Padua and Vicenza, plus several fortified settlements, Veneto has an abundance of sights to keep you entertained. Situated in the northeast of Italy, it stretches from the flat river plains to the Dolomites.

The region has seven provinces:
Belluno, Padova, Rovigo, Treviso, Venezia, Verona and Vicenza

Built on a series of low mud banks amid the tidal waters of the Adriatic, the main thoroughfare through Venice is the Grand Canal. At nearly 4 kilometres long, 30 to 70 metres wide, it divides the city in half. Palaces, churches and historic monuments line the waterway. The Piazza San Marco is the main focal point of the city, with the Oriental splendour of the Basilica di San Marco, the Palazzo Ducale and the Bridge of Sighs. With another famous bridge and bustling markets, the district of Rialto is one of the liveliest spots, while the lagoon islands offer an escape from the crowds. Marana comprises a cluster of small islands, connected by bridges, and has been the centre of the glass-blowing industry since 1291; Burano is the most colourful with brightly painted houses and a long lace-making tradition; while Torcello boasts a 7th century cathedral, the oldest building on the lagoon. Outside Venice, the old university town of Padua is rich in art and architecture and Verona, with its buildings of pink-tinged limestone, is renowned for its Roman ruins including the amphitheatre, which is the third largest in the world. It is also home to Casa di Giulietta, Juliet's house, a restored 13th century inn with a small marble balcony, immortalised in Shakespeare's *Romeo and Juliet*.

Cuisine of the region

Risottos are popular, especially with seafood, plus pork dishes, polenta and heavy soups of beans, rice and vegetables. The region is also home to Italy's famous dessert *tiramisu*, a rich blend of coffee-soaked sponge cake and mascarpone cheese. Locally produced wines include Soave, Merlot, Cabernet, Pinot Grigio and Chardonnay. And Grappa, made from grape husks, juniper berries or plums, is also widely available.

Antipasto di Frutti di Mare: seafood platter

Brodo di Pesce: fish soup

Bussolai: ring shaped cinnamon flavoured biscuits

Radicchio alla Griglia: red salad leaves lightly grilled

Risi e Bisi: soft and liquid risotto with fresh peas and bacon

Risotto alle Seppie: contains cuttlefish ink

Places of interest

Bassano del Grappa: well known for its majolica products and Grappa distilleries

Conegliano: in wine-producing region, renowned wine-growers' school, grape festival in September, well-established wine routes

Euganean Hills: hot suphur springs and mud baths

Montagnana: fortified settledment with medieval town walls

Padua: Basilica di Sant'Antonio, one of the most important pilgrimage destinations in Italy

Treviso: attractive town with medieval, balconied houses overlooking willow-fringed canals

Vicenza: Roman-Renaissance architecture, home of Europe's oldest surviving indoor theatre, 17th century stone bridges

Alan Rogers tip

THE TRADITIONAL GONDOLAS THAT PLY THE WATERS OF VENICE ARE EXPENSIVE. A CHEAPER ALTERNATIVE IS THE *VAPORETTI* (WATER-BUS) OR *TRAGHETTI* (GONDOLA FERRIES).

IT6003 Centro Vacanze Pra' Delle Torri

P.O. Box 176, 30021 Caorle (Veneto)

Pra' delle Torri is another Italian Adriatic site which has just about everything! Pitches for camping, hotel, accommodation to rent, one of the largest and best equipped swimming pools in the country and a golf course where lessons for beginners are also available. Many of the 1,300 grass pitches (with electricity) have shade and are arranged in zones and when you book in at reception you are taken by electric golf buggy to select your pitch. There are two good restaurants, bars and a range of shops arranged around an attractive square. There is a large grass area for ball games but the swimming pool complex is the crowning glory. There is a good children's playground, a babies' car track, and a whole range of sports, fitness and entertainment programmes, along with a medical centre, skincare and other therapies. They have their own sandy beach and Porto Sta Margherita and Caorle are nearby. One could quite happily spend a whole holiday here without leaving the site.

Facilities

Sixteen excellent, high quality toilet blocks with the usual facilities including very attractive 'Junior Stations', units for disabled visitors, washing machines and dryers. Motorcaravan service point. Large supermarket and wide range of shops, restaurants, bars and takeaways. Tennis courts. Football field. Minigolf. Table tennis. Fishing. Watersports. Archery. Basketball and volleyball. Diving. Aqua gym, fitness programmes and keep fit track. Bowls. Mountain bike track. Wide range of organised sports and entertainment. Off site: Riding 3 km.

At a glance

Welcome & Ambience	✓✓✓✓	Location	✓✓✓✓
Quality of Pitches	✓✓✓✓	Range of Facilities	✓✓✓✓✓

Directions

From A4 (Venice - Trieste) motorway leave at exit for Ste Stino di Livenze and follow signs to Caorle then Sta Margherita and signs to site.

Charges 2003

Per person	€ 3.55 - € 7.95
child (1-5 yrs)	€ 2.45 - € 5.95
senior (over 60 yrs)	€ 2.60 - € 6.75
pitch incl. electricity (5A)	€ 6.80 - € 18.70
tent pitch	€ 4.75 - € 14.80
Min. stay 2 nights.	

Reservations

Contact site. Tel: 0421 299063.
Email: torri@vacanze-natura.it

Open

3 April - 25 September.

IT6014 Villaggio Turistico Internazionale

30020 Bibione (Veneto)

This is a large professionally run tourist village which offers all a holidaymaker could want. The Guawzotto family have owned the site since the sixties and the results of their continuous improvements are impressive. The site's large sandy beach is excellent (umbrellas and loungers for a small charge), as are all the facilities within the campsite where English speaking, uniformed assistants will help when you arrive. The tourist village is split by a main road with the main restaurant, cinema and children's club on the very smart 'chalet' side. The most professional hairdressing salon sets the luxury tone of the site. There are 300 clean pitches, many fully serviced, shaded by mature trees and mostly on flat ground. A comprehensive entertainment programme is on offer daily and the large pool provides a great flume and slides and a separate fun and spa pool. The local area is a major tourist resort but for more relaxation try the famous thermal baths at Bibione.

Facilities

Four modern toilet blocks house excellent facilities with mainly British toilets. Excellent provision for children and disabled campers. Washing machines and dryers. Motorcaravan service point. Supermarket. Bazaar. Good restaurant with bright yellow plastic chairs. Snack bar. Pool complex. Fitness centre. Disco. TV. Cinema and theatre. Internet. Play areas. Football. Tennis. Volleyball. Billiards. Electronic games. Doctor's surgery. Off site: Bicycle hire 1 km. Riding 3 km. Golf 6 km. Fishing.

At a glance

Welcome & Ambience	✓✓✓✓✓	Location	✓✓✓✓✓
Quality of Pitches	✓✓✓✓✓	Range of Facilities	✓✓✓✓✓

Directions

Leave A4 east of Venice at Latisana exit on Latisana road. Then take road 354 towards Lingano, after 12 km. turn right to Bavassano and then left to Bibione. Site is well signed on entering town.

Charges 2003

Per adult	€ 5.00 - € 8.75
senior	€ 3.50 - € 8.75
child (1-5 yrs)	free - € 6.75
pitch incl. electricity	€ 9.00 - € 16.50
with electricity and water	€ 12.00 - € 21.50
dog	€ 5.50

Reservations

Made with deposit (min. 1 week, Sat-Sat).
Tel: 0431 442611. Email: info@vti.it

Open

15 April - 25 September.

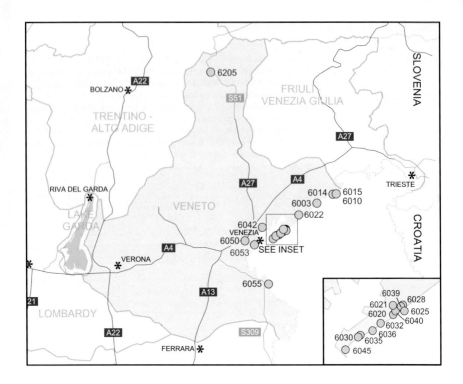

IT6021 Camping Italy

Via Fausta 272, 30013 Cavallino (Veneto)

There are over 30 campsites on the Littorale del Cavallino between Lido di Jesolo and Punta Sabbioni and Camping Italy, under the same ownership as the better known Union Lido which it adjoins, is suggested for those who prefer a smaller site where less activities are available (although those at Union Lido may be used). The 144 tourist pitches are on either side of sand tracts from hard access roads under a cover of trees. Being on the small size (60-70 sq.m), they may be difficult for large units, particularly in high season when cars may have to be parked away from some pitches. All have electricity connections and some have water as well. There is direct access to a gently sloping sandy beach and a good, heated, swimming pool which has a whirlpool at one end. Strict regulations regarding undue noise make this a peaceful site and with lower charges than some in the area, this a good site for families with young children where it is possible to book in advance.

Facilities

Two good quality, fully equipped sanitary blocks include facilities for disabled visitors. Washing machines. Shop. Restaurant. Bar beside beach. Heated swimming pool (17 x 7 m). Small playground, mini-club and children's disco. Weekly dance for adults. Barbecues are only permitted in a designated area. Dogs are not accepted. Off site: Sports centre 500 m. Golf and riding also 500 m.

At a glance

Welcome & Ambience	✓✓✓✓	Location	✓✓✓✓
Quality of Pitches	✓✓✓	Range of Facilities	✓✓✓✓✓

Directions

From Venice - Trieste A4 autostrada leave at exit for airport or Quarto d' Altino and follow signs for Jesolo and Punta Sabbioni. Site on left after Cavallino.

Charges 2004

Per person	€ 4.45 - € 6.90
child (under 6 yrs)	€ 2.90 - € 5.50
pitch with electricity (5A)	€ 7.40 - € 16.70
pitch with electricity and water	€ 7.90 - € 18.00

Three charging seasons.

Reservations

Contact site. Tel: 041 968 090.
Email: info@campingitaly.it

Open

Easter - 16 September.

IT6022 Portofelice Camping Village

Viale Dei Fiori 15, 30020 Eraclea Mare (Veneto)

Portofelice is a typical Italian coastal site with a sandy beach and plenty of well organised activity. It is unusual in being separated from the sea by a protected pine wood with a gravel path between the two. It is of medium size for this part of Italy with 546 tourist pitches and 230 occupied by static caravans, bungalows and tour operators' accommodation. The pitches are arranged in rectangular blocks or zones in regular rows, separated by hedges from hard access roads and with either natural or artificial shade. Cars are parked in numbered places under shade at the side of the zones. All have electricity (6A) and 224 also have water, drainage and TV sockets. The social life of the site is centred around the pool complex where the shops, pizzeria, bar, café and restaurant are also located. A wide range of entertainment and activities are organised for adults and children.

Facilities

Two modern sanitary blocks have the usual facilities with slightly more Turkish style toilets than British. New toilet block for children (0-12 yrs). Facilities for disabled people. Shops. Pizzeria. Restaurant with a good menu at reasonable prices and most tables on a covered terrace with waiter service. Swimming pools with an area specifically equipped for disabled guests, whirlpool massage and sunbathing. Playgrounds. Tennis, football, basket and volleyball, open spaces and a sandy beach. Bicycle hire. Organised activities for children. Activity and entertainment programmes, with evening shows and music. Off site: Riding 200 m. Golf 6 km.

At a glance

Welcome & Ambience	✓✓✓✓	Location	✓✓✓✓
Quality of Pitches	✓✓✓✓	Range of Facilities	✓✓✓✓

Directions

From A4 Venice-Trieste motorway take exit 'S Dona/ Noventa' and go south through S Dona di Piave and Eraclea to Eraclea Mare where site is signed.

Charges 2004

Per person	€ 3.00 - € 8.40
senior (over 60 yrs)	€ 2.40 - € 6.80
child (1-5 yrs)	free - € 6.20
pitch (depending on type)	€ 6.70 - € 17.70

Reservations

Write to site. Tel: 0421 66411. Email: info@portofelice.it

Open

8 May - 19 September.

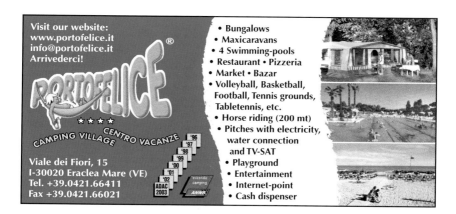

IT6010 Camping-Village Capalonga

Via della Laguna 16, 30020 Bibione-Pineda (Veneto)

A quality site right beside the sea, Camping-Village Capalonga is a large site with 1,350 pitches of variable size (70-90 sq.m). Nearly all marked out, all have electrical connections, some have water and drainage, and there is good shade almost everywhere. The site is pleasantly laid out – roads run in arcs which avoids the square box effect. Some pitches where trees define the pitch area may be tricky for large units. The very wide, sandy beach is cleaned by the site and never becomes too crowded; a concrete path leads out towards the sea to avoid too much sand-walking. The sea bed shelves extremely gently so is very safe for children and the water is much cleaner here than at most places along this coast. A large lagoon runs along the other side of the site where boating (motor or sail) can be practised and a landing stage and moorings are provided. There is also a swimming pool on site. Capalonga is an excellent site, with comprehensive facilities.

Facilities

The seven toilet blocks are well and frequently cleaned. Two newer blocks built side by side have facilities for disabled people and very fine children's rooms with basins and showers at the right height. British and some Turkish style toilets, some washbasins in private cabins and a whole wall of mirrors. Launderette. Motorcaravan services. Large supermarket. General shop for campers and beach goods, cards, papers, etc. Self-service restaurant and separate bar. Swimming pool (25 x 12-5 m; 19/5-15/9). Boating. Fishing. Playground. Large playing field provides exercise stations, football pitch and a general area for ball games and there are play areas with equipment on the beach. Free animation programme with wide range of sport, fitness and entertainment. First-aid room. Dogs are not accepted.

At a glance

Welcome & Ambience	✓✓✓	Location	✓✓✓✓
Quality of Pitches	✓✓✓✓	Range of Facilities	✓✓✓✓

Directions

Bibione is about 80 km. east of Venice, well signed from afar on approach roads. 1 km. before Bibione turn right towards Bibione Pineda and follow camp signs.

Charges 2003

Per person	€ 5.70 - € 9.80
child (1-4 yrs)	free - € 4.50
child (5-10 yrs)	free - € 6.50
pitch with electricity (4/10A)	€ 10.50 - € 19.00
pitch with water and drainage	€ 11.00 - € 20.00
boat	€ 6.50 - € 12.00

Reservations

Advised for July/Aug. and made Sat to Sat only, with large deposit and fee. Tel: 0431 438351. Email: capalonga@bibionemare.com

Open

1 May - 28 September.

IT6025 Camping Residence

Via F. Baracca 47, 30013 Cavallino (Veneto)

The Litorale del Cavallino has a large number of excellent sites, giving a good choice for those wishing to visit and stay in this area near Venice. Camping Residence is a very good site with a sandy beach directly on the Adriatic and is well kept, with many floral displays. Pitches are marked out with small fences or pines, which give good shade, and are laid out in regular rows on level sand. They vary in size, with those for caravans larger than those for tents, and all have electricity connections (6A). A medium size site (for this region) of 300 tourist pitches, it is smaller than 6020 but has the same strict rules regarding noise (no radios or dogs, quiet periods and no unaccompanied under 18s) but is less formal and more personal. The beach fronting has been enlarged and improved and the sea bed shelves gradually making it safe for children. Excellent pools have been added and there is a good animation programme in high season for both children and adults. Venice can be easily reached by bus to Punta Sabbioni and ferry across the lagoon and there are organised excursions to places of interest.

Facilities

The three large sanitary blocks are very clean with full facilities including British style WCs. Although of good quality, they are being refurbished. Supermarket, separate shops for fruit and other goods. Well appointed restaurant with separate bar. Takeaway. Swimming pools with sunbathing areas. Playground. Table tennis. Tennis court. Minigolf. Fitness programme. Video games room. Dancing or disco by beach until 11 pm three times weekly June-August and entertainment programme. Post office. Bureau de change. Doctor will call. Ladies hairdresser. Dogs are not accepted. Off site: Boat moorings for hire at nearby marina. Fishing and bicycle hire 1 km.

At a glance

Welcome & Ambience	✓✓✓✓	Location	✓✓✓✓
Quality of Pitches	✓✓✓✓	Range of Facilities	✓✓✓✓

Directions

From A4 Venice-Trieste autostrada leave at exit for Airport or Quarto D'Altino, follow signs for Jesolo and then Punta Sabbioni. Take first left after Cavallino bridge and site is about 800 m. on right hand side (well signed).

Charges 2003

Per person	€ 3.90 - € 7.90
child (under 5 yrs)	free - € 6.00
pitch	€ 8.20 - € 18.40

Less 10% on pitch fee for over 60s.

Reservations

Made for min. 1 week; contact site. Tel: 041 968027. Email: info@campres.it

Open

24 April - 22 September.

VENEZIA ITALIA

BIBIONE PINEDA IS A PEACEFUL AND RELAXING SEASIDE RESORT LOCATED BETWEEN VENICE AND TRIESTE. ITS SILKY SAND BEACH STRETCHES ALONG THE COASTLINE FOR MORE THAN 3 KM AND IT IS 150 METERS WIDE. ITS MARINA, THE RESTAURANTS, CAFÉS, SHOPS, SPORT FACILITIES AND NIGHT CLUBS, ALL THIS IN A FANTASTIC PINE WOOD SETTING MAKES IT A PARTICULARLY DELIGHTFUL DESTINATION.

DISCOVER A NEW WAY OF GOING CAMPING

★ ★ ★ ★

Capalonga
CAMPING - VILLAGE

NEW 2004 FLY & DRIVE

THE ONLY CAMPSITE IN EUROPE WITH 170 BOAT PLACES.
TEL. +39/0431438351 - TEL. WIN. +39/0431447190 +39/0431447198
FAX +39/0431438986

CAMPING VILLAGE
★ ★ ★ ★

IL TRIDENTE

ESPECIALLY THOUGHT TO SATISFY THE NEEDS OF FAMILIES WITH YOUNG CHILDREN.
TEL. +39/0431439600 - TEL. WIN. +39/0431447393
FAX +39/0431439196

★ ★ ★
Camping Village
Lido

PERFECT FOR THOSE WHO LOVE NATURE AND WANT A PEACEFUL HOLIDAY. CLOSE TO THE SHOPPING CENTRE.
TEL. +39/0431438480 - TEL. WIN. +39/0431447386
FAX +39/0431439193

BIBIONE MARE S.P.A.

I-30020 BIBIONE PINEDA - SAN MICHELE AL TAGLIAMENTO (VE) - VIA DEI GINEPRI, 244

www.bibionemare.com

IT6020 Camping Union Lido Vacanze

Via Fausta 258, 30013 Cavallino (Veneto)

This well known site is extremely large but has first class organisation and it has been said that it sets the standard that others follow. It lies right by the sea with direct access to a long and broad sandy beach which fronts the camp. Shelving very gradually, the beach, which is well cleaned by the site, provides very safe bathing. The site is regularly laid out with parallel access roads under a covering of poplars, pine and other trees typical of this area providing good shade. These mark out the numbered pitches of adequate size (2,600 for touring units), all with electricity and 1,623 also with water and drainage. There are separate parts for caravans, tents and motorcaravans, plus one mixed part. The entrance provides a large off-road overnight parking area with electricity, toilets and showers for those arriving after 9 pm. An aqua-park includes a swimming pool, lagoon pool for children, whirlpool and a slow flowing 160 m. long 'river' for paddling or swimming. Covering 5,000 sq.m. this is supervised by lifeguards and is open mornings and afternoons. There is also a heated pool for hotel and apartment guests, available to others on payment. A selection of sports is offered in the annexe across the road and fitness programmes under qualified staff are available in season. The golf 'academy' has a driving range, pitching and putting greens and practise bunker, and a diving centre has a school and the possibilty of open water dives. There are regular entertainment and activity programmes. Union Lido is above all an orderly and clean site and this is achieved partly by strict adherence to regulations suiting those who like comfortable camping undisturbed by others and good management.

Facilities

Sixteen well kept, fully equipped toilet blocks which open and close progressively during the season include hot water to all facilities, and deep sinks for washing dishes and clothes. Eleven blocks have facilities for disabled people. Launderette. Motorcaravan service points. Gas supplies. Comprehensive shopping area has wide range of shops including a large supermarket (all open till late). Seven restaurants and several pleasant and lively bars. Aqua-park (from 15/5). Tennis. Riding. Table tennis. Minigolf. Skating rink. Bicycle hire. Archery. Two fitness tracks in 4 ha. natural park with play area and supervised play for children. Boat excursions. Recreational events for adults and children. Italian language lessons. Golf academy. Diving centre and school. Windsurfing school in season. Church service in English in July/Aug. Exchange facilities and cash machine. Ladies' and men's hairdressers. First aid centre, doctor's surgery with treatment room and camp ambulance. Dogs are not accepted. Off site: Boat launching 3.5 km.

Directions

From Venice-Trieste Autostrada leave at exit for airport or Quarto d'Altino and follow signs first for Jesolo and then Punta Sabbioni, and camp will be seen just after Cavallino on the left.

Charges 2003

Per person	€ 5.90 - € 8.50
child (under 3 yrs)	€ 3.50 - € 5.90
child (3-12 yrs)	€ 4.90 - € 7.40
pitch with electricity (6A)	€ 10.60 - € 19.10
pitch with water and drainage	€ 13.30 - € 22.00

Three different seasons: (i) high season 29/6-31/8; (ii) mid-season 18/5-29/6 and 31/8-14/9, and (iii) off-season, outside these dates.

Reservations

Made for the letting units only, but site provides 'priority cards' for previous visitors. Tel: 041 2575111. Email: info@unionlido.com

Open

1 May - 30 September, with all services.

At a glance

Welcome & Ambience	✓✓✓✓	Location	✓✓✓✓✓
Quality of Pitches	✓✓✓✓✓	Range of Facilities	✓✓✓✓✓

IT6015 Camping Village Il Tridente

Via Baseleghe 12, 30020 Bibione-Pineda (Veneto)

This is an unusual site as only half the area is used for camping. Formerly a holiday centre for deprived children, it occupies a strip of woodland 200 m. wide and 400 m. long stretching from the main road to the sea. It is divided into two parts by the Residence, an apartment block of first class rooms with air conditioning and full cooking and bathroom facilities which are for hire. The 250 tourist pitches are located amongst tall pines in the area between the entrance and the Residence. Pitch size varies according to the positions of the trees, but they are of sufficient size and have electricity. The ground slopes gently from the main building to the sandy beach and this is used as the recreation area with two swimming pools and a smaller children's pool, tennis courts, table tennis and play places. With thick woodland on both sides, Il Tridente is a quiet site with excellent facilities.

Facilities

The three sanitary blocks, two in the main camping area and one near the sea, are of excellent quality. All have similar facilities with mixed British and Turkish style WCs in cabins with washbasins and facilities for disabled people. Washing machines and dryers. Motorcaravan services. The Residence includes an excellent restaurant, bar and well stocked supermarket. Swimming pools. Playground. Tennis. Table tennis. Mini-football. Volleyball. Animation programme includes activities for children in high season. Boats may be kept at the quay on the sister site, Capalonga (no. 6010), about 1 km. away. Dogs are not accepted.

Directions

From A4 Venice - Trieste autostrada, take Latisana exit and follow signs to Bibione and then Bibione Pineda and camp signs.

Charges 2003

Per person	€ 5.70 - € 9.00
child (under 10 yrs)	free - € 6.30
pitch incl. electricity (4A)	€ 10.50 - € 18.00

Reservations

Contact site. Tel: 0431 439600. Email: tridente@bibionemare.com

Open

12 April - 28 September.

At a glance

Welcome & Ambience	✓✓✓	Location	✓✓✓✓
Quality of Pitches	✓✓✓✓	Range of Facilities	✓✓✓✓✓

Il Parco delle Vacanze

The pleasant holiday park with quality, style and atmosphere in a friendly environment right on to the Venetian Cavallino coast. Open from 1st May to 30th September.

Camping - Caravan - Bungalow

Spacious, fitted pitches on grass under pines, poplars and other typical plants, for tents, caravans and motorcaravans. Many caravan pitches have water and drainage points. Caravans and mobile homes for hire, with shower, WC and air-conditioning. Bungalow "Lido" with kitchen-living room, two double bedrooms (twin beds), shower and separate WC and terrace including some for disabled guests.

Fitness - Sport - Play

Spacious area with games and keep-fit equipment, with trained staff, multi-use sportsground for roller blading and other activities, volleyball, swimming instruction, windsurfing school, diving centre with school and diving excursions at sea, table-tennis, minigolf, tennis and riding school. Archery and football competition. Golf Academy. The Happy Place! Children's play area with much equipment. Climbing games and supervised play programme.

Animation - Entertainment - Activities

Open air theatre for animation. Concerts and music performances. Painting course. Artistic activities. Plays and hobbies with supervisor. Mini club and activities for kids. Scout camp (July and August). Football school from 6 till 15 years. Assistance for children and baby area.

Aqua Park

5000 sq metres of water landscape with a gentle river, a lagoon with waterslide for the children, swimmingpool, a waterfall, wellness facilities with shiatzupool and some whirlpools (15.05 - 20.09 and later weather permitting).

I-30013 CAVALLINO - VENEZIA
Tel. Camping 0039/0412575111
Tel. Hotel 0039/041968043
0039/041968884
Telefax 0039/0415370355

E-mail: info@unionlido.com
Http: www.unionlido.it

Park Hotel Union Lido

The only 4-star-hotel in Cavallino. 78 rooms with air conditioning and all the conveniences. Self-catering complex with 24 two-storey flatlets. Heated swimming pool, with splash and whirlpool also available in the early and late season for our Hotel and self-catering guests. Sauna, massages and physiotherapy.

IT6028 Camping Vela Blu

Via Radaelli, 10, 30013 Cavallino (Veneto)

Thoughtfully landscaped within a natural wooded coastal environment, the tall pines here give shade while attractive flowers and paved roads enhance the setting while giving easy access to the pitches. The 230 pitches vary in size and shape, but all have electricity and many have drainage. A sister site to nos. IT6036 and IT6014, Vela Blu is a relatively new, small, family style site and a pleasant alternative to the other massive sites on Cavallino. The clean, fine sand beach runs the length of one side of the site with large stone breakwaters for fun and fishing. It is fenced making it safer for children and access is via a gate where there a colourful outdoor showers and footbaths. The hub of the site is the charming restaurant and brilliant play area on soft sand, both adjoining a barbecue terrace and enter-tainment area. A well stocked shop is also in this area. For those who enjoy a small quiet site, Vela Blu fits the bill. Venice is easy to access as is the local water park (there is no pool here as yet). The entrance can become congested in busy periods due to limited waiting space.

Facilities
Two excellent modern toilet blocks include baby rooms and good facilities for disabled visitors. An attendant is on hand to maintain high standards. New washing machines and dryers. Dogs are catered for with a fun doggy pool and shower. Motorcaravan service point. Medical room. Shop. Bar. Restaurant and takeaway. Games room. TV room with satellite. Table tennis. Volleyball. Windsurfing. Fishing. Bicycle hire. Entertainment for children and adults by a professional animation team. Off site: Information pack provided to all campers on local entertainment. Theme parks. Bars Restaurants. Shops. Ferry to Venice.

At a glance
Welcome & Ambience	✓✓✓✓✓	Location	✓✓✓
Quality of Pitches	✓✓✓✓	Range of Facilities	✓✓✓✓

Directions
Leave A4 (Venice - Trieste) motorway at exit for Aeroporto and follow signs for Jesolo and Punta Sabbioni. Site is signed after village of Cavallino.

Charges 2003
Per person	€ 3.80 - € 6.80
child (1-5 yrs)	free - € 6.00
seniors (over 60)	€ 2.90 - € 6.00
pitch	€ 8.70 - € 14.60
dog	€ 4.40

Camping Cheques accepted.

Reservations
Made with deposit (Sat-Sat). Tel: 041 968068. Email: info@velablu.it

Open
8 April - 18 September.

IT6205 Camping International Dolomiti

Via Campo di Sotto, 32043 Cortina d'Ampezzo (Veneto)

The Cortina region boasts several good sites and this family run site is one of the nearest to the town. Beside a fast flowing river in a broad flat, grassy area surrounded by mountain scenery, it is a quiet situation three kilometres from the town centre. The 390 good sized pitches are marked out by white stones on either sides of access roads and most have electricity (4A). Half the site is well shaded. There is a heated swimming pool on site. With no reservations made, arrive early in the day in the first three weeks of August.

Facilities
The main toilet block is large and should be adequate, including mainly Turkish style WCs, with some British, and washbasins with hot water sprinkler taps. A heated block has been added providing facilities for disabled visitors. Washing machines and ironing. Gas supplies. Small shop (open long hours) and coffee bar. Swimming pool (1/7-31/8). Basic playground (hard base). Off site: Restaurant 600 m. Fishing 1 km. Golf 2 km. Bicycle hire and riding 3 km.

At a glance
Welcome & Ambience	✓✓✓	Location	✓✓✓
Quality of Pitches	✓✓✓✓	Range of Facilities	✓✓✓

Directions
Site is south of Cortina, to west of main S51. There are signs from the road.

Charges 2003
Per person	€ 4.50 - € 7.50
child (under 6 yrs)	€ 2.50 - € 4.00
pitch	€ 7.00 - € 9.00

Reservations
Not made; contact site for information only. Tel: 0436 2485. Email: campeggiodolomiti@tin.it

Open
1 June - 15 September.

IT6036 Camping Ca'Pasquali

Via A. Poeri, 33, 30010 Cavallino (Veneto)

On the attractive natural woodland coast of Cavallino with its wide sandy beach, Ca'Pasquali is a holiday resort with easy access to Venice. This is an ideal place for a holiday interspersed with excursions to Verona, Padova, the glassmakers of Murano and the local water park. This is a large site affiliated with nos. IT6028 and IT6014. The detail is important here; there are superb pools, a fitness area, an arena for entertainment and a beach-side restaurant. The generously sized pitches are shaded and flat, serviced with drainage and some have spectacular sea views. The fine sandy beach was alive with families playing games, flying kites and enjoying themselves as we watched from the restaurant as the sun set. A family site with many extras, Ca'Pasquali has been thoughtfully designed to a high standard – it is ideal for families as a resort holiday or to combine with sightseeing.

Facilities

Three spotless modern units have excellent facilities with mainly British toilets (paper and thoughtfully, paper seat covers), superb facilities for disabled campers and babies. Washing machines and dryers. Motorcaravan service point. Restaurant with sea views. Snack bar. Supermarket. Very nice pool complex with slides, fun pool and fountains. Aerobics. Fitness centre. Pool bar (happy hour). Play areas. Beach volleyball. Bicycle hire. Small boat launching. Animation. Amphitheatre. Mini-club. Extensive excursion service. Caravan storage. Dogs and other animals are not accepted. Off site: Golf and riding 5 km. Sailing. Fishing. Theme parks.

At a glance

Welcome & Ambience	✓✓✓	Location	✓✓✓✓✓
Quality of Pitches	✓✓✓✓✓	Range of Facilities	✓✓✓✓✓

Directions

Leave autostrada A4 at Sant Dona Noventa exit and head for Sant Dona di Piave, Losolo and on to peninsula of Cavallino. Site is well signed shortly after town of Cavallino.

Charges 2003

Per adult	€ 4.20 - € 7.60
child (1-5 yrs)	free - € 5.70
senior (over 60 yrs)	€ 2.70 - € 7.60
pitch	€ 7.20 - € 21.50

Reservations

Made for min. 7 days with € 130 deposit..
Tel: 041 96 61 10. Email: info@capasquali.it

Open

30 April - 18 September.

IT6032 Camping Cavallino

Via delle Batterie 164, 30013 Cavallino (Veneto)

This large, well ordered site is run by a friendly, experienced family who have other sites in this guide. It lies beside the sea with direct access to a superb beach of fine sand, which is very safe and enjoys the cover of several lifeguards. The site is thoughtfully laid out with large numbers of unusually large pitches shaded by olives and pines. All pitches have electricity. There is a 10% tour operator presence. If you wish to visit Venice a bus service runs to the ferry at Punta Sabbioni, some 20 minutes distance. You then catch an interconnecting ferry which, after a charming journey of 40 minutes, drops you directly at St Marco Square after negotiating its way around the gondolas. A late return will mean a two kilometres walk at the end of a different bus service, but the night views of Venice from the sea are wonderful. Be sure to pay independently at the ferry rather than using the supposed cheap'all-in' tickets which in fact are more expensive.

Facilities

Clean and modern toilet blocks are well spaced and provide a mixture of Turkish and British style WCs with facilities for disabled campers. Launderette. Motorcaravan services. Large shop providing most requirements. Swimming pools (May-Sept). Restaurant with large terrace, offering rapid service and takeaway. The menu is varied and reasonably priced with some excellent shell-fish and pasta dishes. Pizzeria. Table tennis. Minigolf. Play area. Ambitious animation programme is provided, aimed mostly at younger guests. Dogs not accepted.

At a glance

Welcome & Ambience	✓✓✓	Location	✓✓✓✓
Quality of Pitches	✓✓✓	Range of Facilities	✓✓✓✓

Directions

From Venice - Trieste autostrada leave at exit for airport or Quarto and Altino. Follow signs, first for Jesolo and then Punta Sabbiono, and site signs will be seen just after Cavallino on the left.

Latest charges

Per person	€ 3.30 - € 7.30
child (1-6 yrs) or over 60's	€ 2.80 - € 5.90
pitch incl. electricity (4A)	€ 9.30 - € 18.50

Min. stay in high season I week. No credit cards.

Reservations

Made for letting units only, but site provides priority cards for previous visitors. Tel: 041 966133.
Email: info@campingcavallino.com

Open

11 April - 11 October.

Visiting Venice

If you are visiting Italy, a trip to Venice is a must; it is said that you will either love it or find it totally distasteful, but you will walk away enchanted. The city boasts a whole host of sights to keep you entertained, with the Basilica di San Marco and the Palazzo Ducale drawing the largest crowds. One of the best times to visit the city is in the late afternoon, after the crowds have thinned out.

Venice is a grouping of 117 islands, divided into six districts separated by 45 km. of canals. You cross the patchwork of islands and canals on a confusion of footways and attractive bridges. Be sure to allow lots of time for getting around as we guarantee that you will get lost at some point. As a general guide, walking directly from St Marco Square to the bus/train station via the Rialto Bridge will take approximately 45 minutes (without getting lost!).

The Gondolas of Venice

The gondola has been a part of Venice since the 11th century. Measuring 36 feet (10.5 m) long, 4 feet (1.3 m) wide, they are perfectly adapted to negotiating the many narrow, shallow canals of Venice. There is a slight curve to the right, which counteracts the force of the oar, enabling the gondola to travel in a straight path. Apart from the common gondola used for the tourist trade, there is

also the gondola traghetto, which is used to ferry passengers across the grand canal; the gondola regatta, used for racing; and the gondolino, also used for racing, but which is lighter and faster.

A good map of Venice is essential and a compass might prove useful when navigating the fascinating labyrinths of alleys, canals and bridges. There are official signs but enterprising business people here have also erected their own signs to ensure you pass their premises. This makes navigation difficult when attempting to find major features and therefore all signs which are not of the official pattern should be ignored.

When looking for somewhere to eat or drink, beware of overpriced restaurants, as Venice can be very expensive – try to venture to the quieter areas where it is possible to find reasonably priced menus. Local specialities include fish and seafood, and the surrounding area also produces very palatable wines. Just relax, eat and be merry!

73

IT6035 Camping Mediterraneo

Via delle Batterie 38 Ca'Vio, 30010 Cavallino-Treporti (Veneto)

This large site has been considerably improved in recent years and is near Punta Sabbioni from where boats go to Venice. Mediterraneo is directly on the Adriatic Sea with a 480 m. long beach of fine sand which shelves gently and also two large pools (one for adults, the other for children) and a whirlpool. Sporting, fitness and entertainment programmes are arranged and sea swimming is supervised at designated hours by lifeguards. The 750 touring pitches, of which 500 have electricity (from 4A), water and drainaway, are partly in boxes with artificial shade, some larger without shade, with others in unmarked zones under natural woodland equipped with electric hook ups where tents must go. Used by tour operators (145 pitches). This is an organised and efficient site.

Facilities

Eight modern sanitary blocks are of good quality with British type WCs and free hot water in washbasins, showers and sinks. Washing machines. Motorcaravan services. Refrigerator hire. Commercial centre with supermarket and other shops with a restaurant, bars and a pizzeria near the pools. Swimming pool. Playground. Tennis court. Minigolf. Table tennis. Bicycle hire. Surf and swimming school. Regular monthly programme of sports, organised games, excursions etc; dancing or shows 3 times weekly in main season. Fitness programme. Dogs are not accepted. Off site: Riding and golf 3 km.

At a glance

Welcome & Ambience	✓✓✓✓	Location	✓✓✓✓
Quality of Pitches	✓✓✓	Range of Facilities	✓✓✓✓

Directions

Site is well signed from Jesolo-Punta Sabbioni road near its end after Ca' Ballarin and before Ca' Savio. Follow camp signs, not those for Treporti as this village is some way from the site.

Charges 2003

Per person	€ 3.80 - € 8.10
child (3-5 yrs) or senior (60 yrs)	€ 2.60 - € 6.35
pitch with electricity	€ 7.20 - € 18.50
pitch with 3 services	€ 8.00 - € 20.20
tent pitch with electricity	€ 5.80 - € 16.50

Four rates.

Reservations

Made with large deposit. Tel: 041 966721. Email: mediterraneo@vacanze-natura.it

Open

4 May - 22 September.

IT6039 Camping Sant'Angelo

Via F. Baracca 63, 30013 Cavallino (VE) (Veneto)

Sant Angelo Village is aptly named as the site has a central square with an information centre and booking service for excursions. The staff here are fluent in several languages including English. There is a restaurant under a huge canvas canopy and a huge supermarket and fresh vegetable stall. The square an ideal place for relaxing and for bringing campers together to enjoy each others company. An amazing pool complex with round pools interlocked like a series of bubbles is well fenced and supervised. It has its own large round café and amenities block. There are 500 level pitches of good size and shaded by mature trees. The site is well planned and includes a beach bar servicing the playground, sports areas and a fine sandy beach. Unusually a donation is paid to a UNICEF children's education programme for every child who stays at the campsite. This is a large site with a friendly atmosphere, ideal for families with young children and campers with mobility problems. A series of tours booked from the site makes it easy to access Verona, Padova, the glassmakers of Murano and there are day and night tours to Venice.

Facilities

Five modern toilet blocks provide excellent facilities with mainly British toilets and very good facilities for disabled campers and babies. Washing machines and dryers. Motorcaravan service point. Restaurant and snack bar. Supermarket. Great pool complex with spa and fun pool. Aerobics. Fitness centre. Play areas. Beach volleyball. Bicycle hire. Small boat launching. Mini-club, entertainment and excursion service. Dogs and other animals are not accepted. Off site: Sailing 1.5 km. Golf and riding 5 km. Theme parks.

At a glance

Welcome & Ambience	✓✓✓✓	Location	✓✓✓✓✓
Quality of Pitches	✓✓✓✓	Range of Facilities	✓✓✓✓✓

Directions

Leave autostrada A4 at Sant Dona Noventa exit and head for Sant Dona di Piave, Losolo and on to peninsula of Cavallino. Site is well signed shortly after town of Cavallino.

Charges 2003

Per person	€ 4.10 - € 8.45
child (under 5 yrs)	free - € 6.45
senior	€ 2.30 - € 6.45
pitch (incl. electricity and water)	€ 6.60 - € 20.00

Reservations

Made for min. 5 days with deposit. Tel: 041 96 88 82. Email: info@santangelo.it

Open

10 May - 20 September.

IT6040 Camping Village Garden Paradiso

Via Baracca 55, 30013 Cavallino (Veneto)

There are many sites in this area and there is much competition in providing a range of facilities. Garden Paradiso is a very good seaside site also providing three excellent centrally situated swimming pools. Compared with other sites here, this one is of medium size with 835 pitches. Most have electricity (from 6A), water and drainage points and all are marked and numbered with hard access roads, under a good cover of trees. Flowers and shrubs abound giving a pleasant and peaceful appearance. The site is directly on the sea with a beach of fine sand. The restaurant, with self-service at lunch time and waiter service at night, is near the beach with a bar/snack bar in the centre of the site. Used by tour operators (35 pitches).

Facilities

Four brick, tiled toilet blocks are fully equipped with a mix of British and Turkish style toilets. Facilities for babies. Dishwashing and laundry sinks. Washing machines and dryers. Motorcaravan services. Shopping complex. Restaurant (22/4-28/9). Snack bar and takeaway. Swimming pools. Tennis. Table tennis. Minigolf. Play area. Organised entertainment and excursions. Bicycle hire. Dogs are not accepted. Off site: Riding 2 km. Fishing 2.5 km.

At a glance

Welcome & Ambience	✓✓✓✓	Location	✓✓✓✓
Quality of Pitches	✓✓✓✓	Range of Facilities	✓✓✓✓

Directions

Leave Venice-Trieste autostrada either by taking the airport or Quarto d'Altino exits; follow signs to Jesolo and Punta Sabbioni. Take the first road on the left after Cavallino and site is a little way along on the right.

Charges 2003

Per person	€ 4.20 - € 8.25
junior (3-6 yrs) or senior (over 60)	€ 2.65 - € 6.35
baby (1-3 yrs)	free - € 5.30
pitch	€ 9.60 - € 21.00

Less 10% for stays over 30 days (early), or 20 days (late) season. Credit cards accepted.

Reservations

Made with deposit (€ 155) - write to site for details. Tel: 041 968075. Email: garden@vacanze-natura.it

Open

28 March - 30 September.

IT6050 Camping Della Serenissima

Via Padana 334/a, 30030 Oriago (Veneto)

This is a delightful little site of some 140 pitches (all with 16A electricity) where one could stay for a number of days whilst visiting the area's attractions. There is a good service by bus to Venice and the site is situated on the Riviera del Brenta, a section of a river with some very large old villas. It is used mainly by Dutch and British visitors, with some Germans, and is calm and quiet. A long, narrow and flat site, numbered pitches are on each side of a central road. There is good shade in most parts with many trees, plants and grass. The management is very friendly and good English is spoken.

Facilities

The single sanitary block is just adequate, has been and still is being improved, with hot water in washbasins, showers and sinks. Mainly Turkish style WCs. Motorcaravan services. Gas supplies. Shop (all season). Bar. Restaurant and takeaway (1/6-31/10). Play area. Fishing. Bicycle hire. Reduced price bus ticket to Venice if staying for 3 days. No organised entertainment but local markets etc. all well publicised. Off site: Golf and riding 3 km.

At a glance

Welcome & Ambience	✓✓✓✓✓	Location	✓✓✓✓
Quality of Pitches	✓✓✓✓	Range of Facilities	✓✓✓

Directions

From the east take road S11 at roundabout SSW of Mestre towards Padova and site is 2 km. on right. From west, leave autostrada A4 at Dolo exit, follow signs to Dolo, continue on main road through this small village and turn left at T-junction (traffic lights). Continue towards Venice on S11 for site about 6 km on left.

Charges 2003

Per adult	€ 5.60 - € 6.60
child (3-10 yrs)	€ 4.00 - € 5.00
caravan and car	€ 9.80 - € 10.80
tent and car	€ 8.80 - € 9.80
motorcaravan	€ 9.80 - € 10.80
dog	free

Reservations

Are made; contact site. Tel: 041 921850. Email: camping.serenissima@shineline.it

Open

Easter - 10 November.

IT6042 Camping Alba d'Oro

Via Triestina, Ca,Noghera, 30030 Mestre (Veneto)

This well managed site is ideal for visiting Venice and the site's bus service takes you directly to the bus station on the west side of the city. There is always room here and on arrival you can select your own pitch. There is a separate area for backpackers and yet another for families. The 140 pitches, all with electricity, are of reasonable size and separated. The good sized pool is especially welcome after a hot day spent visiting Venice. The site has its own new marina (with crane) and if you wish to bring your own boat you can enjoy the pleasant 40 minute trip into Venice the easy way. The site is close to the airport and loud aircraft noise will be heard on some pitches especially to the east. However, as there is no night flying allowed it is worth staying here to be close to the city. The clientele staying here changes rapidly and is very cosmopolitan, with a very large backpacker element in new tents and mobile homes, but the site is not terribly noisy.

Facilities

The four modern sanitary blocks are kept very clean. One block has facilities for disabled campers. Sinks for washing dishes and clothes. Launderette. Motorcaravan services. Restaurant with a most pleasant terrace overlooking the pool and serving good food at reasonable prices is very busy every night. Part of the same complex, is a lively bar with entertainment in season including pool parties and 'happy hours'. Pizzerias. Table tennis. Bicycle hire. Marina on site. Bus service 1 April - Oct. Shuttle bus to Verona for walking tour (Tuesday and Friday, 1.75 hrs).

At a glance

Welcome & Ambience	✓✓✓✓	Location	✓✓✓✓
Quality of Pitches	✓✓✓✓	Range of Facilities	✓✓✓✓

Directions

From Venice-Trieste autostrada leave at exit for airport and follow signs for Jesolo on the SS14. Site is on right at 10 km. marker.

Charges 2003

Per person	€ 6.40 - € 7.50
child (3-10 yrs)	€ 4.40 - € 5.50
pitch incl. electricity	€ 9.90 - € 10.60
tent	€ 8.50 - € 9.50

Reservations

Contact site. Tel: 041 5415102. Email: albadoro@tin.it

Open

1 February - 30 November.

IT6053 Camping Fusina

Via Moranzani, 79, 30030 Fusina (Veneto)

There are some sites that take one by surprise – this is one. This is old fashioned camping, but what fun, and we met English speaking people who have been coming here for 30 years. Choose from 500 well shaded, flat and grassy informal pitches or a position with views over the lagoon to the towers in St Mark's Square. With water on three sides there are welcoming cool breezes and fortunately many trees hide the industrial area close by. The site owns a large ferry car park and a 700-boat marina which accepts and launches all manner of craft. A deep water channel carries huge ships close by and the water views are never boring. Fusina offers a very easy and comfortable, 20 minute ferry connection to the cultural heart of Venice, Accademia. Several site buildings, including the some of the showers and toilets, were designed by the famous modern architect Scarpa. These are heritage listed and are visited by design students, although this listing makes development and improvement difficult. Those who don't wish to be disturbed by the lively bar can choose from the many superb informal waterside pitches on the far end of the site.

Facilities

Despite planning difficulties sanitary facilities are clean and appropriate, including well equipped new units for disabled campers. Many washing machines and dryers. Motorcaravan service point. Charming restaurant (no credit cards; English breakfast served). Shop (March - 31 Oct). Many of the staff are mature Australian/New Zealand people and English is used everywhere. Playground. Volleyball. Very lively bar entertainment. Boat hire. TV with satellite. Pizzeria and beer garden. Marina with cranes, moorings,and maintenance facilities. Air-conditioned London Cyber bus (really!). Torches useful. ATM. Off site: Excellent public transport and ferry connections to Venice. Boat trips along the Brenta Canal. Ticket office for Croatia, Slovenia, Greece and Turkey. Golf 20 km.

At a glance

Welcome & Ambience	✓✓✓	Location	✓✓✓✓✓
Quality of Pitches	✓✓✓	Range of Facilities	✓✓✓✓

Directions

From SSII Padua - Venice road follow site sign on road east of Mira, turning right as signed. Site is in Fusina at end of peninsula and is well signed (also indicated as 'Fusina parking').

Charges 2003

Per unit	€ 14.00
person	€ 7.00
child (5-12yrs)	€ 4.00

Reservations

No need to book for motorcaravans or tents, otherwise contact site. Tel: 04 15 47 00 55. Email: info@camping-fusina.com

Open

All year.

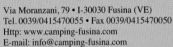

IT6045 Camping Marina di Venezia

Via Montello 6, 30010 Punta Sabbioni (Veneto)

This is a very large site (2,300 pitches) with much the same atmosphere as many other large sites along this appealing stretch of coastline. Marina di Venezia, however, has the advantage of being within walking distance of the ferry to Venice. It will appeal particularly to those who enjoy an extensive range of entertainment and activities, and a lively atmosphere. The site's excellent sandy beach is one of the widest along this stretch of coast and has a pleasant beach bar. The main pool is Olympic sized and there is also a very large children's pool adjacent. Pitches are marked out individually on sandy terrain and most are separated by trees or hedges. They are of an average size for the region (around 80 sq.m). Most are equipped with electricity, and some have water and drainage.

Facilities

Ten modern toilet blocks are maintained to a high standard with good hot showers and a reasonable proportion of British-style toilets. Good provision for disabled visitors. Washing machines and dryers. Shopping facilities include a fish shop, sports shop and a shoe shop, to name but three! Several bars, restaurants and takeaway facilities. Swimming pools (no slides). Several play areas including bouncy castle. Tennis, football, beach volleyball, windsurf and catamaran hire. Wide range of organised entertainment including a good childrens' club in high season. Church on site.

At a glance

Welcome & Ambience	✓✓✓✓	Location	✓✓✓✓
Quality of Pitches	✓✓✓	Range of Facilities	✓✓✓✓

Directions

From A4 motorway, take Jesolo exit. After Jesolo continue towards Punta Sabbioni. Site is clearly signed to the left towards the end of this road, close to the embarkation point for Venice ferries.

Charges 2003

Per person	€ 3.83 - € 7.55
child or senior (under 5 and over 60)	€ 3.26 - € 6.17
pitch incl. services	€ 9.64 - € 18.46
pitch incl. satellite TV connection	€ 11.63 - € 2.13
dog	€ 0.90 - € 2.35

Reservations

Essential for high season – contact site. Tel: 041 530 2511. Email: camping@marinadivenezia.it

Open

20 April - 30 September.

IT6055 Villaggio Turistico Isamar

Isolaverde, via Isamar, 9, 30010 S. Anna di Chioggia (Veneto)

Many improvements have been made here over the years and these continue, making it quite difficult to itemise all the amenities. Although directly by the sea, with its own sandy beach, it is a fair way from the entrance to the sea. The largest camping area, which may be cramped at times, is under pines and grouped around the swimming pool, the large modern sanitary block, shops, etc. near reception. A smaller area is under artificial shade near the beach with an Olympic size, salt-water swimming pool, children's pool and four new pools, a covered entertainment section, pizzeria, bar/restaurant and a small toilet block. Between these sections are well constructed holiday bungalows. A third camping area has been developed mainly for the site's own accommodation. The pitches, on either side of hard access roads, vary in size and all have electrical connections. The site has a much higher proportion of Italian holidaymakers than many other sites. It is also popular with the Germans and Dutch and may become crowded in high season.

Facilities

The main toilet blocks are fully equipped and of good quality with British style WCs (small block has only Turkish style). Dishwashing and laundry sinks. Laundry. Motorcaravan services. Gas supplies. Fridges for hire. Hairdresser. Supermarket and general shopping centre. Large bar/pizzeria and self-service restaurant. Swimming pools. Tennis. Playground. Disco. Games room with pin tables. Riding. Bicycle hire. Extensive entertainment and fitness programme offered for adults and supervised play for children over 4 years of age. Dogs are not accepted. Off site: Fishing 500 m.

At a glance

Welcome & Ambience	✓✓✓✓	Location	✓✓✓✓
Quality of Pitches	✓✓✓	Range of Facilities	✓✓✓✓✓

Directions

Turn off main 309 road towards sea just south of Adige river about 10 km. south of Chioggia, and proceed 5 km. to site.

Latest charges

Per person	€ 3.50 - € 8.80
child (2-5 yrs)	€ 2.50 - € 7.40
pitch with full facilities	€ 5.00 - € 20.00
tent pitch	€ 4.00 - € 10.50

Less 10% for stays in low season for over 2 weeks.

Reservations

Made for min. 7 days with deposit from Sat. Tel: 041 5535 811. Email: info@villaggioisamar.com

Open

13 May - 16 September.

IT6030 Camping dei Fiori

Via Pisani 52, Ca'Vio, 30010 Ca' Vio Treporti (Veneto)

The Lido del Cavallino peninsula, stretching from the outskirts of Lido del Jesolo to Punta Sabbioni, has over 30 good sites directly on the Adriactic sea. Dei Fiori stands out amongst the other small camps in the area. As its name implies, it is aflame with colourful flowers and shrubs in summer and presents a neat and tidy appearance whilst providing a quiet atmosphere. The 420 pitches, with electricity (5/6A), are either in woodland where space varies according to the trees which have been left in their natural state, or under artificial shade where regular shaped pitches are of reasonable size. Well built bungalows for rent enhance the site and are in no way intrusive, giving a village-like effect. About a quarter of the pitches are taken by static units, many for hire. Shops and a restaurant are in the centre next to the swimming pools. Nearby is the hydro-massage bath which is splendidly appointed and reputed to be the largest in Italy. The long beach is of fine sand and shelves gently into the sea. Regulations ensure the site is quiet between 11 pm-7.30 am and during the afternoon siesta period. Venice is about 40 minutes away by bus and boat and excursions are arranged from the site. The site is well maintained by friendly, English speaking management.

Facilities

Three sanitary blocks are conveniently situated around the site and are of exceptional quality with British style WCs, well equipped baby rooms, good facilities for disabled people and washing machines and dryers. Motorcaravan services. Restaurant. Snack bar. Shops. Swimming pools and whirl pool. Fitness centre, hydro-massage bath and programmes (1/5-30/9) under the supervision of qualified staff (a charge is made during middle and high seasons but not in low season). Tennis. Table tennis. Minigolf. Basketball. Children's club and play area. Windsurfing. Organised activities, entertainment and excursions. Dogs are not accepted. Off site: Bicycle hire 2 km. Riding 4 km.

At a glance

Welcome & Ambience	✓✓✓✓	Location	✓✓✓
Quality of Pitches	✓✓✓✓	Range of Facilities	✓✓✓✓

Directions

Leave A4 Venice-Trieste autostrada either by taking exit for airport or Quarto d'Altino and follow signs for Jesolo and then Punta Sabbioni and camp signs just after Ca'Ballarin.

Latest charges

Per person	€ 4.20 - € 8.50
child (1-4 yrs) or senior over 65 yrs	€ 3.20- € 7.50
pitch with 3 services	€ 9.30 - € 19.80
pinewood pitch with electricity	€ 8.00 - € 18.40
tent pitch in pinewood with electricity	€ 6.60 - € 16.50

Min. stay 7 days in high season (4/7-29/8).

Reservations

Advised for high season (incl. Whitsun) and made for min. 7 days. Write for application form as early as possible. Tel: 041 966448.
Email: fiori@vacanze-natura.it

Open

12 April - 4 October.

Friuli-Venézia Giúlia is a beautiful border region nudging Slovenia on the east, Austria and the Carnic Alps to the north with the Adriatic to the south – forming a bridge between the Mediterranean world and central Europe.

The region has four provinces:
Gorizia, Pordenone, Trieste and Udine

Near the Slovenian border lies the atmospheric city of Trieste, with its long bustling harbour. The prime tourist site is the hill of San Giusto; at the summit is the castle and a walk along the ramparts offers sweeping views over the Gulf of Trieste. Across the bay, Múggia is only a short ferry ride from Trieste, whilst outside the city is an area of limestone uplands, known as the Carso. With an abundance of caves, including the Grotta Gigante, the world's largest accessible cave and second largest natural chamber in the world, the Carso can be easily reached by the *tranvia* (cable tramway). Sitting on a group of low islands in the middle of the Adriatic lagoon, Grado is attached to the mainland by a long, narrow causeway. A popular seaside resort, it has a long sandy beach and harbour plus a historic centre. A short distance from here is Aquileia, now a small town but once an important city of the Roman Empire and further inland Udine boasts galleries, fine churches, and well-preserved historic buildings. Towards the Austrian border in the north, is Carnia. With its lush valleys and flower-filled meadows, which give way to Alpine peaks, it is an area popular with walkers.

Cuisine of the region

Fish broths, made from squid, octopus, mackerel, sardines and clams, are common. Gnocchi is a Trieste speciality; gnocchi the size of eggs are stuffed with pitted prune, rolled in breadcrumbs, browned in butter and sprinkled with cinnamon and sugar. Local wines include Tocai, Ribolla Gialla, Merlot and Cabernet Sauvignon.

Brodo di Pesce: fish soup, sometimes flavoured with saffron

Cialzons: ravioli from Carnia, usually stuffed with spinach and ricotta

Jota: a soup of sauerkraut and barley

Spaghetti alle Vongole: spaghetti with fresh clams in a chilli-pepper sauce

Places of interest

Aquileia: Basilica, with mosiac pavement dating from the 4th century

Cividale del Friuli: market town, medieval walls, archaeology museum

Forni di Sopra: thickly wooded area, popular for mountain-biking, horse-riding and hiking

Gorizia: major shopping town, numerous parks and gardens, castle

Pordenon: preserved historic centre

Tarvisio: small mountain resort

tip

VISIT AN *OSMIZZE*, AN INFORMAL EATING PLACE WHERE FARMERS SELL THEIR OWN PRODUCE, USUALLY SITUATED OFF THE BEATEN TRACK. ASK THE LOCAL TOURIST OFFICE FOR DETAILS.

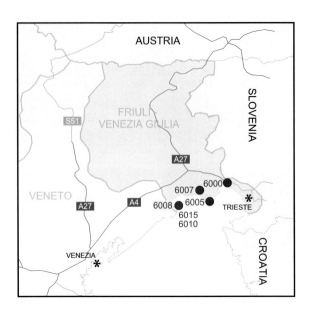

IT6000 Camping Mare Pineta

Sistiana 60 D, Duino - Aurisina, 34019 Trieste (Friuli-Venézia Giúlia)

This site is 18 km. west of Trieste, and is on raised ground near the sea with views over the Sistiana Bay, Miramare Castle and the Gulf of Trieste. A pebbly beach, with a car park, lies just beyond the site, a drive of about one kilometre (a free bus service runs every 40 mins from 9 am-7 pm), and there is a large swimming pool (unheated) on site with a new terrace. The development of this site continues with modern reception buildings and improved sanitary facilities. Over 350 of the 500 individual pitches are available for tourists. They are on gravel hardstanding (awnings possible) in light wood-land, all with electricity (from 3A) and with water nearby. Space is nearly always available (1-15 Aug. is the busiest). For arrivals outside office hours, a waiting area has water and toilet facilities. The Rilke footpath runs along the seaside border of the site. It is reported that a weekend disco on the beach below the campsite involves noisy vehicle departures at 3 am. The site is used by a tour operator.

Facilities

Six toilet blocks of varying quality, some recently modernised and extended, provide some washbasins in cabins and some for children (the hot water supply does not always cope with the demand) and WCs of both British and Turkish style. Facilities for disabled people. Sinks for laundry and dishwashing, most with hot water. Laundry with dryer and ironing. Motorcaravan service point. Shop (all season). Bars. Pizzeria with terrace. Disco. Swimming pool (1/6-15/9) with lessons. Playground. Facilities for football, volleyball and mini-basket. Tennis. Table tennis. Games room. Organised entertainment in season. No dogs or animals are accepted. Off site: Bicycle hire 500 m. Fishing 1 km. Riding 2 km. Golf 10 km.

At a glance

Welcome & Ambience	✓✓✓	Location	✓✓✓✓
Quality of Pitches	✓✓✓✓	Range of Facilities	✓✓✓✓

Directions

From west take Sistiana exit from A4 autostrada, turn right and site is 1 km. on right; from east approach on S14.

Charges 2003

Per person	€ 3.90 - € 7.00
child (3-12 yrs)	€ 3.00 - € 5.50
pitch incl. electricity and water	€ 8.00 - € 16.00
pitch with view of the bay	€ 11.00 - € 20.00

Reservations

Made with 40% deposit and € 15,49 fee.
Tel: 040 299264. Email: info@marepineta.com

Open

12 April - 30 September.

IT6005 Villaggio Turistico Camping Europa

P.O. Box 129, 34073 Grado (Friuli-Venézia Giúlia)

This large flat site beside the sea can take almost 650 units. All the pitches are marked, nearly all with good shade, and there are electrical connections in all areas. The terrain is undulating and sandy in the areas nearer the sea, where cars have to be left in parking places and not by your pitch. There is direct access to the beach but the water is shallow up to 200 metres from beach, with growing seaweed. However, a narrow wooden jetty is provided which one can walk along to deeper water. For those who prefer, there is a swimming pool near the sea and, on the site, a medium sized heated pool and smaller children's pool. This is a good honest site which, after recent improvements, is probably the best in the area.

Facilities

Six toilet blocks are identical and should make up a good supply, with free hot water in all facilities, half British style WCs and facilities for disabled people. Washing machines. Motorcaravan services. Large supermarket; small general shop (May - Sept). Large bar and restaurant/pizzeria, with takeaway (all season). Swimming pools (May - Sept, 10 am -7 pm). Two tennis courts. Football pitch. Table tennis. Fishing. Bicycle hire. Playground. Dancing, at times, in season; some organised activities June/Aug. Dogs are taken only in a special section and in limited numbers. Off site: Golf 500 m. Riding 4 km.

At a glance

Welcome & Ambience	✓✓✓	Location	✓✓✓
Quality of Pitches	✓✓✓	Range of Facilities	✓✓✓✓

Directions

Site is 4 km. east of Grado on road to Monfalcone. If road 35L is taken to Grado from west, continue through the town to Grado Pineta.

Charges 2004

Per person	€ 5.50 - € 8.00
child (3-12 yrs)	free - € 5.50
pitch incl. electricity (4/8A)	
acc. to season and location	€ 8.00 - € 16.00
dog	€ 2.50 - € 6.00

Less 10% for longer stays out of season.

Reservations

Advised for high season and made for min. 1 week from Sat. to Sat., with deposit in high season (50% of total). Tel: 0431 80877. Email: info@villageeuropa.com

Open

10 April - 26 September.

IT6007 Camping Village Belvedere Pineta

33051 Grado (Friuli-Venézia Giúlia)

Belvedere Pineta is situated on the edge of an almost entirely land-locked lagoon, five kilometres from Grado on the northern Adriatic Sea. A minor road runs between the site and the lagoon and a bridge over this connects the site with the beach of fine sand. It is a large site with 900 tourist pitches arranged in regular rows with most under shade provided by the many tall pine trees which cover the site. Most are of reasonable size and all have electricity (4/6A). An area of letting accommodation is to one side of the camping area. With two pools, an area for ball games, tennis courts, minigolf, table tennis and the beach there are plenty activities to enjoy and during high season (July/Aug) there is a large programme of sport and entertainment for both children and adults organised.

Facilities

Most of the six toilet blocks have been refurbished to a good standard with all the usual facilities including some for children and free hot water in all basins, showers and sinks. Facilities for disabled visitors. Motorcaravan service point. Range of shops. Restaurant, pizzeria and takeaway. Swimming pools. Sports facilities. Play areas. Organised entertainment in high season.

At a glance

Welcome & Ambience	✓✓✓✓	Location	✓✓✓✓
Quality of Pitches	✓✓✓✓	Range of Facilities	✓✓✓✓

Directions

Leave A4 (Venice - Trieste) motorway at exit for Palmanova and go south on SS352 towards Grado. Camp is signed after Aquileia and is on the left.

Charges 2003

Per person (10-60 yrs)	€ 3.20 - € 8.00
senior (over 60 yrs)	€ 2.70 - € 6.70
child (2-10 yrs)	free - € 5.70
pitch	€ 7.60 - € 19.00
dog	€ 2.60 - € 6.50

Camping Cheques accepted.

Reservations

Contact site. Tel: 0431 91007. Email: info@belvederepineta.it

Open

1 May - 30 September.

IT6008 Camping Sabbiaddoro

Via Sabbiadoro 8, 33054 Lignano Sabbiadoro (Friuli-Venézia Giúlia)

This is a large, quality site with a huge entrance and efficient reception. It has over 1,250 pitches and is ideal for families who like all their facilities to be close by. The local resort town is just 200 m. away and buzzes with activity in high season The fine beach is 250 m. distant and safe for children. The pitches vary in size, are shaded by attractive trees and have electricity. The amenities are all in excellent condition and well thought out especially the pool complex. Everything here is very modern, safe and clean. You may wish to cover your car and unit to prevent sap covering it over time. A second site close by is opened for younger customers in high season – they use the main site facilities.

Facilities

Well equipped sanitary facilities include superb facilities for disabled visitors. Washing machines and dryers. Huge supermarket (12/4-29/9). Bazaar. Newspapers. Good restaurant and snack bar (31/5-29/9). Heated outdoor pool complex with separate fun pool area, slides and fountains (late May - Sept). Table tennis. Disco. TV Room. Internet. Play areas. Tennis. Fitness centre. Volleyball. Billiards. Electronic games. Motorcaravan service point. Car work shop. Petrol station. Small boat launching. Surgery. Range of entertainment in the main season. Dogs are not accepted in high season. Discount shopping cards issued to campers with local offers. Off site: Fine beach near particulary good for children. Windsurfing. Volleyball. Minigolf. Bicycle hire. First aid. Shops, restaurants and bars. Riding, sailing and golf 2 km. Various theme parks.

Directions

Leave A4 at Latisana exit, west of Triest and head to Latisano. From Latisano follow road to Lignano and then Sabbiadoro. Site is well signed as you approach the town.

Charges 2003

Per adult	€ 3.90 - € 7.30
child (3-12 yrs)	€ 2.60 - € 4.20
pitch	€ 6.20 - € 11.40
pitch with electricity (6/10A)	€ 7.00 - € 12.20

Reservations

Made for min. 15 days with € 50 deposit.
Tel: 0431 71455. Email: campsab@dns.netanday.it

Open

23 March - 29 September

At a glance

Welcome & Ambience	✓✓✓✓	Location	✓✓✓✓
Quality of Pitches	✓✓✓✓	Range of Facilities	✓✓✓✓

Ligúria is a long, thin coastal strip nestling at the foot of olive and vine clad mountains. The Italian Riviera boasts an abundance of sandy beaches and charming seaside villages, while inland the mountain resorts offer plenty of walking and a respite from the crowds.

The region has four provinces:
Genova, Imperia, La Spezia and Savona

Ligúria divides neatly into two distinct stretches of coastline; to the west is the Riviera di Ponente and to the east is the Riviera Levante. Between the two lies Genoa, Italy's biggest port. It has a fascinating old town with medieval alleyways, and numerous palaces and churches to explore. It was also once the home of Christopher Columbus. The surrounding hills offer a quiet retreat from the city: the picturesque Valle Scrivia has several hiking routes and is easily accessible from the small town of Casella. Stretching across to the French border the Riveria di Ponente has a number of places of interest: the pretty wine-producing town of Dolceacqua; the pleasant resort of San Remo; the charming seafront village of Cervo; and the medieval hilltown of Toirano. There are more coastal resorts along the Riviera Levante including Portofino, the most exclusive harbour and resort town in Italy. With sandy beaches and small coves, this attractive area also offers good walking. Further along is the coastline of the Cinque Terre (Five Lands). The name refers to five tiny villages which appear to cling dramatically to the edge of sheer cliffs: Monterosso al Mare, Vernazza, Corniglia, Manrola and Riomaggiore.

Cuisine of the region

The best known speciality is *pesto*: made with chopped basil, garlic, pine nuts and grated cheese with olive oil, it was invented by the Genoese to help their long term sailors fight scurvy. Fish and seafood is readily available, often eaten with pasta. Chickpeas grow in abundance, and make *farinata*, a kind of chickpea pancake. Genoa is famous for its *pandolce*, a sweet cake laced with dried fruit, nuts and candied peel.

Burrida di seppie: cuttlefish stew

Cacciucco: rich stew of mixed fish and seafood cooked with wine, garlic and herbs

Carpione: fish marinated in vinegar and herbs

Cima alla Genovese: cold stuffed veal

Torta pasqualina: spinach and cheese pie

Trenette al Pesto: noodles with pesto

Places of interest

Albenga: small market town

Camogli: attractive resort

Cinque Terre: wine-growing region, picturesque villages, sandy coves and beaches

Dolceacqua: medieval stone bridge and ruined castle

La Spezia: museum with medieval and Rennaissance art, ferry trips to Bastia in Corsica

Lévanto: beachside resort

Portovénere: village with three islets offshore

Toirano: caves at the Grotte della Basura and Grotta di Santa Lucia

Villa Hanbury: impressive botanical gardens

tip

THE WATERS OFF THE LIGURIAN COAST COMPRISE AN INTERNATIONAL WHALE SANCTUARY, HOME TO 12 SPECIES OF WHALE PLUS DOLPHINS. BOAT TRIPS ARE AVAILABLE.

85

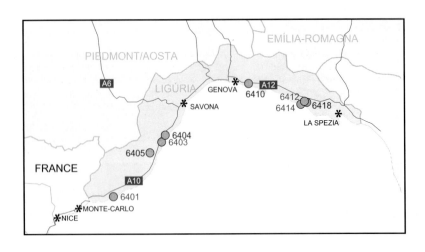

IT6401 Camping Villaggio dei Fiori

Via Tiro a Volo 3, 18038 San Remo (Ligúria)

Open all year round, this open and spacious site has high standards and is ideal for exploring the Italian Riviera or for just relaxing by the enjoyable, filtered sea water pools. If you prefer, there is a path to a secluded and pleasant beach overlooked by a large patio area. The beach surrounds are excellent for snorkelling and fishing. Unusually, most of the pitch areas at the site are totally paved and there are some extremely large pitches for large units (ask reception to open another gate for entry). There is ample shade from mature trees and shrubs, which are constantly watered and cared for in summer, and pleasant views over the sea from the western pitches. All pitches have electricity (only 3A) and there is an outside sink and cold water for every four Some super pitches overlook the beach edge. The friendly management speak excellent English and will supply detailed tourist plans. Excursions are offered (extra cost) along the Italian Riviera dei Fiori and the French Côte d'Azur. Buses run from outside the site to Monte Carlo, Nice, Cannes, Eze and many other places of interest.

Facilities

Three clean and modern sanitary blocks have British and Turkish style WCs and hot water throughout and two private cabins in each. Facilities for disabled campers. Washing machines, dryer and irons. Motorcaravan services. Large restaurant with fine menu and extensive terrace with giant children's toys close by. Bar sells essential supplies. Pizzeria and takeaway (all year). Sea water swimming pools (one for children, and both with a small extra charge in high season) and sophisticated whirlpool spa (June-Sept). Tennis. Table tennis. Volleyball. Play area. Fishing. Animation for children and adults in high season. Excursions. Bicycle hire. Dogs or other animals are not accepted. Off site: Shop 150 m. Riding and golf 2 km.

At a glance

Welcome & Ambience	✓✓✓✓	Location	✓✓✓✓
Quality of Pitches	✓✓✓	Range of Facilities	✓✓✓✓

Directions

From main SS1 Ventimiglia - Imperia road, site is on right side of road just before town of San Remo. There is a sharp right turn if the site is approached from the west. from autostrada A10 take San Remo Ouest exit. Site is well signed.

Charges 2003

Per pitch incl. up to 4 persons	€ 25.00 - € 46.00
half pitch incl. 2 persons, no car	€ 16.00 - € 28.00
electricity	€ 2.00

Some charges due on arrival. Discounts for stays in excess of 7 days. Discount for readers 10% in low season. Camping Cheques accepted.

Reservations

Contact site for details. Tel: 0184 660635.
Email: info@villaggiodeifiori.it

Open

All year.

IT6403 Camping Baciccia

Via Torino 19, 17023 Ceriale (Ligúria)

This friendly, family run site is a popular holiday destination. There is always a family member by the gate to greet you, and Vincenzina and Giovanni, along with their children Laura and Mauro, work tirelessly so ensure that you enjoy your stay. Tall eucalyptus trees shade the 120 tightly packed pitches which encircle the central facilities block. The pitches are on flat ground and all have electricity. Baciccia was the nick-name of the present owner's grandfather who grew fruit trees and tomatoes on the site. The informal restaurant overlooks a large swimming pool. The menu is simple and the traditional Italian food is freshly cooked. There is a half size tennis court and boule as well as organised water polo and pool games. If you have forgotten anything by way of camping equipment just ask and the family will loan it to you. The beach is a short walk and the town has the usual seaside attractions but it is worth visiting the tiny traditional villages close by. This may suit campers who wish for a family atmosphere and none of the brashness of large seaside sites.

Facilities

Two clean and modern sanitary blocks near reception have British and Turkish style WCs and hot water throughout. Washing machines, dryer and irons. Motorcaravan services. Restaurant/bar. Pizzeria and takeaway (all year). Sea water swimming pools (June-Sept). Tennis. Table tennis. Volleyball. Play area. Fishing. Animation for children and adults in high season. Excursions. Bicycle hire. Off site: Shop 150 m. Riding and golf 2 km.

At a glance

Welcome & Ambience	✓✓✓	Location	✓✓✓✓
Quality of Pitches	✓✓✓	Range of Facilities	✓✓✓

Directions

From the A10 (E80) between Imperia and Savona, take Albenga exit. Turn left towards Ceriale and Savona, turning left after 3 km. at traffic lights and follow signs to site.

Charges 2003

Per unit incl. up to 3 persons (over 2 yrs)	€ 22.00 - € 42.00
extra person	€ 4.00 -€ 8.00
half pitch incl. 2 persons, no car	€ 14.50 - € 27.50
dog	€ 2.00 - € 4.00

Discounts for stays in excess of 7 days. Discount for readers 10% in low season.

Reservations

Contact site. Tel: 0182 990 743.
Email: info@campingbaciccia.it

Open

All year.

500 m from the sea, situated immersed in the green and completely quiet. Comfortable bungalows-chalets and mobile homes for 2-6 persons with kitchenette, WC and one or two bedrooms. Heating and linen. **2 swimming pools, open from 1st April to 31 October.** Tennis, bocce, children's playground, animation, barbecue, bar, washing and drying machines and shopping possibilities. Modern sanitary facilities with hot water. **Special offers**

bungalow camping baciccia

Via Torino, 19 • I-17023 CERIALE (Savona) • Riviera dei Fiori
Tel. 0039/0182990743
Fax 0039/0182993839
Http: www.campingbaciccia.it
Http: web.tiscalinet.it/baciccia
E-mail: info@campingbaciccia.it

IT6405 Camping C'era una Volta

Localita Fasceti, 17038 Villanova d'Albenga (Ligúria)

An attractive campsite, C'era una Volta is about eight kilometres back from the sea, situated on a hill-side with panoramic views. Pitches are on terraces in different sections of the site, with 120 for tourers (45 for tents). Varying in size, most pitches have shade from the young trees harbouring crickets with their distinctive noise. Some of the upper pitches have good views. Cars are required to park in separate areas at busy times. There are electricity connections (6A), with water and a drain close by. The charming creeper covered restaurant has a large sheltered terrace. Amenities include four excellent swimming pools in different parts of the site, open in the main season. One is large (30 m) with a children's pool in the upper area, another, also with a large children's pool is by the restaurant and is overlooked by the entertainment area. A small concealed section at the top of the site is fenced off for naturists to sunbathe in privacy. Charges are high in season but the site has an enjoyable atmosphere. A private beach is one kilometre (reduced cost to campers), and a bus runs to the beach. This is a good site for families.

Facilities

The main toilet block is modern and above average with hot water throughout. Four additional smaller blocks are spread around the site. Maintenance can be variable. Shop. Bar and pizzeria (15/5-10/9). Restaurant with good traditional menu. Takeaway (high season). Disco (July/Aug). Swimming pool complex (15/5-20/9). Tennis. Large adventure playground. Fitness track with exercise points. Small, modern gym and fitness track. Organised sports and other events in season, also dancing or entertainment some nights. Boule. Electronic games. Table tennis. Off site: Riding 500 m. Golf 2 km.

At a glance

Welcome & Ambience	✓✓✓✓	Location	✓✓✓✓
Quality of Pitches	✓✓✓	Range of Facilities	✓✓✓

Directions

Leave autostrada A10 at Albenga, turn left and left again at roundabout for the SS453 for Villanova. Follow Villanova signs to T-junction, turn left towards Garlenda, turn right in 200 m. and follow signs to site.

Charges 2003

Per pitch incl. up to 3 persons	€ 19.00 - € 36.00
tent pitch incl. up to 3 persons	€ 16.00 - € 30.00
extra person	€ 6.00 - € 10.00

Credit cards not accepted. Electricity included. Discounts for longer stays in low season.

Reservations

Made for min. of a few days with 30% advance payment. Tel: 0182 580461. Email: camping@uno.it

Open

1 April - 30 September.

IT6410 Camping Genova Est

Via Marconi-loc Cassa, 16031 Bogliasco (Ligúria)

This wooded site is set on very steep slopes close to the Genoa motorways coming from the north or west and, although it has very limited facilities, it is quite near the town. There is a regular free bus service to the beach in high season, or if you are extremely fit a set of steep stairs will take you there in 15 minutes. The Buteros who run and own the site both speak good English and are enthusiastic and anxious to please. The approach from the main road twists and climbs steeply with a tight final turn at the site entrance. There are 54 touring pitches with electricity available. The small play area is set on a narrow terrace and children should be supervised. A pretty small bar and a little restaurant with a terrace give fine views over the sea. Torches are needed at night in several parts of the site. This is a site to be used for exploring Genoa and Riviera di Levante, rather than for extended stays.

Facilities

One of the two sanitary blocks provides free hot showers and en-suite cabins (WC, washbasin and shower). Washing machine. Motorcaravan services. Shop and bar/restaurant (both Easter - 30/9). Essential daily goods form restaurant. Towing vehicle available. Gas supplies. Site is not suitable for disabled people. Off site: Fishing 1.5 km.

At a glance

Welcome & Ambience	✓✓✓✓	Location	✓✓✓✓
Quality of Pitches	✓✓✓	Range of Facilities	✓✓

Directions

From autostrada A10 take Nervi exit and turn left (south) on the SS1 towards La Spezia. In Bogliasco look for a sharp left turn with a large sign for the site. Follow narrow winding road for 2 km. to site.

Charges 2003

Per person	€ 5.00 - € 5.30
child (3-10 yrs)	€ 3.30 - € 3.60
caravan	€ 5.40 - € 5.70
small tent	€ 4.60
car	€ 2.80
motorcaravan	€ 7.50
electricity (3/5A)	€ 1.70

Less 5% discount for holders of the current Alan Rogers Guide.

Reservations

Contact site. Tel: 010 3472053. Email: camping@dada.it

Open

15 March - 20 October.

IT6404 Camping Dei Fiori

Viale Riviera, 11, 17027 Pietra Ligure (Ligúria)

This is an unsophisticated site with basic facilities situated around 500 metres from the beach. The main road runs past the entrance and the restaurant terrace is overlooked by an elevated section of this road. There are 232 pitches here, mainly seasonal for Italian campers who dominate most of the site. The 60 flat touring pitches are on the lower terrace of the site, with little shade and have a two bar fence on one side with a four metre drop into a river (possibly dangerous for young children). They can be difficult for manoeuvring with larger units. The swimming pool is pleasant and there is a small elevated toddler's pool. All food and drink is served from one small building and a covered terrace across the main site road is used for eating and as a bar. The site is unsuitable for young children, infirm and disabled campers.

Facilities

The three blocks are quite old and provide a mixture of British and Turkish toilets. Showers are token operated but hot water may be in short supply. The facilities are under pressure during the morning and evening rush. Sinks have cold water only. Very basic facilities for disabled campers. Swimming pool, solarium, bar, pizzeria, Play area and a games room, There is an entertainment programme in season. Bicycle hire. Off site: Fishing and boat launching 1 km. Riding 8 km. Golf 10 km.

At a glance

| Welcome & Ambience | ✓✓✓ | Location | ✓✓✓ |
| Quality of Pitches | ✓✓ | Range of Facilities | ✓✓✓ |

Directions

Take the Pietra Ligure exit from the A10 autostrada. The campsite is clearly signed and is around 1 km. from the junction.

Charges 2003

Per pitch incl. 3 persons	€ 18.00 - € 33.00
child (4-10 yrs)	€ 3.00 - € 4.00
electricity	€ 2.00
dog	€ 1.00 - € 2.00

Reservations

Made with € 110 deposit. Tel: 019 62 56 36. Email: info@campingdeifiori.it

Open

All year.

Camping Villaggio DEI FIORI ★★

Riviera delle Palme

V.le Riviera, 11 - I-17027 Pietra Ligure (SV)

The camping site is situated at only 500 meters from the sea in a peaceful and quiet position, surrounded by green. It is the ideal place for a relaxing holiday. AVAILABLE FACILITIES ON THE CAMPING SITE: swimming pool- market- snack bar- training paths - washing & drying machines - telephones- fax- games room- bungalows, mobile homes and caravans for hire – camper service – children's play area – archery – entertainment, dance and gymnastic in particular periods.

Tel. 0039 019625636
Fax 0039 0196294105
Tel. Win. 0039 019625260
e-mail: info@campingdeifiori.it - www.campingdeifiori.it

IT6414 Camping Arenella

Loc. Arenella, 19013 Deiva Marina (Ligúria)

Situated at the back of the town of Deiva Marina, Camping Arenella is accessed from the A12 autostrada via a reasonable but twisting 15 km. stretch of road. The site is on a hillside amongst pines and there are some good views. There are around 70 'permanent' pitches and a further 50 pitches for tourists with electricity available. Cars are required to be parked in a separate area. The most interesting tourist option is a visit to Cinque Terre, five villages which can only be reached by rail, boat or cliff footpath. Their history is one of fishing but they now also specialise in wines. There are very pleasant walks and treks in the Ligurian woods nearby.

Facilities

Two centrally situated, and quite dated sanitary blocks have predominantly Turkish style WCs and free hot water in showers and washbasins. Small snack bar and shop (June - Sept). Free bus service to the beach. Off site: Beach 1.5 km.

At a glance

| Welcome & Ambience | ✓✓✓ | Location | ✓✓✓ |
| Quality of Pitches | ✓✓ | Range of Facilities | ✓✓ |

Directions

Leave A12 autostrada at Deiva Marina exit and follow signs to Deiva Marina. Site is well signed and can be found to the right.

Charges 2003

per pitch incl. 2 persons	€ 13,50 - € 22,50
extra person	€ 2,80 - € 5,00
child (2-10 yrs)	€ 1,90 - € 3,00
electricity (3/5A)	€ 2,50 - € 3,80
dog	free - € 3,00

Reservations

Recommended in high season. Tel: 01 87 82 52 59. Email: campingarenella@libero.it

Open

January - October.

Ligúria

IT6412 Villaggio Camping Valdeiva

Loc. Ronco, 19013 Deiva Marina (Ligúria)

A mature and peaceful site three kilometres from the sea between the famous Cinque Terre and Portofino, Valdeiva is open all year. It is situated in a valley amongst dense pines so views are restricted. On flat ground and separated, most of the 125 pitches are used for permanent Italian units, the remaining 30 or so shared between tourers and tents (some tent pitches are on high terraces) with shade in most parts. Of varying size, they have electricity (3A) connections. Cars may be required to park in a separate area depending on the pitch. The site does have a small swimming pool, which is very welcome if you do not wish to take the free bus to the beach. The play area has dated metal equipment with sharp edges and we strongly recommend the closest parental supervision if you choose to use the area. The beach is pleasant and the surrounding village has several bars and restaurants. We see this as a transit site rather than for extended stays.

Facilities

Three sanitary blocks are provided for the tourers and tents, and they are all very different. One block is more modern, the others are dated. WCs are mainly Turkish, but there are some of British style. Washbasins have hot water and there are free hot showers. Shop for basics only (15/6-15/9). Bar/restaurant with reasonable menu and pizzas cooked in a traditional wood fired oven (15/6-15/9). Small swimming pool. New play area. Table tennis. Electronic games. Excursions. Free bus to the beach. Torches required. Bicycle hire. Off site: Fishing and boat launching 3 km.

At a glance

Welcome & Ambience	✓✓✓	Location	✓✓✓✓
Quality of Pitches	✓✓✓	Range of Facilities	✓✓✓

Directions

Leave autostrada A12 at Deiva Marina exit and follow signs to Deiva Marina. Signs are clear at the first junction and site is on left approx. 3 km. down this road.

Charges 2003

Per pitch incl. 2 persons	€ 14.98 - € 22.21
3 persons	€ 18.08 - € 29.95
4 persons	€ 21.17 - € 34.09

Reservations

Contact site. Tel: 0187 824174. Email: camping@valdeiva.it

Open

All year.

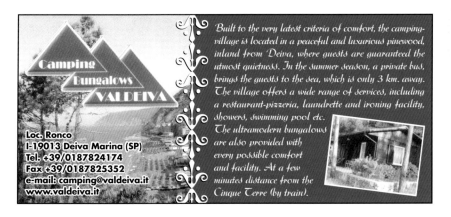

IT6418 Camping Framura

Località La Spiaggetta, 19014 Framura (Ligúria)

Framura is a small cliff-side site of 160 pitches including just 12 pitches for tourers. The touring pitches are wedged in between seasonal units and are on the site of the old railway line as is the whole steeply terraced site. The supporting amenities here are basic and although the views are directly over the sea from the 12 pitches, the route to the sea and a rough stony beach is over huge sea defence rocks. Access to the site is through an old railway tunnel and there is absolutely no shade. The site is unsuitable for children, the infirm and has no facilities for disabled campers, but it might suit the more adventurous camper, who needs little support and enjoys a challenge. The site is twinned with the Hotel Riviera through the tunnel and the pleasant restaurant here can be used, if you have missed the supermarket in town.

Facilities

Five very mixed blocks offer basic toilets, mostly Tukish but some British style. Innovation has been used here and one miniature shower block is carved into the rock face. Cold water at sinks. Washing machine. Very basic snack bar and bar. Tiny shop. Canoeing and windsurfing is possible for the stout hearted. Fishing. Off site: Boat launching 1 km. Bicycle hire 3 km.

At a glance

Welcome & Ambience	✓✓✓	Location	✓✓✓✓
Quality of Pitches	✓✓✓✓	Range of Facilities	✓✓

Directions

From A12 autostrada take nearest exit to Deiva Marina (depending on approach direction) east of Portofino. Although the address is Framura do not go towards Framura as the road is impassable for larger units! In the town of Deiva Marina follow campsite signs until you end up facing a railway tunne – drive through to the site.

Charges 2003

Per person	€ 7.50 - € 9.50
child (4-12 yrs)	€ 5.00 - € 7.00
pitch	€ 5.00 - € 10.50
electricity	€ 1.00

Reservations

Contact site. Tel: 0187 815030.
Email: hotelriviera@hotelrivieradeivamarina.it

Open

1 April - 15 October.

Once two regions, Emilia-Romagna stretches from the Adriatic coast almost to the shores of the Mediterranean. A prosperous area with historical cities and thriving industry, it also home to two of Italy's most famous food exports: Parma ham and parmesan cheese.

Emilia-Romagna is comprised of nine provinces:
Bologna, Ferrara, Forli, Modena, Parma, Piacenza, Ravenna, Reggio Emilia and Rimini

One of the richest regions of Italy, Emilia and Romagna only become united in 1947. Its landscape is varied, with the flat fields of the northern plain giving way to the forest covered Apennine mountains in the south. Carving a route through the heart of the region is the Via Emilia, a Roman military road built in 187 BC that linked the garrison town of Piacenza to Rimini on the coast. Most of the major towns lie along this route including Bologna, the region's capital. The historic city boasts a rich cultural heritage with its famous porticoes, old university buildings and medieval palaces clustered around bustling town squares. North of Bologna, Ferrara is one of the most important Renaissance centres in Italy, while further inland Modena and Parma are home to some of the regions finest architecture. Parma also boasts one of the country's top opera houses. In the east, Ravenna is renowned for the Byzantine mosaics that decorate its churches and mausoleums, and along the Adriatic coast lie various beaches and the seaside resorts of Cervia, Cesenatico and Rimini. A popular summer destination, Rimini has sandy beaches, a lively nightlife, an abundance of bars and restaurants plus a charming old quarter with cobbled streets and Roman remains.

Cuisine of the region

Bologna is regarded as the gastronomic capital of Italy. Famous regional specialities include parmesan cheese (*parmigiano-reggiano*), egg pasta, Parma ham (*prosciutto di Parma*) and balsamic vinegar. Local dishes include lasgane, tortellini stuffed with ricotta and spinach, *bollito misto* (boiled meats), *zampone* (stuffed pig's trotter). Fish is also popular along the coast of Romagna.

Cannelloni: large pasta tubes stuffed with meat or cheese and spinach, covered in tomato or cheese sauce

Ciacci: chestnut-flour pancakes filled with ricotta cheese and sugar

Spaghetti al Ragù: pasta with beef and tomato sauce

Torta di Limone: tart made with lemon and fresh cream

Places of interest

Faenza: home of faience ceramic-ware

Ferrara: walled town with impressive medieval castello

Modena: the home of fast cars, both Ferrari and Maserati have factories on the outskirts

Montese: wild black cherry festival in July, medieval singing, dancing and classical concerts in August

Piacenza: historic Roman town, medieval and Renaissance architecture

Valli di Comacchi: a wetland area, good for bird watching

Vignola: best known for its cherries and cherry-blossom, spring festival, 15th-16th century castle

 tip

VISIT THE VILLAGES IN THE FOOTHILLS OF THE APENNINES, SOUTH OF MODENA, TO SAMPLE THE LOCAL CUISINE *ALLA TUA NONNA* (LIKE GRANDMOTHER USED TO MAKE).

93

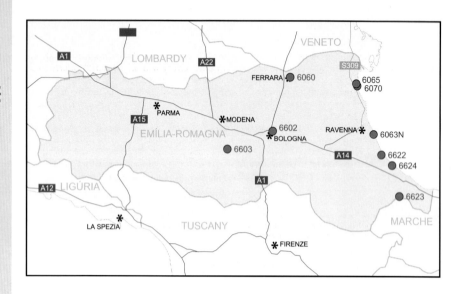

IT6060 Camping Communale Estense

Via Gramicia 76, 44100 Ferrara (Emilia-Romagna)

This pretty municipal campsite on the northern outskirts offers comfortable facilities for all types of units and includes 50 fairly large, grass pitches, with numerous electrical connections. Trees are used to provide shade and to screen the site. Unusual concrete portals around the site are covered in roses. And shrubs and other flowers give a cheerful atmosphere. The site is good for exploring local attractions, reception staff are professional with English spoken and prices are reasonable. On-site facilities are limited, with machines for snacks and cold drinks, but there is an excellent trattoria within walking distance (one km) and a wide choice of other eating places in the city itself. If you have an interest in opera, talk to Christina in reception as she is an accomplished singer with much information on Italian opera.

Facilities

Two acceptable, adjacent toilet blocks are fully equipped, one heated with British and Turkish style toilets. Separate facilities for disabled visitors. Drinks and snacks machines. Torches required in places. Off site: Restaurant close by. Golf 100 m. Fishing 500 m. Riding 3 km.

At a glance

Welcome & Ambience	✓✓✓✓	Location	✓✓✓✓
Quality of Pitches	✓✓✓✓	Range of Facilities	✓✓

Directions

Site is well signed from the city and is on the northern side of the ring road.

Charges 2003

Per person (over 8 yrs)	€ 4.50
pitch	€ 6.50
dog	€ 1.50
electricity	€ 1.50

No credit cards.

Reservations

Not required. Tel: 0532 752396.
Email: campeggio.estense@libero.it

Open

All year.

IT6063N Camping Classe

Lido di Dante, 48020 Ravenna (Emilia-Romagna)

Lido di Dante is not a major tourist resort and is therefore more peaceful than many locations along Italy's eastern coastline. Between the site and the shoreline (200 m) a large, delightful natural area provides a habitat for many species of birds and other wildlife. On the site a variety of well spaced trees offer shade over 430 good sized flat grass pitches each with electricity (4A). The underlying soil has a high sand content allowing good drainage and no problems for pegs. Part of the campsite (2.5 ha) is screened devoting 225 places for those that enjoy naturism (electricity only 2A). This area has a sanitary block and a small bar. Naturists must dress to visit any other part of the site, to make use of the 'free' facilities or when walking to the sandy beach. Italy does not have any official naturist beaches although this particular section of the coast is recognised as being such. Having walked through the nature reserve, those that prefer to remain clothed should walk to the left while those that enjoy nude sunbathing walk in the opposite direction (naturists require an INF card and no singles allowed).

Facilities

Sanitary facilities in six blocks are not modern but are adequate and generally clean. Toilets are a mix of British and Turkish style. Baby bath and mini toilet. One small block is reserved for disabled visitors. Dishwashing and laundry sinks. Washing machine. Shop. Restaurant (all season, all day). Swimming pool (bathing hats required). Minigolf, tennis and gym. Fitness programmes and sporting competitions. Fitness trail. Play areas. English spoken. High season animation programme for adults and children.
Off site: Small village adjacent to site has a couple of shops and very popular restaurants.

At a glance

Welcome & Ambience	✓✓✓✓	Location	✓✓✓
Quality of Pitches	✓✓✓✓	Range of Facilities	✓✓✓✓

Directions

Travelling south from Ravenna towards Rimini on S16, after passing 'Ravenna Sud' service area, take next exit signed Classe (km. 157). Continue on this road passing over S16. Do not turn right into Classe. Prior to humpback bridge turn right signed Lido di Dante and site is signed from this junction.

Charges 2003

Per person	€ 5.68 - € 7.30
child (0-8 yrs)	€ 4.60 - € 5.00
tent pitch	€ 6.00 - € 14.00
caravan	€ 10.33 - € 15.00
motorcaravan	€ 9.00 - € 14.00
dog	€ 3.10
electricity	€ 2.32

Reservations

Necessary in high season. Low season address: Via del Fringuello 10, 47900 Rimini. Tel: 0544 492005. Email: info@campingclasse.it

Open

1 April - 30 September.

IT6602 Camping Hotel Città di Bologna

Via Romita 12 - 4A, 40127 Bologna (Emilia-Romagna)

This spacious site was established in 1993 on the edge of the Trade Fair Centre of Bologna and is very clean and modern. The reception is impressively efficient and friendly with excellent English spoken. Although near enough to the motorway to be aware of vague traffic hum, the site is surrounded by fields and trees giving a peaceful atmosphere. The intention was not only to make a campsite, but to provide high quality motel-type rooms for use by those visiting trade fairs. The 120 pitches are numbered and marked out by trees giving some shade. On level grass with hardstandings (open fretwork of concrete through which grass can grow) in two areas, there are electrical connections (6A) in all areas. You will always find space here as there is huge over capacity. The site is excellent for an overnight stop or for longer stays to explore the attractions in the area.

Facilities

Modern sanitary blocks (some WCs are Turkish style). Excellent provision for disabled visitors (some British style WCs with free showers and alarms that ring in reception). Washing machines. Motorcaravan services. Smart bar with adjoining terrace where snacks are offered. Superb new heated and supervised swimming pool (small charge). Small play area. Table tennis. Football. Minigolf. Volleyball. Medical room – doctor will call. Off site: Bus service to city centre from site. Shops and restaurant 500 m.

At a glance

Welcome & Ambience	✓✓✓✓	Location	✓✓✓
Quality of Pitches	✓✓✓✓	Range of Facilities	✓✓✓✓

Directions

Site is well signed from 'Fiera' (fair) exit on the autostrada on the northeast of the city.

Charges 2004

Per person	€ 4.00 - € 7.00
child (5-9 yrs)	€ 3.00 - € 4.50
pitch	€ 8.00 - € 12.00
single person and tent	€ 8.00 - € 13.00
dog	€ 2.00

Electricity included. Camping Cheques accepted.

Reservations

Write to site. Tel: 051 325016. Email: info@hotelcamping.com

Open

All year (except 10 days at Christmas).

IT6065 Camping Bungalow Park Tahiti

Viale Libia 133, 44020 Lido delle Nazioni (Emilia-Romagna)

Tahiti is an excellent, extremely well run site, thoughtfully laid out less than a mile from the sea (a continuous small fun road-train link is provided). Flowers, shrubs, ponds and attractive wooded structures enhance its appearance and, unlike many campsites of this size, it is family owned and run. They have thought of everything here and the manager Stefano is a dynamo who seems to be everywhere, ensuring the impressive standards are maintained. The staff are smart and attentive. As well as the 25 x 12 m. swimming pool, there is a 'Atoll Beach' Caribbean style water-play fun area with palms, plus a jacuzzi, bar and terrace (small extra charge for 'wet' activities). A new 'Thermal Oasis' offers health and beauty treatments. The 400 pitches are of varying size, back to back from hard roads and defined by trees with shade in most areas. There are 30 pitches with a private unit containing a WC and washbasin. Electricity (6A) is available throughout. English is spoken by the friendly management, although the British have not yet really discovered this site, which is popular with other European campers. The site is very busy in season with much to-ing and fro-ing. It is also keen on recycling and even has a facility for exhausted batteries.

Facilities

All sanitary blocks are of a very high standard, nicely decorated with plants and potted shrubs. They have a mix of British and Turkish style WCs and free hot water for washbasins, sinks and showers. The new block has a baby room and hairdressing room. Two waiter service restaurants with extensive menus. Bar. Pizzeria, takeaway. Large supermarket and kiosk. Swimming pools. New fitness centre with beauty and fitness treatments. Several playgrounds and mini-club, bouncy castles and mini go-carts. Well equipped gym. Archery. Tennis. Floodlit sports area. Table tennis. Minigolf. Basketball. Volleyball. Football pitch. Bicycle hire. Electronic games. Free transport to the beach. Organised entertainment in ourdoor theatre and excursions in high season. New 'disco-pub'. Daily medical service. ATM. Internet terminals. Dogs are not accepted. Torches needed in some areas. Off site: Fishing 300 m. Riding 500 m.

At a glance

Welcome & Ambience	✓✓✓✓	Location	✓✓✓✓
Quality of Pitches	✓✓✓✓	Range of Facilities	✓✓✓✓✓

Directions

Turn off SS309 35 km. north of Ravenna to Lido delle Nazioni (north of Lido di Pomposa) and follow camp signs.

Charges 2004

Per person	€ 4.50 - € 8.10
child (2-8 yrs)	free - € 6.10
pitch acc. to season and type and facilities	€ 8.20 - € 26.90
pitch with sanitary facility	€ 22.90 - € 35.90

Reservations

Made for min. 1 week (2 weeks in high season) with deposit. Tel: 0533 379500.
Email: info@campingtahiti.com

Open

3 April - 26 September.

IT6624 Camping Villaggio Rubicone

Via Matrice Destra 1, 47039 Savignano (FO) (Emilia-Romagna)

This is a sophisticated, professionally run site where the very friendly owners, Sandro and Paolo Grotti are keen to fulfil your every need. The reception area is most attractive, spacious and efficient, operating an effective security system and offering a booking service for local attractions including trips to Venice, Rimini and other places of interest. Rubicone covers over 30 acres of thoughtfully landscaped, level ground by the sea and has a large private beach where guests can enjoy the luxurious facilities, including free parasols. There is shade from poplar trees for some of the 600 touring pitches which vary in size (up to 90 sq.m). Arranged in back to back double rows, in some areas the central pitches are a little tight for manoeuvring larger units. All the pitches are kept very neat with hedges and all have electrical connections (5A), 40 with water and waste water facilities, and 20 with private sanitary facilities. There are many bars around the site from beach bars to night club bars and the restaurant offers excellent food and efficient service at very reasonable prices. The animation programme is for both young and old and is staged in a circular terraced area near the main bar. The site has an amazing array of activities on offer (e.g. judo lessons) and many sporting opportunities including a smart modern double tennis court. Across the railway line (via an underpass) is a huge complex including excellent swimming pools for adults and children.

Facilities

In addition to the 20 private sanitary units, there are modern toilet blocks with hot water for the showers and washbasins (half in private cabins), mainly British style toilets, baby rooms and two excellent units for disabled visitors. Washing machines. Motorcaravan services. Bars. Restaurant, snack bar and excellent shop (from 10/5). Pizzeria (all season). Swimming pools (from 1/5; bathing caps mandatory). Children's play equipment. Tennis. Solarium. Jacuzzi. Mini racing track. Water motorbikes. 'Powered' trampolines. Beach with lifeguard and showers. Fishing. Boat launching. Sailing and windsurfing schools. Gas supplies. Dogs are not accepted. Off site: Bicycle hire 500 m. Riding 2 km. Golf 15 km.

At a glance

Welcome & Ambience	✓✓✓✓	Location	✓✓✓✓
Quality of Pitches	✓✓✓✓	Range of Facilities	✓✓✓✓✓

Directions

Site is 15 km. northwest of Rimini. From Bologna exit the A14 at Rimini north and head for the S16 to Bellaria and San Mauro a Mare; site is well signed.

Charges 2004

Per person	€ 4.60 - € 8.50
child (2-8 yrs)	€ 3.50 - € 7.00
pitch (small, medium, large)	€ 9.80 - € 14.70
electricity	€ 2.10
No credit cards.	

Reservations

Contact site. Tel: 0541 346377.
mail: info@campingrubicone.com

Open

1 May - 30 September.

IT6603 Camping Ecochiocciola

Via Testa 70, 41050 Maserno di Montese (Emilia-Romagna)

Tucked away in the Apennines in a small village, this interesting little campsite is open all year and has many surprises. 'Ecochiocciola' (named after the snail wearing his house on his back) is being developed by the owner Ottavio Mazzanti as a place to enjoy the natural geographic, geological, botanical and zoological features of the area. Comforts such as the swimming pool are designed to enhance the experience. Ottavio speaks excellent English and there are mementos of his extensive travels in the reasonably priced restaurant, which serves Indian as well as Italian dishes. The 50 small touring pitches are on level or gently sloping ground with some terraces, many enjoying superb views. Ottavio has begun to develop many of his unique ideas into features which will entertain and interest his guests, including a guided tour through the adjacent 'didactic' park complete with illustrative boards, which analyse the environment. There is also an orchard with ancient fruits and a garden with kitchen and medicinal herbs. This is a peaceful site with a distinctly rustic feel for people who enjoy natural settings.

Facilities

Two mature but clean sanitary blocks have some British style WCs and coin-operated hot showers. Facilities for disabled campers. Washing machine. Motorcaravan services. Restaurant. Bar. Pizzeria. Games room, large multipurpose room for entertainment. Swimming pool with shallow area for children (14/6-31/8) with nearby barbecue and grill. Football, volleyball tennis and skating area. Bicycle hire. Torches necessary. Off site: Riding trails, guided tours and mountain biking. No shop on the site but the village is 300 m. Local bus stop in village. Riding 3 km.

At a glance

Welcome & Ambience	✓✓✓	Location	✓✓✓✓
Quality of Pitches	✓✓✓	Range of Facilities	✓✓✓

Directions

From tha A1 take Moderna South exit through Vignola, Montese, Sesta la Fanano, to Maserno di Montese. Site is 200 m. from the village, well signed.

Charges 2004

Per person	€ 4.00 - € 6.00
child (2-8 yrs)	€ 3.00 - € 5.00
pitch	€ 8.00 - € 12.00
electricity (6A)	free
dog	€ 1.50 - € 3.00
Camping Cheques accepted.	

Reservations

Contact site. Tel: 059 980065.
Email: info@ecochiocciola.com

Open

All year excl. 3/2- 7/3 and 10/11 - 19/12.

IT6622 Camping Adriatico

Via Pinarella 90, 48015 Cervia (Emilia-Romagna)

Adriatico, on the Italian Riviera, is owned and run by the pleasant Fabbri family. It is a busy seaside type of site popular with the Italians. English is spoken and all facilities are clean and well kept. As you would expect there is some noise from the local resort (nearest disco is 200 m), and on the western side you will be serenaded by the voluble frogs in the adjacent allotment. The pitches vary in size, are on flat ground, well shaded with lots of room to manoeuvre. The self service restaurant and bar complex is close to the entrance, as are the supervised pools. In a pleasant situation and a short walk from the busy Adiatic beach, this site would be good for families who enjoy bustling seaside sites. There are limited sports here and some live music in the bar during high season, but the town of Cervia offers all you could want in this sort of holiday area. Reasonably priced food and wine can be found in the town, along with spa treatments which are popular here. Any incoming mail is delivered to your pitch.

Facilities

Four sanitary blocks, two large two small, have some British style WCs, individual washbasins with cold water and free hot showers. One hot tap in washing areas. Baby rooms. Washing machines and a dryer. Facilities for disabled campers. TV room. Restaurant/bar, snack bar and takeaway. Swimming pool (15/5-12/9; charged). Market. Electronic games. Table tennis. Play area. Excursions to local areas of interest. Off site: Fishing, boat launching and bicycle hire within 1 km. Riding 3 km. Golf 4 km.

At a glance

Welcome & Ambience	✓✓✓✓	Location	✓✓✓✓
Quality of Pitches	✓✓✓✓	Range of Facilities	✓✓✓

Directions

Site lies midway between Ravenna and Rimini. From A14 autoroute take exit for Cesena or Ravenna and head for Cervia on SS16. Site is south of Cervia, well signed. Drive along the sea-front and the signs are between the 167/169 markers. From the sea front to the site (800 m) there are some interesting turns away from the sea and corners with cars parked in very casual Italian style everywhere.

Charges 2004

Per person	€ 4.60 - € 7.30
child (2-8 yrs)	€ 3.50 - € 5.50
pitch	€ 9.60 - € 13.20
tent pitch	€ 7.50 - € 11.50
dog	€ 3.00 - € 5.00

Camping Cheques accepted.

Reservations

Made with deposit. Tel: 0544 71537.
Email: info@campingadriatico.net

Open

24 April - 12 September.

IT6623 Centro Turistico San Marino

Strada San Michele 50, Cailungo, 47893 Repubblica di San Marino (Emilia-Romagna)

According to one guide book, the Republic of San Marino is 'an unashamed tourist trap which trades on its falsely preserved autonomy'. However, tourists do seem to find it interesting, particularly those with patience to climb to the battlemented castles on the three highest ridges. Centro Turistico San Marino is four kilometres below this, standing at 400 m. above sea level and spreading gently down a hillside, with lovely views across to the Adriatic. This excellent, modern site has a variety of well cared for trees offering shade. The main grass pitches are roomy, on level terraces accessed from tarmac or gravel roads. Separated by hedges, all have water, waste and electricity connections (5A), ten with satellite TV connections. There are smaller pitches on lower terraces for tents. The irregularly shaped swimming pool has an pretty flower bedecked island. There is a pleasant open feel to this site. Used by a tour operator (30 pitches).

Facilities

Four high quality heated sanitary blocks, kept very clean, are well located around the site with British and Turkish style WCs and hot water in washbasins, sinks and showers. Washing machines and dryers. Motorcaravan services. Gas supplies. Shop with limited supplies (all year, closed Tuesday in winter). Kitchen with fridge and gas cooker for use by campers and TV room (satellite). Attractive restaurant/ pizzeria with good menu and pleasant terrace overlooking the pools (all year). Swimming pool (20/5-31/8) with jacuzzi and solarium. Several play areas. Video games. Table tennis. Volleyball. Football. Archery. Boules. Tennis. Bicycle hire. Small amphitheatre for entertainment. Animation programme for children (high season). Bus service on market days and Sundays. Minibus and car hire at extremely competitive rates (local taxis are very expensive).

At a glance

Welcome & Ambience	✓✓✓✓	Location	✓✓✓✓
Quality of Pitches	✓✓✓✓	Range of Facilities	✓✓✓✓

Directions

Leave autostrada A14 at exit Rimini-Sud (or SS16 where signed), follow SS72 west to San Marino. Site is signed from about 15 km. This is the only camping site in this strange little republic.

Latest charges

Per person	€ 5.00 - € 8.00
child (4-10 yrs)	€ 3.00 - € 6.00
caravan	€ 4.00 - € 11.00
tent	€ 3.00 - € 8.00
car	€ 2.00 - € 4.00
motorcaravan	€ 6.00 - € 13.00
dog	€ 1.00 - € 4.00

Camping Cheques accepted.

Reservations

Write to site. Tel: 0549 903964.
Email: info@centroturisticosanmarino.com

Open

All year.

Tuscany probably represents the most commonly perceived image of Italy, with its classic rolling green countryside, lush vineyards and olive groves with a backdrop of medieval hilltowns and historical cities, where Renaissance art and beautiful churches abound.

Tuscany is comprised of the following provinces:

Arezzo, Florence, Grosseto, Livorno, Lucca, Massa Carrara, Pisa, Pistoia, Prato and Siena

One of the most beautiful cities in Italy, much of Florence was rebuilt during the Renaissance, although there are parts which still retain a distinctly medieval feel. The city boasts a wealth of historical and cultural sights, including the Cathedral, the Baptistry, the Campanile, and the church of Santa Croce to name but a few. It is also home to the Uffizi Gallery, which holds Italy's greatest art collection. Siena is another popular draw. At the heart of the city is the Piazza del Campo, one of the loveliest Italian squares, which plays host to the famous Palio, a bareback horse race which takes place twice a year in summer. Overlooking the piazza is the Gothic town hall of Palazzo Pubblico and bell tower, which is the second highest medieval tower ever built in Italy. Elsewhere in Tuscany, the medieval hilltown of San Gimignano is famed for its thirteen towers, built during the 12th and 13th centuries, which dominate the landscape. Lucca's old town is set inside a ring of Renaissance walls fronted by gardens. Another medieval hill town, Monteriggioni also has beautifully preserved walls, while Volterra is dramatically sited on a high plateau which offers fine views over the surrounding hills. And Pisa with its famous leaning tower needs no introduction.

Cuisine of the region

Soups are very popular particularly *ribollita* (stew of vegetables, beans and chunks of bread) and the best place to try *cacciucco* (spiced fish and seafood soup) is in Livorno, the town of its birth. Meat is often grilled and kept plain. Local cheeses include *pecorino*, made with sheep's milk, and *marzolino* from the Chianti region, which is also renowned for producing some of the best wines in Italy. Tuscan desserts include *panforte* (a dense cake full of nuts and fruit) and *cantuccini* (hard almond-flavoured biscuits), which are often served together with Vinsato, a traditional dessert wine.

Bistecca alla Fiorentina: rare char-grilled steak

Pol alla diavola: marinated chicken, grilled with herbs

Scottiglia di Cinghiale: wild boar chops

Torta di Riso: rice cake with fruit sauce and fruit

Places of interest

Alpi Apuan Natural Park: protected area offering good hiking trails through wooded valleys

Arezzo: 13th century San Francesco church houses famous frescoes by Piero della Francesca

Bagni di Lucca: spa town

Cortono: oldest hilltown in Tuscany with maze of old streets and medieval buildings

Elba: largest island off Tuscan coast with white sandy beaches and woodlands, good for walking.

Fiesole: idyllic hilltop town offering superb views of Florence

Viareggio: coastal town boasting Art Nouveau architecture

Vinci: birthplace of Leonardo da Vinci, with museum celebrating his works

tip

WHEN VISITING MUSEUMS IN FLORENCE BOOK IN ADVANCE TO AVOID THE LONG QUEUES (NOTE MANY CLOSE ON MONDAYS). MUSEUM PASSES ALSO OFFER GOOD VALUE FOR MONEY.

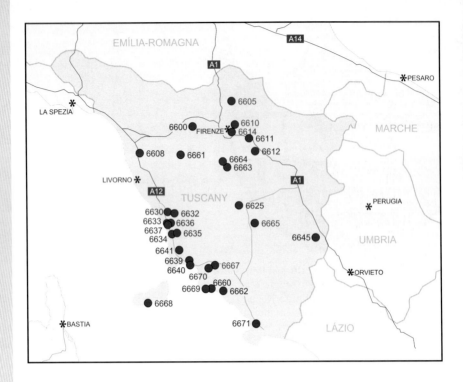

IT6605 Camping Mugello Verde

Via Massorondinaio 39, 50037 San Piero a Sieve (Tuscany)

Mugello Verde is a country, hillside site with long curving terraces and one tarmac access road. Some pitches offer good views. English is spoken at reception where much tourist information is available – ask for the dates of the Ferrari team practices and the racing on the nearby International Mugello racing track! There are 200 good sized pitches for motorcaravans and caravans with smaller areas for tents. All pitches have 6A electricity and mature olive and other trees provide shade. Some permanent pitches are scattered among the tourist pitches.

Facilities

Two sanitary blocks on the terraces have been refurbished to a good standard and facilities are clean and relatively modern with mixed British and Turkish style WCs. Most washbasins have hot water. Dishwashing and laundry facilities (hot water throughout). Comprehensive facilities for disabled campers. Shop. Restaurant/bar with varied menu and pizzeria (all season). Swimming pool (15/6-15/9; no paddling pool). New play area. Electronic games. Tennis. Off site: Riding, golf, bicycle hire and fishing all within 5 km.

At a glance

Welcome & Ambience	✓✓✓	Location	✓✓✓✓
Quality of Pitches	✓✓✓	Range of Facilities	✓✓✓✓

Directions

From A1 autostrada take Barberino del Mugello exit and follow SS65 to San Piero a Sieve. Site is well signed from the town.

Latest charges

Per person	€ 5.40 - € 8.30
child	€ 2.60 - € 5.16
pitch	€ 6.20 - € 13.90

Camping Cheques accepted.

Reservations

Write to site. Tel: 055 848 511.
Email: mugelloverde@florencecamping.com

Open

All year.

IT6600 Camping Barco Reale

Via Nardini 11 - 13, 51030 San Baronto (Tuscany)

This site is beautifully situated high in the Tuscan hills close to the town of Pistoia. Part of an old walled estate, there are impressive views of the surrounding countryside and pleasant walks available in the grounds. It is a quiet site of 15 ha. with 250 pitches with good shade from mature pines and oaks, Some pitches are huge with great views and others are very private. Most are for tourers, but some have difficult access (site provides tractor assistance). All have electrical connections (10A) and 50 have water and waste water drainage. The site has an attractive bar, a very smart leased restaurant with terraces (try the brilliant traditional dishes), a leased shop (prices are a little high). The pools have really stunning views to the west (on a clear day you may see the island of Capraia) This is a most attractive and popular site, which will appeal to those who prefer a quiet site but with plenty to do for all age groups. In high season there is an information kiosk which supplies tourist information, makes bookings and help in general. Used by tour operators.

Facilities

Two modern sanitary blocks are well positioned and kept very clean. They have free hot water throughout, good facilities for disabled people (dedicated pitches close by) and a pretty baby room. Laundry facilities. Motorcaravan services. Restaurant. Bar. Disco. Shop. Supervised swimming pool and children's pool (caps required; 1/5-15/9). Ice cream shop (1/6-31/8). Playgrounds. Table tennis. Volleyball. Football. Chess. Bowls. Bicycle hire. Internet point. Entertainment and adventure park. The large Roman style amphitheatre provides a full programme of animation for children in high season. Cooking lessons for Tuscan style food. Excursions on foot and by bus (all season). No charcoal fires are permitted. Off site: Village and shops 1 km. Disco and indoor pool 5 km. Fishing 8 km. Golf 15 km.

At a glance

Welcome & Ambience	✓✓✓	Location	✓✓✓✓
Quality of Pitches	✓✓✓	Range of Facilities	✓✓✓✓

Directions

From Pistoia take Vinci - Empoli - Lamporecchio signs to San Baronto. From Empoli follow signs to Vinci and San Baronto. Final approach is around a sharp bend and up a steep slope. The drive from the autoroute is pretty but very winding and extremely time consuming!

Charges 2004

Per person	€ 6.70 - € 8.70
child (0-3 yrs)	€ 3.00 - € 4.00
child (3-12 yrs)	€ 4.00 - € 5.30
caravan	€ 6.20 - € 8.00
tent	€ 5.50 - € 7.00
car	€ 3.70 - € 4.80
motorcaravan	€ 9.90 - € 12.80
water and drainage	€ 1.20

Credit cards accepted for amounts over € 155.
Discounts for longer stays.
Camping Cheques accepted.

Reservations

Write to site. Tel: 0573 88332.
Email: info@barcoreale.com

Open

1 April - 30 September.

IT6610 Camping Panoramico Fiesole

Via Peramonda 1, 50014 Fiesole (Tuscany)

This is a mature but pleasant site in a fine hilltop situation offering wonderful views over Florence. The site is appreciably fresher and quieter than those nearer the very busy city. It can become crowded in the main season and a very steep final access can be difficult for larger units although the site will assist with a jeep. Pitches are separated, motorcaravans and caravans in the upper area and tents on the lower terraces. The last approach to the site take you through the charming village of Fiesole but there are some challenging turns and tight squeezes (look for the helpful wall mounted mirrors) A shuttle bus service operates one way from the site to the centre of town (8.45 - 11.45 am) to connect with the service to Florence (tickets from site office). However, it is an extremely long uphill walk back to the campsite from the town and thus the local bus (to within 300 m) or taxi may be essential. The 120 pitches, all with electricity, are on terraces and steep walks to and from the various facilities could cause problems for people with mobility or breathing problems. There is shade in many parts. At the entrance, a large aviary houses a mixture of sad looking birds, tortoises, pigeons and guinea pigs. Dine on the terraces of the pleasant restaurant and enjoy the romantic views over Florence.

Facilities

Two tastefully refurbished toilet blocks have mainly British style WCs, free hot water in washbasins and good showers. Washing machines and dryers. Shop (1/4-31/10). Bar and restaurant (1/4-31/10). Swimming pool (1/6-30/9). New play area reported. Electronic games. Fridges, irons and little cookers available for campers' use. English spoken. Torches required in some parts.

At a glance

Welcome & Ambience	✓✓✓	Location	✓✓✓✓
Quality of Pitches	✓✓✓	Range of Facilities	✓✓✓

Directions

From A1 take Firenze-Sud exit and follow signs to Fiesole (which lies NNE of central Firenze). From Fiesole centre follow camping signs out of town for approx. 1 km; the roads are very narrow both through the town and the final steep access. Site is signed on the right. If approaching from the north in a large unit you will need to pass the entrance road, proceed to the town and turn at the bus terminus as the access road is too sharp and steep for a left turn.

Charges 2003

Per person	€ 9.00
child (3-12 yrs)	€ 6.50
pitch incl. electricity (5A)	€ 14.50
Credit cards accepted.	

Reservations

Not taken and said to be unnecessary if you arrive by early afternoon. Tel: 055 599069.
Email: panoramico@florencecamping.com

Open

All year.

IT6608 Camping Torre Pendente

viale delle Cascine 86, 56122 Pisa (Tuscany)

Torre Pendente is a friendly site, well run by the Signorini family who speak good English and make everyone feel welcome. It is within walking distance of the famous leaning tower of Pisa (but via a dimly lit underpass). Obviously its position means it is busy throughout the main season. A medium sized site, it is on level, grassy ground with tarmac or gravel access roads and some shade. There are 220 touring pitches, 160 with 5A electricity. All site facilities are near the entrance. There is a most pleasant swimming pool complex with pool bar and a large terrace. Here you can relax after hot days in the city and enjoy drinks and snacks or find more formal fare in the restaurant. This is a very busy site in high season with many nationalities discovering the delights of Pisa.

Facilities

Three toilet blocks (two new) are clean and smart with British and Turkish style toilets with new facilities for disabled campers. Hot water at sinks. Washing machine. Motorcaravan services. Mini market. Restaurant, bar and takeaway. Swimming pool with pool bar, children's pool and spa. Playground. Boules. New efficient reception building. Accomodation. Off site: Bicycle hire. Riding 3 km.

At a glance

Welcome & Ambience	✓✓✓✓	Location	✓✓✓✓✓
Quality of Pitches	✓✓✓	Range of Facilities	✓✓✓✓

Directions

From autostrada A12, exit at Pisa Nord and follow signs for 5 km. to Pisa. Do not take first sign to town centre. Site is well signed at a later left turn into the town centre (Viale delle Cascine) and is then a short distance on the left hand side.

Charges 2004

Per adult	€ 7.50
child (3-10 yrs)	€ 3.10 - € 3.50
pitch	€ 9.50 - € 11.30
dog	€ 1.60

Reservations

Contact site. Tel: 050 561704.
Email: torrepen@campingtoscana.it

Open

Week before Easter - 15 October.

IT6614 Camping Michelangelo

Viale Michelangelo, 50125 Firenze (Tuscany)

If you want to see Florence, this is the place, partly because the city is laid out like a tapestry 100 metres below and partly because it is easy to get into the city. A busy, bustling all year site with lots of backpackers, there are 240 flat pitches, half are for tourers. All have electricity (3A) and the pitches for motorcaravans and caravans are pleasant. The small bar (with snack bar and takeaway) has a large terrace giving unrivalled views over the Duomo – what a backdrop for the entertainers who perform here regularly. For a restaurant meal or pizza, the campsite has a huge pleasant restaurant across the busy road (10% discount for campers). The Cardini family plan a continuous programme of improvements over the next three years. The city is a charming fifteen minute walk via the Ponte Vecchio and the famous Piazzale Michelangelo is 300 m. from the site.

Facilities

Three dated blocks struggle with the numbers at peak periods and offer a mixture of Turkish and British style toilets with new facilities for disabled campers. Washing machines and dryers. Motorcaravan service point. Supermarket. Gas. Good restaurant. Cocktail bar. Snack bar. TV. 5-a-side football and tennis (over the road). Play area. Electronic games. Live music 5 times a week. Internet. ATM. Bicycle hire. Electrical bicycle or electric car hire (allowed in the pedestrian area of city). Bus service to city. Torches useful.

At a glance

| Welcome & Ambience | ✓✓✓ | Location | ✓✓✓✓✓ |
| Quality of Pitches | ✓✓✓✓ | Range of Facilities | ✓✓✓ |

Directions

Leave autoroute A1 and head for the city centre. Site is south of the river near Piazzale Michelangelo. We suggest that on coming to the river 0.5 km. east of the Ponte Vecchio, then moving east along the river bank until the signs for Piazzale Michelangelo. There are then camping signs (no name) and the site is off the main road on the right down a steep incline.

Charges 2003

Per person	€ 8.00
child (5-12 yrs)	€ 4.60
pitch	€ 5.00 - € 10.70

Reservations

Made only for tents and groups in winter. Tel: 055 6811880. Email: michelanglo@ecvacanze.it

Open

Facilities/directions text

IT6611 Camping Il Poggetto

Via Il Poggetto 143, 50010 Troghi (Tuscany)

This superb new site has a lot to offer. It benefits from a wonderful panorama of the Colli Fiorentini hills with acres of the Zecchi family vineyards to the east adding to its charm. It is just 15 km. from Florence. The charming and hard-working owners Marcello and Daniella have a wine producing background and you can purchase their fine wines at the site's shop. Their aim is to provide an enjoyable and peaceful atmosphere for families. All 90 pitches are of a good size and have electricity (7A) and there are a few in excess of 100 sq.m for larger units. On arrival you are escorted to view available pitches then assisted in taking up that place. The restaurant offers some fine Tuscan fare along with pizzas, pastas and delicate 'cucina casalinga' (home cooking). An attractive large terrace overlooks the two pools. A regular bus service runs directly from the site to the city (discounted tickets). English is spoken. There are plans to extend the site in 2004.

Facilities

Two spotless sanitary blocks with subtle piped music are a pleasure to use with a mix of British and Turkish style WCs, washbasins and showers. Three private sanitary units for hire. Five very well equipped units for disabled campers and pretty baby room. Hot water throughout including for dishwashing. Washing machines, dryers, irons and clean ironing boards. Motorcaravan services. Gas supplies. Shop. Bar. Restaurant. Takeaway. Volleyball. Swimming pools and jacuzzi (15/5-30/9). Games room. Table tennis. Bicycle and scooter hire. Playground and animation for children all season. Excursions twice weekly and organised trekking. Internet point. Site barrier closed 13.00-15.00 hrs. Off site: Tennis 100 m. Fishing and riding 2 km. Golf 12 km.

At a glance

| Welcome & Ambience | ✓✓✓✓✓ | Location | ✓✓✓✓ |
| Quality of Pitches | ✓✓✓✓✓ | Range of Facilities | ✓✓✓✓✓ |

Directions

Leave A1 at 'Incisa Valdarno' exit and turn left towards Incisa after 400 m turn right on Sp1 towards Firenze. Site is 5 km. at Troghi, well signed.

Charges 2004

Per person	€ 7.20
child (0-12 yrs)	€ 5.00
pitch	€ 12.50
small tent pitch	€ 9.00

Reservations

Contact site. Tel: 055 8307323. Email: poggetto@tin.it

Open

1 March - 15 October.

IT6668 Camping Ville degli Ulivi

Marina di Campo, 57034 Elba (Tuscany)

Set in an olive grove, just 500 metres from a beautiful sandy bay, Ville degli Ulivi offers a wide range of amenities. There is a variety of accommodation on offer including rooms, caravans and chalets to rent, in addition to 120 touring pitches. These are small (less than 80 sq.m.) but some are hedged, electricity connections are available and there is a fair amount of shade. Facilities include a restaurant and bar, a pizzeria and a shop. The pool is an attractive feature, complete with slides and a jacuzzi. Excursions and entertainment are organised or you could try diving in the clear Elba waters from the site's own small diving centre.

Facilities

Toilet facilities are good with hot showers and facilities for disabled visitors. Laundry facilities.Bar/restaurant. Pizzeria. Shop. Swimming pool. Play area. Bicycle and scooter hire. Diving centre. Entertainment in high season. Excursions. Off site: Marina di Campo village has restaurants and bars.

At a glance

| Welcome & Ambience | ✓✓✓✓ | Location | ✓✓✓✓ |
| Quality of Pitches | ✓✓✓✓ | Range of Facilities | ✓✓✓✓ |

Directions

From the ferry port at Portoferraio, follow signs for Procchio, then Marina di Campo. Before the village of Marina di Campo, turn left towards 'La Foce - Lacona'. In about 800 m. turn right to site.

Charges 2004

Per adult	€ 6.50 - € 13.00
child (0-9 yrs)	€ 1.50 - € 9.00
tent	€ 6.00 - € 15.00
caravan	€ 7.50 - € 15.00
motorcaravan	€ 8.50 - € 17.00
electricity (6A)	€ 2.00 - € 2.50
car	€ 2.00 - € 4.00

Reservations

Contact site. Tel: 0565 976098. Email: info@villedegliulivi.it

Open

15 May - 13 September.

IT6625 Camping La Montagnola

53018 Sovicille (Tuscany)

An agreeable alternative to sites closer to the centre of Siena, La Montagnola is set in secluded wood-land to the north of the village of Sovicille. The owners have worked hard to provide a good basic standard of amenities. The 66 pitches are of good size (80 sq.m) and offer considerable privacy. Clearly marked with shade, all are suitable for caravans and motorcaravans, and have electrical connections (6A). However, there are just three water points on the site. Some higher pitches are around a central barbecue area along with mobile homes. There is a large wooded area and an overflow field for tents with no electricity and another field has a Play area. A friendly bar/shop area offers snacks and many provisions including wines. This unsophisticated site could make an excellent touring base for central Tuscany and is not too far from the motorway and Siena (ten kilometres with an hourly bus service from the site).

Facilities

A single toilet block provides free hot showers and sufficient washbasins and mainly British style toilets – not luxurious, but adequate and clean. Small well stocked shop and bar. Play area. Volleyball. Table tennis. Torches definitely required in tent areas. Off site: Large supermarket 6 km. (San Rocco a Pilli or Rosia), and a small one 6 km (Sovicille). Two restaurants in the village.

At a glance

| Welcome & Ambience | ✓✓✓ | Location | ✓✓✓ |
| Quality of Pitches | ✓✓✓ | Range of Facilities | ✓✓✓ |

Directions

From north on Firenze - Siena motorway take Siena Ovest exit, turn left on SS73, at the village Voltebass turn right following signs for Sovicille from where site is signed. From south (Grosseto) take SS223 turning at crossroads to Rosia from where site is also signed.

Charges 2003

Per person	€ 6.00
child (4-12 yrs)	€ 4.00
pitch	€ 8.00

Reservations

Not necessary. Tel: 0577 314473.

Open

Easter - 30 September.

IT6630 Camping Montescudaio

Via del Poggetto km 2, 56040 Montescudaio (Tuscany)

This well developed site, south of Livorno, is fashioned out of a very extensive area of natural undulating woodland (with low trees) and has its own character. The fact that the site is cleverly divided into separate areas for families and couples, including those in tourers, shows the owner's desire to reduce any possibility of noise for families on site. There are 372 pitches for touring units with shade, most of a good size, plus 170 seasonal units, bungalows or large caravans, in separate clearings. Electricity (5A) is available in all parts, long leads required in some pitches. The comprehensive range of amenities includes a commercial centre with all manner of shops with many goods from the area including an excellent choice of wines. The restaurant is extremely good with a Tuscan menu. A piano bar operates through the season along with various other entertainment in July/August. This is an ttractive site which is being developed with great style. The owner is keen to please his clients and has tried to think of most needs. It is four kilometres from the sea at the nearest point but there is a pleasant large free pool on the site with a separate children's pool. A miniature botanical garden is at the centre of the site and further small gardens around the centre and pool areas. Used by tour operator (25 pitches).

Facilities

Top quality sanitary blocks are comprehensively appointed and have hot water in all the blocks. Baby baths in the two main blocks. This is one of the few sites we have seen using steam cleaning as a matter of routine. Motorcaravan services. Freezer for campers. Excellent laundry service. Shops. Bar. Restaurant and takeaway in main season. Open-air pizzeria with bar and small dance floor (from mid-June). Swimming pool. Tennis. Several comprehensive play areas scattered around the site. Table tennis. Fitness field. Excursions. Organised events programme in main season. Medical service. Dogs are not accepted (kennels available outside). Torches required in some areas.

At a glance

Welcome & Ambience	✓✓✓	Location	✓✓✓✓
Quality of Pitches	✓✓✓	Range of Facilities	✓✓✓✓

Directions

From the Genova - Livorno autostrada take exit for Rosignano Marittimo. Take the highway (Livorno-Grosseto) towards Roma and exit for Cecina. Follow signs for Guardistallo (not Montescudaio) and site is located on the Cecina-Guardistallo road, 2 km. from Cecina.

Charges 2004

Per person (any age)	€ 5.30 - € 7.30
pitch incl. electricity	€ 11.30 - € 20.30

Reservations

Min. stay in July/Aug. 7 days. Write with € 50 deposit. Tel: 0586 683477.
Email: info@camping-montescudaio.it

Open

9 May - 21 September.

IT6632 Camping Valle Gaia

Via Cecinese 87, 56040 Casale Marittimo (Tuscany)

Valle Gaia is a delightful family site with a friendly, laid back atmosphere, which is in marked contrast to some of the busy sites on the coast. Yet it is located just nine kilometres from the sandy beaches at Cecina. This pretty site has two enticing pool complexes, both with children's pools and generous sunbathing terraces, and is just a short drive away from the mediaeval Manhattan of San Gimignano, Volterra and Siena. The 150 pitches are of a reasonable size (90 sq.m.), well shaded by pine or cypress trees and surrounded by oleanders. Most have electrical connections (4/6A). The bar and restaurant are very popular, the latter located in a splendidly converted farmhouse, and specialising in local cuisine.

Facilities

Three toilet blocks of modern construction are maintained to a high standard with mainly British style toilets. Some washbasins in cubicles. Washing and drying machines. Shop stocks a good range of provisions including local produce. Tennis courts, 5-a-side pitch, table tennis and games room. Bicycle hire. Only gas barbecues are permitted.
Off site: Shops at Casale Marittimo 3.5 km. Riding 4 km.

At a glance

Welcome & Ambience	✓✓✓	Location	✓✓✓✓
Quality of Pitches	✓✓✓✓	Range of Facilities	✓✓✓✓

Directions

From A12 autostrada, take Rosignano Marittimo exit, following signs to Roma, joining the E80. Take Casale Marittimo exit and follow signs to the town. The site is clearly signed from here.

Charges 2004

Per pitch	€ 8.10 - € 13.40
adult	€ 4.30 - € 7.40
child (under 10 yrs)	€ 3.18 - € 5.43
Camping Cheques accepted.	

Reservations

Essential for high season – made with deposit. Tel: 0586 681 236. Email: info@vallegaia.it

Open

3 April - 16 October.

IT6634 Camping Continental

Via I Maggio, Marina di Castagneto, 57024 Donoratico (Tuscany)

Recommended by our Italian Agent, Continental will be inspected in 2004. Situated by the 'blue flag' beach and with lots of shade from a pine wood, there are over 500 pitches, a restaurant, pizzeria and bar. Just a couple of hundred metres away is the lively Marina di Castagneto.

Directions
From SS1/E4 between Livorno and Grosseto exit at Donoratico to Marina di Castagneto where site is signed.

Open
1 April - 30 September.

Charges 2003	
Per person	€ 5.00 - €8.50
child (2-8 yrs)	€ 3.50 - € 7.00
pitch	€ 7.50 - € 13.00

Reservations
Contact site. Tel: 0565 744014
Email: info@campingcontinental.it

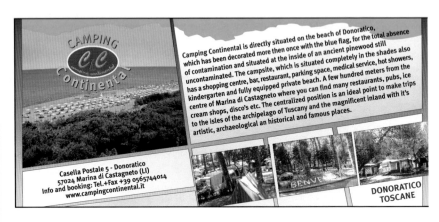

Camping Continental is directly situated on the beach of Donoratico, which has been decorated more then once with the blue flag, for the total absence of contamination and situated at the inside of an ancient pinewood still uncontaminated. The campsite, which is situated completely in the shades also has a shopping centre, bar, restaurant, parking space, medical service, hot showers, kindergarten and fully equipped private beach. A few hundred meters from the centre of Marina di Castagneto where you can find many restaurants, pubs, ice cream shops, disco's etc. The centralized position is an ideal point to make trips to the isles of the archipelago of Tuscany and the magnificent inland with it's artistic, archaeological an historical and famous places.

Casella Postale 5 - Donoratico
57024 Marina di Castagneto (LI)
Info and booking: Tel.+Fax +39 0565744014
www.campingcontinental.it

DONORATICO TOSCANE

IT6641 Blucamp

57021 Campiglia Marittima (Tuscany)

Blucamp is a relatively new, simple site in a tranquil setting near the pretty village of Campiglia Marittima. Owned and run by a partnership of two charming Italians who are keen to welcome British guests, good English is spoken. The famous islands of Elba and Capraia can be sighted whilst checking in at the new reception block, and there are fabulous views over green hills and the sea from the upper pitches. The 100 pitches (all with 3A electricity, 12 fully serviced) are terraced and on steep slopes; one area is for tents only and has the most amazing views. There is a tractor (free) to help you install your unit if required. Cars are parked off the pitches in numbered bays. All pitches have young trees that provide some shade but others are more open. The site is entirely for tourists, with just four bungalows for rent. It is busy in high season, but is very quietly situated, eight kilometres back from the sea, just 700 m. from the old medieval village of Campiglia Marittima. There is a ferry connection to Elba and Corsica 19 km. distant and many areas of interest in the area.

Facilities
Two satisfactory sanitary blocks have British and Turkish style WCs, individual washbasins with cold water and free hot showers. Six private sanitary units for hire. Washing machine. Small friendly restaurant/bar with a pretty terrace is run by a separate family and offers wonderful Tuscan cuisine specialising in fish. Attractive medium-sized swimming pool. Electronic games. Table tennis. Internet. Torches required in some areas. Off site: Riding 2 km. Fishing 8 km.

At a glance			
Welcome & Ambience	✓✓✓✓	Location	✓✓✓✓
Quality of Pitches	✓✓✓	Range of Facilities	✓✓✓

Directions
Take exit for S. Vincenzo Sud off the main S1 road Livono to Follonica. Follow signs for Campiglia Marittima where site is signed.

Latest charges	
Per person	€ 7.10
child (0-8 yrs)	€ 4.90
pitch	€ 9.00 - € 13.00
with water and drain	€ 4.30
private sanitary unit	€ 8.00
dog	€ 5.00
Less 30% outside July/Aug.	

Reservations
Made with deposit; contact site. Tel: 0565 838553.
Email: info@blucamp.it

Open
17 May - 7 September.

IT6639 Camping Riotorto

Loc. Campo al Fico, 15, 57020 Riotorto (Tuscany)

Riotorto is a simple no frills campsite with a pleasant pool, basic entertainment area, terrace and bar. The restaurant serves a good value menu of the day based on a fish or meat dish. The site will arrange low cost tours to Rome, Florence and Elba (all under € 40). The 150 pitches are grassed and some have shade. They are arranged in rows with some hedging and are somewhat cramped. It is a low key family site three kilometres from the beach and a free shuttle bus operates twice daily. Some noise is experienced from the road along the front boundary. Upon arrival here visitors must pay for a € 3 deposit for a wrist band. The deposit is returned when the band is cut off on departure. We see this more as a transit site than one for an extended stay.

Facilities

Two old but clean, large blocks have mainly British style WCs and cold water in washbasins and hot showers. Facilities for disabled people in one block. Washing machines. Motorcaravan services. Mini-market. Bar close to pool. Simple restaurant. Pizzeria and takeaway (all season). Swimming pool (25 x 15 m; not supervised, open May - Sept). Tennis. Football. Table tennis. Play area. Simple evening entertainment for adults. Mountain bike hire. Free shuttle bus to beach twice daily. Off site: Beach 1.5 km. Golf and riding 10 km. Fishing. Excursions. Sailing.

At a glance

Welcome & Ambience	✓✓✓✓	Location	✓✓✓
Quality of Pitches	✓✓✓✓	Range of Facilities	✓✓✓

Directions

Site is on the coast opposite Elba. It is 6 km. from Follonica and 10 km. from Piobino on the minor (no number) coast road towards Mte. Massoncello where the site is signed off the road.

Charges 2003

Per adult	€ 5.50 - € 16.00
child	€ 4.00 - € 12.00
pitch	€ 12.00 - € 24.00
dog	€ 3.00 - € 6.50

Camping Cheques accepted.

Reservations

During July/Aug. made for min. 2 weeks.
Tel: 0565 21008. Email: info@campingriotorto.com

Open

1 April - 30 September.

IT6635 Camping Le Pianacce

Via Bolgherese, 57022 Castagneto Carducci (Tuscany)

In a quiet situation in the Tuscan hills, six kilometres from sea at Donoratico, this high quality site has an attractive medium-sized pool, overlooked by the restaurant/bar terrace that also has commanding views over the area. The site is on steeply rising ground and has 48 pitches for touring units, all with electricity (3A) and shade, in tiered rows on fairly narrow terraces. Access to most is not easy because the limited space between the small dividing hedges and the high bank of the next terrace restricts manoeuvring so installation is now made by the site's tractor. The site is likely to be full from about mid-July to 20 Aug though it remains a quiet site and peaceful at night. There is a nature reserve next to the site and the nearby sandy beach it is 20 km. long and beautiful. A new addition to the site is a park with a small lake, ideal for peaceful walks. Used by tour operators (40 pitches).

Facilities

There are three toilet blocks, including a small one at the top of the site, all refurbished to a high standard. British style WCs, individual washbasins with hot water and free hot showers. Baby room with bath and child sized facilities. Motorcaravan services. Shop. Restaurant/bar. Swimming pool and children's pool with water games. Archery. Tennis. Minigolf. Bicycle hire. Playground. Information point. Internet point. Free bus service to beach. Gas supplies. Animation is provided in season for children and adults. Barbecues are only permitted on the communal area. Torches required in some areas. Dogs are not accepted. Off site: Fishing and riding 6 km.

At a glance

Welcome & Ambience	✓✓✓✓	Location	✓✓✓✓
Quality of Pitches	✓✓✓	Range of Facilities	✓✓✓✓

Directions

Turn off main S1 just north of Donoratico in hamlet of Il Bambolo at sign to Castagneto Carducci. After 3 km. turn left at signs to Bolgheri and site, then follow camp signs. Single track final approach.

Charges 2003

Per person	€ 4.50 - € 8.30
child (0-10 yrs)	€ 3.30 - € 6.60
pitch	€ 7.80 - € 13.60
2 man tent incl. motorcycle	€ 5.50 - € 10.00

Some special offers in low season. No credit cards.

Reservations

Made with deposit; contact site. Tel: 0565 763667. Email: info@campinglepianacce.it

Open

3 April - 10 October.

IT6636 Camping Le Capanne

Via Aurelia Km 273, 57020 Bibbona (Tuscany)

Marina di Bibbona is a relatively little known resort situated a little to the south of Livorno and close to the better known resort of Cecina. The area retains much charm and a number of popular beaches are close at hand. Le Capanne is a member of the 'Camping di Charme' group and the site's new owners have some ambitious development plans, many of which are already fulfilled. There are 320 good sized pitches, most with electricity. The pitches are nearly all well shaded by pine, olive and eucalyptus trees. A modern mobile home area has a sunnier, more open setting with around 75 pitches taken up with mobile homes or chalets belonging to the site or to tour operators.

Facilities

Toilet blocks are of a traditional design but kept clean, with plenty of hot water. Toilets are mixed British and Turkish style. Dishwashing and laundry sinks. Washing machines. Mini-market and 'bazaar'. Bar and popular restaurant away from camping area near site entrance specialising in Tuscan cuisine. Large swimming pool and large play area. Bicycle hire. Entertainment programme in high season.
Off site: Beach 2 km. with bus from the site in high season. Riding 2 km. Fishing 2.5 km.

At a glance

Welcome & Ambience	✓✓✓✓	Location	✓✓✓✓
Quality of Pitches	✓✓✓✓	Range of Facilities	✓✓✓✓

Directions

Take A12 autostrada (Livorno - Rosignano Marittimo) to its end and join the Via Aurelia (S1) heading south. Exit at Bibbona and follow signs to the campsite.

Charges 2004

Per adult	€ 4.50 - € 8.30
child (under 10 yrs)	€ 3.30 - € 6.60
per pitch (incl. 5A electricity)	€ 7.80 - € 13.60

No credit cards.

Reservations

Necessary for the high season. Tel: 0586 600 064. Email: info@campinglecapanne.it

Open

1 April - 30 September.

IT6637 Camping Il Gineprino

Via dei Platani, 56a.b.c, 57020 Marina di Bibbona (Tuscany)

Il Gineprino, a small, new family run site is on the edge of Bibbona but not directly on the coast. The friendly owner, Roberto was an architect and designed the entire site, which has a nice family atmosphere. When we visited there was lots of fun and dancing by the floodlit pool. Trees planted in 1995 now provide shade for most of the pitches. There are 70 pitches (ten with private sanitary facilities) on the main site plus 50 bungalows, watch for low branches if you are around 3.5 meters high. A further area for 50 motorhomes, with electricity and another sanitary block is directly across the quiet beach access road. The site has an unusually shaped pool and an excellent restaurant with terrace, serving superb local cuisine. Cars have to be parked in a separate area opposite the site entrance. The 130 touring pitches are numbered and marked by trees at the corners and all have a water tap and electricity (4A). Entertainment is provided on two or three evenings each week in high season and excursions can be arranged. The beach is about 400 m. away and can be reached on foot through a pinewood. British guests are welcome and English is spoken.

Facilities

Three sanitary blocks have British and Turkish style WCs, hot water in washbasins and showers, with cold for dishwashing and laundry. Family room (on payment) with WC, washbasin and shower and facilities for disabled people. Motorcaravan services. Shop, restaurant with terrace (both 1/5-15/9). Swimming pool with children's pool and aquagym (1/5-15/9). Games room. TV room. Table tennis. Bicycle hire. Football ground. 'Bocce'. Volleyball. Some entertainment in high season. Excursions.
Off site: Fishing 500 m. Riding 1 km.

At a glance

Welcome & Ambience	✓✓✓✓	Location	✓✓✓✓
Quality of Pitches	✓✓✓✓	Range of Facilities	✓✓✓✓

Directions

Site is signed on the approach from the main SS1 coast road between La California and Marina di Bibbona. Follow signs to Marina di Bibbona where there are no campsite signs.

Charges 2003

Per person	€ 5.00 - € 10.00
child (0-8 yrs)	€ 3.00 - € 6.00
pitch with electricity	€ 7.00 - € 13.00
dog	€ 2.00 - € 5.00

No credit cards.

Reservations

Write to site. Tel: 0586 600550. Email: ilgineprino@tiscalinet.it

Open

April - end September.

IT6660 Camping Maremma Sans Souci

Grosseto, 58043 Castiglione della Pescaia (Tuscany)

This seaside site is owned and run by the Perduca family and sits in natural woodland on the coast between Livorno and Rome. The minimum amount of undergrowth has been cleared to provide 400 individually marked and hedged, flat pitches for camping enthusiasts. This offers considerable privacy in individual settings. A positive feature of this site is that there are no seasonal pitches. Some pitches are small and cars may not remain with tents or caravans but must go to a numbered, shaded and secure car park near the entrance. There is a wide road for motorhomes but other roads are mostly narrow and bordered by trees (this is a protected area, and they cannot fell the trees). Access to some parts is difficult therefore for caravans and each pitch is earmarked either for caravans or for tents. There are electrical connections (3A) for all caravan pitches. An excellent sandy beach is less than 100 m. from one end of the site (400 m. from the other) and is used only by campers. The waters here won the highest award in Italy for cleanliness in 2001 and the beach is very safe for swimming. The restaurant with several terraces is in the centre of the site and offers outstanding Italian food at extremely good prices along with a fine choice of wines. Maremma is a most friendly site right by the sea which should appeal to many people who like a relaxed style of camping and a real personal touch.

Facilities

Five small, mature toilet blocks are well situated around the site. Free showers and hot water at the sinks, plus lots of little extras such as hair dryers and soap dispensers, etc. Three blocks have additional, private cabins each with WC, basin and shower and there are separate facilities for disabled campers. Baby showers and baths. Washing machines. Motorcaravan services. Laundry. New reception incl. doctor's surgery and facilities for disabled visitors. Cash point. Shop. Excellent restaurant (self service in season) serving a range of local fish and fresh pasta. Bar with pizzas and other snacks. Well stocked shop. Free freezer. Volleyball. Car wash. Sailing school. Good English spoken. Torches required in some areas. No dogs are taken between 16/6-31/8. Off site: Excursions organised to Elba and Rome.

Directions

Site is 2.5 km. northwest of Castiglione on road to Follonica.

Latest charges

Per person	€ 5.00 - € 7.75
child (2- 6 yrs)	€ 4.00 - € 5.15
pitch and car	€ 6.50 - € 13.00

Reservations

Necessary for July/Aug. and will be made for min. 1 week with deposit (€ 2,58). Tel: 0564 933765. Email: info@maremmasanssouci.it

Open

1 April - 31 October.

At a glance

Welcome & Ambience	✓✓✓✓	Location	✓✓✓✓
Quality of Pitches	✓✓✓✓	Range of Facilities	✓✓✓✓

IT6640 Camping Pappasole

Carbonifera 14, 57020 Vignale Riotorto (Tuscany)

This lively site offers plenty of sporting activities and is located 250 m. from its own sandy beach facing the island of Elba. It is a large site on flat, fairly open ground offering 409 pitches of 90 sq.m. many with electricity (3A) and water, others with electricity, water and waste water connections. Some 344 pitches have their own cosy individual sanitary facility with WC, shower and washbasin, and next to these a compartment with four burner gas stove, fridge, sink with H&C water, drainer, and cupboards (extra cost for this about £5 per night). Pitches are separated by bushes with shade from mature trees and artificial shade in other areas. There may be some road or rail noise in certain parts. The excellent swimming pools are a strong feature (the children's pool is huge). However, the central focus of the site is an attractive covered area (a very tall, open marquee type structure, floodlit at night) for dancing, music and entertainment that is surrounded by the main buildings. The animation programme is impressive and varied. There are many sporting opportunities including windsurfing and sailing, tennis, activities and excursions are organised. The beach is superb and a short walk, this site is popular with the Italians and is good for families.

Facilities

The three modern sanitary blocks have free hot water for washbasins and showers and mainly Turkish, but with some British style WCs. These facilities may be a fair walk from some pitches. Laundry facilities. Motorcaravan services. Gas supplies. Fridge hire. Unisex hairdresser. Restaurant. Snacks. Bar. Shop. Swimming pools (from 26/4). Play area. Tennis. Table tennis. Bowls. Handball. Watersports. Minigolf. Bicycle hire. Fishing. Medical services. Safety deposit boxes. Off site: Riding 5 km. Sub aqua diving. Excursion programme (26/5-8/9).

Directions

Site is north of Follonica just off the SS1 (Follonica Nord exit). Follow signs for 'Torre Mozza' and site. You must cross the bridge over the railway line to access the site.

Charges 2004

Per person	€ 5.00 - € 11.50
child (3-10 yrs)	€ 3.50 - € 8.00
pitch	€ 9.50 - € 24.00
pitch with services	€ 14.00 - € 38.00
small tent pitch	€ 6.00 - € 15.50
dog	€ 2.50 - € 9.00

Reservations

Made for whole weeks, Sat-Sat. Write to site. Tel: 0565 20420. Email: info@pappasole.it

Open

5 April - 13 October.

At a glance

Welcome & Ambience	✓✓✓	Location	✓✓✓✓
Quality of Pitches	✓✓✓✓	Range of Facilities	✓✓✓✓

IT6662 Camping Le Marze

Strada Provinciale 158, km 30,200, 58046 Marina di Grosseto (Tuscany)

This natural site is situated four kilometres north of Marina di Grosseto and has 180 generously sized pitches for touring units. Separated by hedges, all have electricity (3A) and most enjoy natural shade from mature pine trees. On sand and with easy access, there is a background noise of cicadas from the lofty pines and squirrels entertain high above. A private beach is across the main road. Bicycles are an asset and you can also enjoy a cycle ride to the town along a beach track. The beach is worth the walk as it is the strongest feature here, being soft sand which shelves slowly. There are secluded dunes, and a lifeguard. The beach bar is excellent and operates as a disco at night thus protecting the site from noise. The site layout is circular with the restaurant, bar and shop complex in the centre. There is a large tour operator presence but these are on the outer ring of the site and not intrusive.

Facilities

The four sanitary facilities are of a good standard, two of them new and excellent with British style WCs (some Turkish in the older blocks). Facilities for disabled campers in the new blocks along with baby facilities and private bathrooms. Motorcaravan service point. Market with amazing choice of goods and a bazaar alongside. Bar, restaurant, pizzeria and takeaway. Two identical swimming pools, unusual in that they are in supported structures (1.3 m. deep). Two play areas. Ambitious entertainment programme in season, excursions and activities including gym with a personal trainer (extra charge). Barbeque areas. Evening entertainment. Swimming pools with aqua-aerobics and watersports. Torches required in some areas. Bicycle hire. Off site: Riding and boat launching 3 km. Golf 5 km.

At a glance

Welcome & Ambience	✓✓✓	Location	✓✓✓✓
Quality of Pitches	✓✓✓✓	Range of Facilities	✓✓✓✓

Directions

At Grosseto on S1 Livorno - Rome road take road signed to Marina di Grosseto. Take S327 road to Castiglione della Pescaia, 1.4 km before the Marina. Site is well signed on the right about 3 km. towards Castiglione della Pescaia.

Charges 2003

Per person	€ 5.68 - € 8.26
child (2-12 yrs)	€ 3.36 - € 6.61
caravan	€ 5.16 - € 7.33
car	€ 4.75 - € 6.61
motorcycle	€ 2.84 - € 3.87
motorcaravan	€ 8.88 - € 11.05

Reservations

Contact site. Tel: 0564 35501.
Email: lemarze@ecvacanze.it

Open

1 May - 3 October.

IT6645 Parco Delle Piscine

Via del Bagno Santo 29, 53047 Sarteano (Tuscany)

On the spur of Monte Cetona, Sarteano is a spa, and this large smart site utilises that spa in its very open environs. The novel feature here is the three unique swimming pools fed by the natural thermo-mineral springs. Two of these pools (the largest is superb with water cacade and hydro-massage, and the other large shallow pool is just for children) are set in a huge park-like ground with many picnic tables. They are free to all those staying on the site. A third excellent pool is on the camping site itself and is opened in main season for the exclusive use of campers. A very big building alongside the spa-pool houses a select restaurant on the first floor and a pizzeria on the second floor, the terrace gives fine views over the local area. Delle Piscine is really good as a sightseeing base or as an overnight stop from the Florence-Rome motorway (site is six kilometres from the exit). Access to the attractive town is directly outside the site gate. The views from the town are unusual, over both Umbria and Tuscany. This spacious site is well run, the infrastructure is excellent and there is lots of room to manoeuvre everywhere. There are 450 individual, flat pitches, all of good size and fully marked out with high neat hedging giving really private pitches. There is a friendly welcome from the English speaking staff.

Facilities

The two heated toilet blocks are of high quality with mainly British style WCs, and numerous sinks for laundry and dishwashing (with hot water). Motorcaravan services. Restaurant/pizzeria/bar. Takeaway. Coffee bar. Newspaper kiosk. Swimming pools (one all season). TV room, satellite TV room and mini-cinema with 100 seats and a very large screen. Tennis. Soccer field. Table tennis. Volleyball. Exchange facilities. Free guided cultural tours. Local market on Fridays. Internet. Gas supplies. Dogs are not accepted. Off site: Bicycle hire 100 m. Riding 3 km.

At a glance

Welcome & Ambience	✓✓✓✓	Location	✓✓✓✓
Quality of Pitches	✓✓✓✓✓	Range of Facilities	✓✓✓✓

Directions

From autostrada A1 take exit for Chiusi and Chianciano, from where Sarteano (6 km) and site are signed.

Charges 2004

Per adult	€ 9.50 - € 12.00
child (3-10 yrs)	€ 5.50 - € 7.50
tent or caravan	€ 9.50 - € 12.00
car	€ 3.50 - € 6.00
motorcaravan	€ 13.00 - € 18.00
electricity	€ 3.50

Reservations

Write to site, or book by Email Tel: 0578 26971.
Email: info@bagnosanto.it

Open

1 April - 30 September.

The Leaning Tower of Pisa

Situated in the Campo dei Miracoli, alongside the Cathedral, Cemetery and the Baptistry, the Tower of Pisa (*Torre Pendente*) is rather a comic sight, attracting thousands of visitors from all over the world, who pose for the family photographs holding up the structure. Local vendors line the street, selling an assortment of tower souvenirs – you won't come away empty handed!

A brief history

Begun in 1173, the bell tower was built as a symbol of Pisa's weath and power, on the sandy silt subsoil of a former estuary. It was in 1178, when the tower was three storeys high, that the tilt first became obvious and work was halted. Modern analysis reveals that had work continued, before the underlying soils had settled, the tower would certainly have toppled.

Nearly a century after the tower was first started, work recommenced. Initially the tower lent to the north 0.2 degrees but after architects added three more storeys, tilted to counterbalance the tower, it lent to the south about one degree (approximately 2.7 feet).

Over the next 90 years the inclinations increased to about 1.6 degrees. During that time the seventh floor was completed (1319) and the bell tower added (1350). In 1655 the largest of the tower's seven bells was installed, weighing three and a half tonnes.

In the mid-nineteenth century an ill-advised attempt to correct the lean was started. This involved digging a trench all the way round the base of the tower, which in fact complicated things – not only was there an increase in the lean by half a degree, but as the cellar lies below the water table on the south side, the excavation triggered an inrush of water. Matters were made worse in 1934 when cement was injected into the base, accelerating the lean even more. The crisis came to a head in 1990, when leaning more than five metres, the tower was closed to the public.

Lead ingots were placed to stabalise the tower and engineers began the painstaking process of soil extraction; carefully removing soil from beneath the north side of the tower to help ease it slightly back toward the vertical. The tower was re-opened to the public in December 2001, and the work, at a cost of more than € 27 million, has decreased the inclination of the tower by approximately 43 cm.

Ticket Information

Entry fee: € 15,00 per person. Tickets can be purchased at the Ticket Office next to the Leaning Tower or booked online (http://www.opapisa.it) in advance only (allow at least 16 days). Tickets booked online cost € 17.00 per person.

Opening hours: daily from 8:30 am to 8:30 pm (opening times vary according to season).

Tours take place every 40 minutes and last 35 minutes. Children must be accompanied by an adult (no entry for children under 8 years).

IT6665 Camping Le Soline

via delle Soline, 51, 53010 Casciano di Murlo (Tuscany)

Le Soline is a country hillside site with wonderful views of the Tuscan hills from its steep slopes. Just 20 km. south of Siena and 800 m. from the village of Casciano, it has 80 neat pitches for large units and 60 tents on seven terraces with 6A electricity. Many trees including olives provide shade for the pitches, most having views. Ducks wander the site whilst geese are the gatekeepers. There is a full entertainment programme in high season and some free guided tours of the area (includes a dip in the lake). The kind and attentive Broggini family spare no efforts in making your stay a pleasant memory and are extremely hard working to this end. The elegant restaurant has an excellent menu and the terraces look over the pool to the colourful hills beyond. The heated pools are clean with sunbathing areas loungers and umbrellas. The site will suit families who wish for a peaceful break.

Facilities

A good quality, heated sanitary block (recently refurbished) is on the third terrace, providing mixed British and Turkish style WCs, facilities for disabled campers and hot water in the basins but showers are on payment. A few small private sanitary blocks are for hire. Motorcaravan services. Gas supplies. Laundry. Freezer for campers use. Restaurant. Pizzeria (all season). Well stocked shop (15/3-10/11). Swimming pools (Easter-15/10). Playground. Volleyball. Mini-football field. Archery. Bicycle hire. Organised excursions (June-Aug). Barbecue area (not allowed on pitches). Car wash area. Mobile homes and bungalows to rent. Cats are not accepted. Off site: Riding 600 m. Fishing 3 km.

At a glance

Welcome & Ambience	✓✓✓✓	Location	✓✓✓✓
Quality of Pitches	✓✓✓✓	Range of Facilities	✓✓✓✓

Directions

From Siena, turn off SS223 (Siena - Grosseto) to the left to Fontazzi (about 20 km) and keep right for Casciano, following signs. Alternatively, from Via Cassia SS2 turn at Lucignano d'Arbia for Murlo.

Charges 2003

Per person	€ 7.00
child (2-12 yrs)	€ 5.00
caravan	€ 6.50
tent	€ 5.00 - € 6.00
motorcaravan	€ 7.00
car	€ 1.50
motorcycle	€ 1.00
dog	€ 1.00
electricity	€ 1.50

Reservations

Contact site. Tel: 0577 817410. Email: camping@lesoline.it

Open

All year.

IT6661 Toscana Village

Via Fornoli, 56020 Montopoli (Tuscany)

Five years ago a forest stood here and was part of the attractive medieval Tuscan village of Montopoli. Toscana Village has been thoughtfully carved out of the mature pines and it is ideal for a sightseeing holiday in this central area. The 150 level pitches (some large) are on shaded terraces and are carefully maintained. Some pitches have full drainage facilities and water, most have electricity (3A). The amenities are centrally located in a pleasant modern building and the restaurant has a terrace where there are views of the forest. For a swim or sunbathe and to relax, the unusually shaped pool is in a separate area of the site. This site is being improved and enlarged each year, and it is a quality site tucked away from the hustle and bustle of the cities.

Facilities

One modern central block has excellent facilities including British style toilets, hot water at all the stylish sinks, private cabins and new facilites for disabled campers. Washing machines and a dryer. Motorcaravan service point. Shop. Gas. Restaurant with terrace (limited menu). Takeaway. Bread to order. Swimming pool (lifeguard 11.30-18.30 hrs; disclaimer signed if you use the pool out of these times; open May - Sept). Play area. 5-a-side football. Bicycle hire. Organised activities. Doctor's room. Torches useful. Off site: Fishing 6 km. Golf and riding 7 km. Walk to Montopoli village (1 km).

At a glance

Welcome & Ambience	✓✓✓✓✓	Location	✓✓✓✓
Quality of Pitches	✓✓✓✓	Range of Facilities	✓✓✓✓

Directions

From A12 autostrada (Genove - Florence) take Pisa Centro exit. Take the F1,P1,L1 and then the Montopoli exit. Look for a large cemetery on the right just before the town. Opposite is Via Masoria leading to Via Fornoli and the campsite. It is well signed.

Charges 2003

Per person	€ 5.00 - € 6.30
child (2-10 yrs)	€ 4.00 - € 5.00
pitch	€ 10.00 - € 11.50
electricity	€ 1.50
water and drainage	€ 2.50

Camping Cheques accepted.

Reservations

Made with 20% deposit. Tel: 0571 449032. Email: info@toscanavillage.com

Open

Easter - 15 October.

IT6664 Camping Toscana Colliverdi

Via Marcialla 349, Loc. Marcialla, 50020 Certaldo (Tuscany)

Very much a 'no frills' country hillside site, Toscana Colliverdi has space for 60 large units on deep terraces and two small areas for tents. All the terrace pitches have electricity. One part of the access road is tarmac the other rough gravel – large units should use the tarmac for ease of access on the steep slopes. There are excellent panoramic views of the surrounding countryside (unfortunately marred by overhead wires and a pylon supporting them sitting at the bottom of the site). This site's strength is the owner, Constantino who is there to please whatever the situation. You are greeted with a bottle of free Chianti and a big smile. He is an expert on the local history and culture and has an extensive array of tourist information and many fascinating snippets that are not in the guide books. Nothing is too much trouble and a comprehensive pack is given to all. There are no supporting facilities but he is in close liaison with suppliers in the local village and all requisites are available. The site is dark at night and the centre steps are a challenge as some are of differing depths, thus a good torch is required. If you are content to be self-supporting and want expert assistance in exploring Tuscany along with the advantage of reasonable campsite fees, then this could be for you.

Facilities

A small, but clean and good quality sanitary block is on the second terrace, and we are told a second block has been added. British and Turkish syle toilets, showers, external washbasins, dishwashing and laundry sinks all have hot and cold water. The new block should mean that facilities are no longer stretched at peak periods. No facilities for disabled campers. Washing machine. Bar. Shop. Play area. Bicycle hire. No other on site facilities but see text.

Off site: Restaurant, shop, butcher, greengrocer, post office 1 km.

At a glance

Welcome & Ambience	✓✓✓✓✓	Location	✓✓✓✓
Quality of Pitches	✓✓✓	Range of Facilities	✓✓

Directions

From A1 autostrada Florence - Siena, take Tavarnelle exit and head for Tavarnelle. At the village follow signs for Marcialla. Site entrance is on the left approximately 700 m. after the village of Marcialla.

Charges 2003

Per person	€ 6.00 - € 6.50
child (1-9 yrs)	€ 4.00 - € 4.50
motorcaravan	€ 9.50 - € 10.00
tent or caravan	€ 5.50 - € 6.00
car	€ 2.00
electricity (3/5A)	€ 2.00
dog	€ 1.50 - € 2.00

No credit cards.

Reservations

Write to site. Tel: 0571 669334.
Email: toscolverdi@virgilio.it

Open

1 April - 30 September.

IT6667 Camping La Finoria

Via Monticello, 66, 58023 Gavorrano (Tuscany)

An unusual site set high in the mountains with incredible views, La Finoria is a rugged site with a focus on nature. Italian schoolchildren attend education programmes here. The three motorcaravan pitches are at the top of the site for those who enjoy a challenge, with a dozen caravan pitches on lower terraces accessed by a steep gravel track. Under huge cheastnut tress there is a very pretty terraced area for tents. These have a private natural feel which some might say is what camping is all about. If you visit in November you can help collect the olives and make olive oil or a little earlier gather chestnuts for puree. Campers are invited to take part in the educational programmes in the 'LEA' building (Laboratario di Educazione Ambientale). The restaurant reflects the owner's attention to detail; the food here is wonderful and all the pasta is home-made. After an exhausting day communing with nature, or exploring the area, there is a large pool for a refreshing swim before enjoying the night views.

Facilities

Two blocks provide British and Turkish style toilets, hot showers and cold water at washbasins and sinks. Facilities for disabled campers. Washing machines. Small shop (closed Jan/Feb). Good restaurant and bar (closed Jan/Feb). Swimming pool (May - Sept), Lessons on the environment. TV. Excursions to Rome, Florence and Elba. Torches essential. Off site: Riding 2 km. Local village 3 km. Tennis 3 km. Bicycle hire 6 km. Golf 8 km. Fishing 12 km. Beach 12 km.

At a glance

Welcome & Ambience	✓✓✓✓	Location	✓✓✓✓
Quality of Pitches	✓✓✓	Range of Facilities	✓✓✓

Directions

From SS1 Follonica - Grosseto road take Gavorrano exit. Then take road to Fenoria. This is a steady climb for some 10 minutes, and as soon as you start to descend at a junction (the only one) look left downhill for a large slightly faded large white sign indicating the site off to the left.

2003

Per pitch	€ 4.00 - € 10.00
person	€ 2.50 - € 8.50
child (1-6 yrs)	€ 2.00 - € 4.50

Reservations

With only a few motorcaravan or caravan pitches it is best to phone ahead in high season.
Tel: 0566 844381. Email: finoria@ouverture.it

Open

All year.

IT6669 Camping Village Baia Azzurra

Le Rocchette, 58043 Castiglione della Pescaia (Tuscany)

Encircled by hills, Baia Azzurra is a cool green site with lots of trees. A new lagoon shaped pool has a pretty bridge feature and lots of loungers but, more importantly, a lifeguard on a raised platform at all times. Also within the fenced pool complex is an entertainment area, a playground and small café. The lawn and garden here make it a pleasant place to relax. The 120 average sized, grassy pitches are shaded by tall trees and artificial shade. The site has fairly basic amenities including the restaurant and bar near the entrance. The high spot of the site is the new pool and entertainment complex. Cross a minor road and a 400 m. walk brings you to the fine yellow sand beach with safe waters. This beach may be difficult for disabled guests. The site has a pleasant open feel but you will need to choose your pitch carefully to access the best of the sanitary blocks. We see this as a site for short visits only.

Facilities

Three old sanitary blocks offer a slightly confusing range of unisex facilites with British style toilets in one block only, plus units for disabled visitors in one block. Hot showers but otherwise the water is cold at sinks. Washing machines. Shop (all season). Restaurant, bar and pizzeria. Swimming pools (May - Sept). Large play area. Bicycle hire. Evening entertainment and animation. Mini-club (high season). Two freezers for visitor's use. Barbecues are not permitted. Off site: Beach 400 m. Boat launching 7 km. Riding 10 km. Golf 17 km.

At a glance

Welcome & Ambience	✓✓✓✓	Location	✓✓✓✓
Quality of Pitches	✓✓✓✓	Range of Facilities	✓✓✓✓

Directions

From SS1 Livorna - Roma road take Grosseto exit on SS322. Follow SS322 north from Castiglione della Pescaia and turn left at sign for Rochette. Site is 3 km. on the right.

Charges 2003

Per person	€ 6.50 - € 11.00
child (under 6 yrs)	€ 5.00 - € 6.50
pitch	€ 8.00 - € 13.50
dog	€ 5.50

Reservations

Advisable in high season; contact site.
Tel: 05 64 94 10 92. Email: info@baiaazzurra.com

Open

1 April - 31 October.

IT6663 Camping Semifonte

Via Ugo Foscolo 4, 50021 Barberino Val d'Elsa (Tuscany)

Camping Semifonte is a small basic, terraced site with fine views over the surrounding hills. The 90 pitches (76 for caravans and motorcaravans, the remainder without electricity for tents) are on steep terraces, small and tight for manoeuvring. Each terrace has a tap and electricity connections (4A). There is a very small shop selling basics. The small pools are separate and of the supported type, neither has security fencing and the paddling pool is alongside the play area, so children must be supervised at all times here. The prices are reasonable but the facilities are limited and you would be advised to arrive with full cupboards. The site is unsuitable for disabled campers and infirm visitors. A good restaurant is 500 m. from the site with another in the small village a short walk away.

Facilities

Two small sanitary blocks have a mixture of British and Turkish toilets, few showers and are under much pressure at peak periods. Motorcaravan service point. Small supported swimming pool for adults – no safety barrier. Children's supported pool with no safety fence, next to small play area. Off site: Regular bus route to/from Florence and Siena. Bicycle hire 0.5 km. Riding 1 km. Golf 15 km.

At a glance

Welcome & Ambience	✓✓✓	Location	✓✓✓✓
Quality of Pitches	✓✓✓✓	Range of Facilities	✓✓

Directions

From Florence-Siena autostrada take Tavarmelle exit to Barberina Val Elsa. Take first left on entering village and site is 500 m.

Charges 2003

Per person	€ 6.00 - € 6.50
child (3-10 yrs)	€ 4.00 - € 4.50
pitch	€ 5.50 - € 9.00
electricity (4A)	€ 2.00

Reservations

Made with € 5,50 fee (non refundable).
Tel: 055 807 5454. Email: semifonte@semifonte.it

Open

1 April - 20 October.

IT6671 Camping International Argentario

Localita Torre Saline, 58010 Albinia (Tuscany)

Argentario is really two separate campsites with a large holiday villa complex, all sharing the common facilities. The pools, animation area and bar area, like the villa complex are new and elegantly designed. The large irregular shaped pool and smaller circular children's pool are very inviting. Animation is organised daily by the team where there is something for everyone, young and old. The 404 pitches are smaller than usual, but mostly flat and on a surface of dark sand and pine needles being shaded by tall pines. The area is quite dusty and many of the pitches are a very long way from the amenities. Motorcaravans are parked in a large separate open square. Some campers may find the long walks trying, especially as the older style facilities are tired and stressed during peak periods. A basic restaurant and pizzeria is remote froom the touring section and has no views. The beach of dark sand has attractive views across to the mountains. We see this site more for short stays than extended holidays and unsuitable for disabled campers.

Facilities

Three mature blocks have mostly Turkish style toilets, a few cramped showers with hot water and cold water at the sinks (showers are very busy at peak periods). There are facilities for disabled campers but we think this site would prove very difficult because of the sand surface and remoteness of some facilities. Washing machines. Motorcaravan service point. Shop. Restaurant, bar and takeaway. Swimming pools. Tennis. Boat hire. Minigolf. Volleyball. Basketball. Archery. Tennis. ATM. Cars are parked in a separate car park in high season. Dogs are not accepted. Torches very useful. Off site: Boat launching and riding 1 km. Golf 20 km. Bar and restaurant on beach.

At a glance

Welcome & Ambience	✓✓✓✓	Location	✓✓✓
Quality of Pitches	✓✓✓	Range of Facilities	✓✓✓✓

Directions

Site is off the SS1 at the 150 km. mark, signed Porto S. Stefano. It is on the right, clearly marked but be careful to ignore the first 'combined' campsite sign and proceed another 300 m. to the main entrance with reception.

Charges 2003

Per unit incl. 2 adults	€ 16.00 - € 23.90

Reservations

Made for the full month only in August (no deposit). Tel: 0564 870 302.

Open

Easter/1April - 30 September.

IT6633 Camping Village Free Time

Via dei Cipressi, 57020 Marina di Bibbona (Tuscany)

Free Time is a modern site just 700 metrers from an attractive sandy beach and 500 metres from the little resort of Marina di Bibbona. Pitches are on level ground, most with electricity connections, and are reasonably shaded. There is a good, well-stocked supermarket and a ba/restaurant/pizzeria complex overlooking the pool. The main pool is large and there is a separate, smaller childrens' pool.

Facilities

The sanitary blocks are modern and well maintained. Special disabled facilities. Some pitches are available with private sanitary facilities (extra charge). Motorcaravan service point. Lively 'animation' programme in peak season (including aqua gym in the pool and disco evenings). Five a-side football pitch. Fishing lake. Childrens' play area. Dogs only accepted in low season. Off site: Beach 700m. Cecina 5km.

At a glance

Welcome & Ambience	✓✓✓	Location	✓✓✓✓
Quality of Pitches	✓✓✓✓	Range of Facilities	✓✓✓

Directions

Exit Livorno - Civitavecchia road ('superstrada') at the La California exit and follow signs to Marina di Bibbona. The site is well signposted.

Charges 2003

Per pitch	€ 9.00 - € 13.00
adult	€ 6.00 - € 10.00
child (1-9 years)	€ 4.00 - € 6.00
electricity (3A)	€ 0.50

Reservations

Contact site. Tel: .0335 762 6086 or 0586 600934 E-mail: freetime@camping.it

Open

11 April - 5 October.

TOSCANA
COSTE DELLA MAREMMA - COSTA D'ARGENTO · LAZIO

Pavilions · Bungalows · Caravans · Camping sites

TALAMONE
Camping Village

58010 TALAMONE (GR)
TEL 0564 / 88 70 26 FAX 0564 / 88 71 70
www.talamonecampingvillage.com
info@talamonecampingvillage.com

Direct access to the sea

ARGENTARIO
Camping Village

58010 ALBINIA (GR)
TEL 0564 / 87 03 02 FAX 0564 / 87 13 80
www.argentariocampingvillage.com
info@argentariocampingvillage.com

Direct access to the sea

IL GABBIANO
Camping

58010 ALBINIA (GR)
TEL 0564 / 87 02 02 FAX 0564 / 87 02 02
www.ilgabbianocampingvillage.com
info@il gabbianocampingvillage.com

Direct access to the sea

CLUB DEGLI AMICI
Camping Village

01010 PESCIA ROMANA (VT)
TEL 0766 / 83 02 50 FAX 0766 / 83 02 50
www.clubdegli amicicampingvillage.com
info@clubdegliamicicampingvillage.com

Direct access to the sea

CALIFORNIA
Camping Village

01014 MARINA DI MONTALTO (VT)
TEL 07664 / 80 28 48 FAX 0766 / 80 12 10
www.californiacampingvillage.com
info@californiacampingvillage.com

FORMULA CLUB ALL INCLUSIVE

Private beach
Sunshades and deck chairs
Swimming pool
Whirlpool
Archery
Golf (practice range)
Canoes, kayaks, paddle surfboards
Mini football and volleyball
Fitness
Tennis and basketball
Sailing and diving
Entertainment
Miniclub Dance school, ...

The Gitav group's establishments are situated along the coast, under secular pinewoods.

They are placed in a very popular area rich of natural, historical and archaeological appeals (oasis, natural parks and sea parks, medieval villages, Etruscan necropolis...)

Wherever the "All Inclusive Club Formula" does not apply the Gitav group's offers special arrangements for boats docking facilities, fishing-tourism, horseback ridings, ...

GITAV 6

For further information, see the editorials of each camping.

CENTRO PRENOTAZIONI GITAV C.P. 67 I - 58010 ALBINIA (GR)
TEL 0039 - 0564 870068 FAX 0039 - 0564 870470
www.gitav.com   E-MAIL: info@gitav.com

IT6670 Camping Village Vallicella

Loc. Vallicella, 58020 Scarlino (Tuscany)

Cleverly set into two sides of a valley like an amphitheatre, the pitches here have glorious views over Tuscany to the sea and across the mountains to incredible hilltop villages. The very steep access slopes are surfaced with bitumen for ease of movement and the terracing is designed for privacy and views. Stone walls and attractive wooded safety rails are features around the site. The mostly shaded pitches are flat with a gravel/sand surface and cars are parked away from pitches. Thought has gone into the design of the beautiful restaurant, pool and recreational area, which all share the superb vistas. The extensive animation programme includes visiting professional entertainment. Vallicella is a friendly, family owned and oriented site for those who like plenty of exercise.

Facilities

Three blocks (one older, two modern) have mixed Turkish and British style toilets. A very difficult site for disabled visitors because of the steep terrain but thoughtfully designed, good facilities are near a long terrace giving easy access to the hub of the site. Mini-market. Bar. Restaurant Wine bar. Pizzeria. Swimming pools (an additional pool and play-park is planned for 2004). Hydro-massage. Sauna. All day animation programme for children. Evening adult entertainment programme. Play area (supervision required.) Babyfoot. Bicycle and scooter hire. Internet point. Off site: Riding 3 km. Fishing and boat launching 6 km. Golf 9 km.

Directions

From autostrada E80, take Follonica exit and follow signs for Scarlino. Site is well signed as you climb the hill.

Charges 2003

Per adult	€ 6.20 - € 10.30
child (3-12 yrs)	€ 3.10 - € 6.20
pitch	€ 6.70 - € 16.70
animal	€ 4.10

Reservations

Contact site. Tel: 0566 37229. Email: info@vallicella.it

Open

20 April - 19 October.

At a glance

Welcome & Ambience	✓✓✓✓✓	Location	✓✓✓✓
Quality of Pitches	✓✓✓✓✓	Range of Facilities	✓✓✓✓✓

IT6612 Camping Norcenni Girasole Club

Via Norcenni 7, 50063 Figline Valdarno (Tuscany)

The Norcenni Girasole Club is an excellent, busy and well run site in a picturesque, secluded situation with great views of Tuscan landscapes 19 km. south of Florence. Owned by the dynamic Cardini-Vannucchi family, care has been taken in its development and the buildings and infrastructure are most attractive and in sympathy with the surrounds. Absolutely everything is to hand and guests will only need to leave the site if they wish to explore the local attractions. There is an amazing choice of superb swimming pools on site and at the 'Lagoon' in the sister site which is 100 m. walk. Children can ride the large, exciting water flume free, play in the waterfall and feature pool or revert to other themed pools with slides. A modern health complex provides saunas, jacuzzi, steam bath, a fitness centre, hydro-massage, Shiatzu massage or a straight massage (extra cost). Three attractive restaurants with terraces serve wonderful food. One of these restaurants is at the sister site and offers more cosmopolitan food. There are 470 clean and roomy pitches for touring units, all with electricity (4A) and water, most shaded by well tended trees. The ground is hard and stony (tent pegs can be difficult). Although on a fairly steep hillside, pitches are on level terraces accessed from good, hard roads. Tour operators occupy another 150 pitches and there are a few (20) permanent pitches. An extensive animation programme is published each week with music on three evenings and lots of activities for children. Courses in the Italian language, Tuscan cooking and wine tasting are provided. There are many English visitors and all information and most of the animation is in English.

Facilities

Sanitary facilities are very good with mixed British and Turkish style WCs. Hot water is available throughout. Five family bathrooms are for rent but, being very popular, these need to be booked in advance. Facilities for disabled visitors. Washing machines and dryers. Supermarket and gift shops. Wine shop. Bar and superb restaurants with terrace. Pizzeria. Gelateria. Two flood-lit tennis courts. Riding. Wonderful swimming pools, one covered and heated (supervised; hats required). Fitness centre with jacuzzi and Turkish bath (charged). Soundproof disco. Riding. Internet café. ATM. Off site: Several excursions are on offer with one evening tour of Florence that includes a five course dinner in an historic palace. Daily bus direct to Florence and shuttle buses to the local railway station.

Directions

From Florence take Rome A1/E35 autostrada and take Incisa exit. Turn south on route 69 towards Arezzo. In Figline turn right for Greve and watch for Norcenni signs - site is 4 km up a twisting, climbing road. If approached from the west it is a very long narrow winding road.

Charges 2004

Per person	€ 6.80 - € 9.70
child (2-12 yrs)	€ 4.10 - € 5.70
caravan or trailer tent	€ 6.10 - € 8.40
tent	€ 5.70 - € 7.80
car	€ 3.90 - € 5.40
motorcaravan	€ 10.00 - € 13.80

Reservations

Made with deposit. Tel: 055 915141. Email: girasole@ecvacanze.it

Open

30 March - 2 November.

At a glance

Welcome & Ambience	✓✓✓✓	Location	✓✓✓✓
Quality of Pitches	✓✓✓✓	Range of Facilities	✓✓✓✓✓

Known as the 'Green Heart of Italy' Umbria is a beautiful region of rolling hills, woods, streams and valleys that gives way to high mountain wilderness. It is well known for the beauty and profusion of its medieval hilltowns.

Umbria has two provinces: Perugia and Terni

Umbria's main attraction is the Vale of Spoleto and the hilltowns of Assisi and Spoleto. The birthplace of Saint Francis, Assisi attracts vast numbers of art lovers and pilgrims throughout the year who visit his burial place, the Basilica di San Francesco, built in 1228 two years after his death. Within a scenic woodland setting, Spoleto was once an important Roman colony. The town has the remains of a Roman amphitheatre, reputedly where ten thousand Christian martyrs were slaughtered, and a variety of Romanesque churches. It also boasts an impressive 14th century aqueduct, which offers good views of the surrounding countryside. Near Perugia, the regional capital, is Lake Trasimeno, the fourth largest lake in Italy. It has plenty of opportunities for fishing, swimming and watersports. The lakeside town of Castiglione del Lago is a good place to relax and unwind on the small sandy beaches; from here boats make regular trips to the Isola Maggiore, one of the lake's three islands. Further north is Gubbio, the most thoroughly medieval of all the Umbrian towns. A charming place full of twisting streets with soft-pink stone houses and terracotta-tiled rooftops, its beauty is enhanced by the forest-clad Apennines mountains looming up behind.

Cuisine of the region

Simple pastas and roast meats are popular, especially pork and *la porchetta* (whole suckling pig stuffed with rosemary or sage, roasted on a spit). Truffles can be found in abundance, particularly in Noria, which also produces some of the country's best hams, sausages and salamis. The rivers yield fish such as eel, pike, trout and crayfish. Locally grown vegetables include lentils, beans, celery and cardoons. Good quality olive oil is readily available. Orvieto is a popular Umbrian white wine.

Agnello alla cacciatora: lamb with a sauce of anchovies, garlic and rosemary

Crescionda: rich traditional cake prepared with almond biscuits, lemon rind and bitter chocolate

Fichi: candied figs with almonds and cocoa

Tartufo nero: black truffles

Places of interest

Deruta: town renowned for its ceramics

Monte Cucco Regional Park: offers organised trails and outdoor activities

Monti Sibillini: national park with good walking trails

Norcia: mountain town, birthplace of St Benedict

Orvieto: boasts one of the greatest Gothic churches in Italy

Spello: renowned for frescoes in the 12th-13th century church of Santa Maria Maggiore, Roman ruins

Todi: striking hilltown, 13th century church and palaces

tip

UMBRIA HOSTS TWO POPULAR EVENTS IN SUMMER: THE FESTIVAL OF TWO WORLDS IN SPOLETO AND THE JAZZ FESTIVAL IN PERUGIA. CONTACT THE TOURIST OFFICE FOR DETAILS.

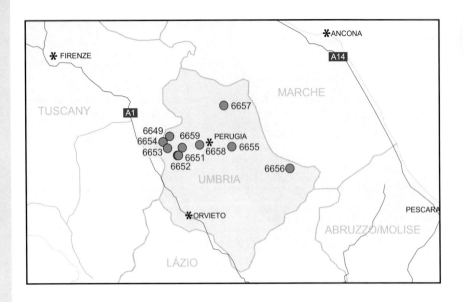

IT6652 Camping Villaggio Italgest

Via Martiri di Cefalonia, 06060 Sant Arcangelo di Magione (Umbria)

Directly on the shore on the south side of Lake Trasimeno, Sant Arcangelo is ideally placed for exploring Umbria and Tuscany. The area around the lake is fairly flat but has views of the distant hills and can become very hot during summer. Villaggio Italgest is a pleasant site with 248 tourist pitches on level grass and, except for the area next to the lake, under a cover of tall trees. All pitches have electrical connections (6A) and cars are parked away from the pitches. The site offers a wide variety of activities, tours are organised daily and there is entertainment for children and adults in high season. The bar/disco remains open until 2 am. There is a good sized swimming pool area with one pool with slides, a smaller children's pool and a whirlpool. Whether you wish to use this site as a base for exploration, as a place to relax, you will find this a most pleasant place to stay. English is spoken.

Facilities

The one large and two smaller sanitary block have mainly British style WCs and free hot water in the washbasins and showers. Facilities for disabled people. Motorcaravan services. Washing machines and dryers. Community room with stoves, fridges and freezers. Bar, restaurant, pizzeria and takeaway (all season). Mini-market. Swimming pool (25 x 12.5 m). Tennis. Football. Volleyball. Table tennis. Play area. Wide range of activities, entertainment and excursions. Marina for boats with crane. Entertainment for adults and children (July/Aug). Italian language and civilisation couses. Excursions. TV (satellite) and games rooms. Disco. Films. Watersports, motor boat hire and lake swimming. Fishing. Mountain bike and scooter hire. Internet point. Private area with beach for dog owners and dog-sitting service. Off site: Golf, parachuting, riding, canoeing and sailing close by.

At a glance

Welcome & Ambience	✓✓✓✓✓	Location	✓✓✓✓
Quality of Pitches	✓✓✓✓✓	Range of Facilities	✓✓✓✓

Directions

Site is on the southern shore of Lake Trasimeno. Take Magione exit from the Perugia spur from the Florence - Rome autostrada, proceed southwest round the lake to S. Arcangelo where the site is signed.

Charges 2003

Per person	€ 5.70 - € 7.70
child (3-9 yrs)	€ 4.00 - € 5.70
pitch	€ 6.00 - € 9.50
small tent pitch	€ 5.00 - € 6.50
car	€ 1.80 - € 2.50
dog	€ 1.80 - € 2.50

Reservations

During winter telephone 075/5847422 or write to site with 30%. Tel: 075 848 238.
Email: camping@italgest.com

Open

1 April - 30 September.

IT6651 Camping Polvese

06060 S. Arcangelo sul Trasimeno (Umbria)

A lakeside site, Polvese takes its name from the island which can be seen clearly from the site. The 80 tourist pitches are in two areas, generally separated from the very permanent pitches rented by Italians and Germans guests. On flat ground, the older pitches are reasonably sized and shaded, with some by the lake. The new area has young trees and relies on artificial shading. Children have a separate shallow pool in which to play and the adult pool is clean and pleasant. The restaurant with its lake views and a pleasant terrace, is run as a separate business, whilst the very small bar doubles as a shop selling basics for campers. There is a mini-club in high season plus a little entertainment for adults in the evening, and a slightly tired outdoor cinema. Tours are organised along with food tastings. We see this as a site for short visits rather than extended stays.

Facilities

Single, basic sanitary block with a tired exterior. The inside is dated with a few minor cosmetic problems but is relatively clean with free hot showers. British and Turkish style toilets and cold water at all the sinks. Facilities for disabled campers. Washing machine. Motorcaravan service ponit. Restaurant (not owned by site). Basic bar - doubles as shop. TV. Outdoor cinema (basic). Swimming and paddling pools. Bicycle hire. Soccer. Volleyball. Boule. Mini-club. Freezers for campers. Barbecue area. Torches required. Off site: Riding 2 km.Golf (8 hole) 5 km.

At a glance

Welcome & Ambience	✓✓✓	Location	✓✓✓✓
Quality of Pitches	✓✓✓	Range of Facilities	✓✓✓

Directions

Site is on south side of Lake Trasimino. From Florence - Rome autostrada take Magione exit and the lakeside road south to S. Arcangelo where the site is well signed.

Charges 2003

Per person	€ 4.50 - € 5.50
child (3-10 yrs)	€ 3.50 - € 4.00
pitch	€ 3.50 - € 7.00
animal	€ 2.00 - € 2.50

Camping Cheques accepted.

Reservations

Reservations taken (min. 1 week in high season). Tel: 0758 48078. Email: polvese@polvese.com

Open

1 April - 1 October.

IT6649 Camping Punta Navaccia

06069 Tuoro sul Trasimeno (Umbria)

Situated on the north side of Lake Trasimeno, this park is run by the friendly and welcoming owners, The area surrounding the site also has a lot to offer, The main attraction is of course the lake, ideal for swimming and a variety of watersports. The campsite is large with over 70,000 square metres and 400 touring pitches, (200 with 4A electricity) and all with shade. The campsite has a long (stony) beach with moorings and carthaginians for launching your boat or sunbathing. The site has 60 mobile homes with airconditioning available for rent.

Facilities

Sanitary block with British style WC's, showers and some private cabins. Washing machine and dryer. Motor caravan service point. Heated swimming pool and paddling pool. Shop, restaurant and take away (April - November). Large covered amphitheatre. Disco. Cinema screen. Miniclub. Animation is organised in high season (in Italian, English, German and Dutch). Play area. Tennis. Basketball. Beach volleyball. Mini football. Table tennis. Motor caravan service point. Boat launching on site. Off site: Sandy beach (200 m). Windsurfing, sailing and canoeing 200 m.

At a glance

Welcome & Ambience	✓✓✓✓	Location	✓✓✓✓
Quality of Pitches	✓✓✓✓	Range of Facilities	✓✓✓✓

Directions

Going south from Florence (Firenze) to Rome on the A1, take the S326 to Perugia near Bettolle. After approx. 30 km take the exit for Tuoro sul Trasimeno. The site is well signposted.

Charges 2004

Per unit incl. 2 persons	€ 17.00 - € 24.00
extra person	€ 5.50 - € 8.00
child (2-9 yrs)	€ 4.00 - € 6.00

Camping Cheques accepted.

Reservations

Contact site. Tel: 075 826357. Email: navaccia@camping.it

Open

15 March - 31 October.

IT6653 Camping Listro

Via Lungolago, 06061 Castiglione del Lago (Umbria)

This is a simple, pleasant, flat site with the best beach (private to the campsite) on Lake Trasimeno. As the lake is very shallow with some reeds (seven metres at its deepest), it has very gradually sloping beaches making it very safe for children to play and swim. This also results in very warm water, which is kept clean as fishing and tourism are the major industries hereabouts. Camping Listro is a few hundred yards north of the historic town of Castiglione and the attractive town can be seen rising up the hillside from the site. It provides 110 pitches all with electricity (3A) with 70% of the pitches enjoying the shade of mature trees. Younger campers are in a separate area of the site, ensuring no noise disturbance and some of the motorcaravan pitches are right on the lakeside giving stunning views out of your windows. Facilities on the site are fairly limited with a small shop and bar and snack bar, and there is no organised entertainment. English is spoken and British guests are particularly welcome. If you enjoy the simple life and peace and quiet in camping terms then this site is for you.

Facilities

Two screened sanitary facilities are very clean with British and Turkish style WCs. Facilities for disabled visitors. Washing machine. Motorcaravan services. Bar. Shop. Snack bar. Play area. Table tennis. Volleyball. Private beach. Off site: The town is 800 m. and many bars and restaurants are near, as are sporting facilities including a good swimming pool and tennis courts (discounts using the camp-site card).

At a glance

Welcome & Ambience	✓✓✓✓	Location	✓✓✓✓
Quality of Pitches	✓✓✓	Range of Facilities	✓✓✓

Directions

From A1/E35 Florence-Rome autostrada take Val di Chiana exit and join the Perugia (75 bis) superstrada. After 24 km. take Castiglione exit and follow town signs. Signs to site are clearly marked just before the town.

Charges 2003

Per person (over 3 yrs)	€ 3.50 - € 4.20
pitch	€ 3.50 - € 4.20
car	€ 1.10 - € 1.60
motorcycle	€ 0.80 - € 1.05

Less 10% for stays over 8 days in low season.

Reservations

Contact site. Tel: 075 951193. Email: listro@listro.it

Open

1 April - 30 September.

IT6656 Camping Il Collaccio

Azienda Agricola 11 Collaccio, 06047 Castelvecchio di Preci (Umbria)

Il Collaccio is owned and run by the Baldoni family who bought the farm over 30 years ago, rebuilt the derelict farmhouse in its original style and then decided to share it with holiday makers by developing a campsite and accommodation for rent. The farming aspect was kept, along with a unit producing salami (they run very popular salami making and Umbrian cookery courses over Easter and New Year) and its products can be bought in the shop and sampled in the excellent restaurant. The camping area has been carved out of the hillside which forms a natural amphitheatre with splendid views. At first sight the narrow steep entrance seems daunting (the owner will assist) and the road which leads down to the somewhat steep camping terraces takes one to the exit. A pleasant restaurant and bar over-looks the upper pools and a bar is alongside the lower pools. The 93 large pitches are on level terraces with stunning views. Electrical connections (6A) are available; long leads useful. Thousands of trees, planted to replace those cut down by the previous owner, are maturing and provide some shade. An interesting feature is a tree plantation on a lower slope where they are experimenting in cultivating truffles. Small, but not intrusive, tour operator presence.

Facilities

Three modern sanitary blocks are spaced through the site with British and Turkish styled WCs, cold water in washbasins and hot, pre-mixed water in showers and sinks. Facilities for disabled visitors. Washing machine. Motorcaravan service point. Restaurant (all season). Shop (basics, 1/7-31/8). Two new swimming pools both with children's pool (15/5-30/9). Play area. Tennis. Volley and basketball. Football. Table tennis. Boules. Entertainment in high season. Excursion opportunities with small numbers on gourmet visits to olive oil and wine making organisations. Off site: Cycling and walking. Canoeing and rafting 2 km. Fishing 10 km.

At a glance

Welcome & Ambience	✓✓✓✓✓	Location	✓✓✓✓
Quality of Pitches	✓✓✓✓	Range of Facilities	✓✓✓✓

Directions

From SS77 Foligno-Civitonova Marche road turn south at Muccia for Visso from where Preci is signed. There is a direct route (saving a long and extremely winding approach) through a new tunnel, if the site is approached north of Eggi which is approx. 10 km. north of Spoleto. The tunnel exit is at Sant Anatolia di Narco SS209, where a left turn will take you to Preci.

Charges 2003

Per person	€ 5.50 - € 7.25
child (3-12 yrs)	€ 2.25 - € 3.50
caravan or motorcaravan	€ 6.50 - € 8.50
tent	€ 5.50 - € 7.25

Electricity included. Camping Cheques accepted.

Reservations

Write to site. Tel: 0743 939005.
Email: info@ilcollaccio.com

Open

1 April - 30 September.

IT6654 Camping Badiaccia

Via Trasimeno 1, Voc. Badiaccia 91, 06061 Castiglione del Lago (Umbria)

A lakeside site, Camping Badiaccia has excellent views of the surrounding hills and the islands of the lake. Being directly on the lake gives an almost seaside atmosphere. There is a protected swimming area along the beach with lots of sunbathing space and sunloungers and some reed areas close by and a jetty that provides a base for fishing. The site also has a protected mooring for small boats and offers a good selection of sporting opportunities with four special staff in high season to organise activities for children and adults. Well tended and maintained, Badiaccia has a pleasant appearance enhanced by a variety of plants and flowers and English is spoke by the friendly staff. Some of the 150 numbered pitches are smaller than average but there is good shade in most parts, all have 4A electricity and are separated by trees and bushes in rows from hard access roads. A very pleasant, large swimming pool is by the restaurant and a children's pool in the beach area. Guided excursions to Rome and Florence are organised in high season and a list detailing local markets is displayed.

Facilities

The two centrally positioned sanitary blocks can be heated and are fully equipped. Washing machines. Motorcaravan services. Gas supplies. Restaurant, snack bar and shop – all open all season. Gelateria. Swimming pool (20 x 10 m) and children's pool (1/6-30/9). Play areas. Tennis. Table tennis. Minigolf. Boules. Minigolf. Volleyball. Football. Beach volley-ball. Windsurfing. Watersports. Fishing. Boat hire. Entertainment and excursions in high season. Large barbecue area by lake. English spoken. Torches required in places. Dogs accepted but not by the lakeside. Off site: Riding 3 km. Golf 20 km.

At a glance

Welcome & Ambience	✓✓✓✓	Location	✓✓✓✓
Quality of Pitches	✓✓✓✓	Range of Facilities	✓✓✓✓

Directions

From A11 Milan-Rome autostrada take Val di Chiana exit and turn east towards Perugia on the SS75bis. Leave this at Castiglione exit and go south on SS71 in the direction of Castiglione where site is well signed about 5 km. north of the town.

Latest charges

Per person	€ 4.65 - € 5.68
child (under 10 yrs)	€ 3.10 - € 4.65
caravan	€ 5.16 - € 5.68
tent	€ 4.65 - € 5.16
car	€ 1.55
motorcaravan	€ 5.68 - € 6.20

Electricity included.

Reservations

Write to site. Tel: 075 9659097.
Email: camping@badiaccia.com

Open

1 April - 30 September.

123

IT6655 Camping Internazionale Assisi

S Giovanni in Campiglione 110, 06081 Assisi (Umbria)

Camping Internazionale is situated on the west side of Assisi and has high grade facilities which provide tourers with a good base to visit the area. The excellent restaurant has a large terrace which can be completely enclosed serving reasonably priced meals, ranging from pizzas to local Umbrian dishes. Finish off with a drink in the enjoyable 'Stonehenge Bar' which stays open a little later. The city is lit up in the evenings to provide a beautiful backdrop from some areas in the site. The 175 pitches are large and clearly marked on flat grass, all with electricity (3A). There is shade as it can be very hot in this part of Italy, and a welcome relief is the site's pleasant, large swimming pool. The site is pleasantly out of the city bustle and heat and offers a regular shuttle bus service. The site organises many tours in the area for individuals and groups. In terms of value this is one of the cheapest sites we have seen in Northern Italy.

Facilities

The well appointed and clean toilet block has free hot showers, plenty of washbasins, mainly Turkish style WCs (only 4 British style in each block) and facilities for disabled people. Washing machine. Motorcaravan services. Restaurant/pizzeria with self-service section (closed Weds). Bar with snacks. Shop. Ice cream bar. Group kitchen for campers with tables and benches. Free swimming pool, jacuzzi and circular children's pool (bathing caps mandatory). Table tennis. Bicycle hire. Tennis. Volleyball. Roller skating area. Gas supplies. Off site: Riding 2 km. Excursions to Assisi centre, Rome and Siena. Bus service to city three times daily from outside the site (one on Sundays except Easter).

At a glance

Welcome & Ambience	✓✓✓	Location	✓✓✓✓
Quality of Pitches	✓✓✓	Range of Facilities	✓✓✓

Directions

Site is on the south side of the SS147, which branches left off SS75 Perugia - Foligno road. Follow Assisi signs and, since there are several campsite signs in the town, look for the un-named camping sign going off to the left (downhill) as you enter the city. The site is approx. 4 km. from the city. At Violi a village just before Assisi there is a warning of a low bridge of 3.3 m – in fact it is much higher at the centre of the curved bridge and even the highest units will pass through.

Charges 2003

Per adult	€ 6.00 - € 7.00
child (3-10 yrs)	€ 4.00 - € 5.00
caravan	€ 6.00 - € 7.00
tent	€ 5.00 - € 6.00
car	€ 2.00 - € 3.00
motorcaravan	€ 8.00 - € 9.00

Electricity included. Credit cards accepted for min. € 50.

Reservations

Made for 1 week stays in high season, but not really necessary. Tel: 075 813710. Email: info@campingassisi.it

Open

1 April - October.

IT6659 Villaggio Parco dei Pini

Via Gandhi 1, San Feliciano, 06060 Magione (Umbria)

A pretty new site on the lakeside, this is a great alternative to the larger sites in the area. It is set in the grounds of the oldest villa on the lake (restoration is in progress) and the whole site has been refurbished to a very high level using the existing historic buildings to provide the high quality amenities. A very nice pool at the lakeside overlooks the island of Polvese and meals taken at the new restaurant share this prime view. The 40 flat, good sized pitches are under enormous trees giving excellent shade and there is a very peaceful atmosphere with some pitches enjoying lake views. A section of permanent pitches is placed unobtrusively in a separate area of the site. English is spoken but it is a great place to practice your Italian especially at weekends when professional entertainment is provided. The staff also organise tours of beautiful Umbria but there is a temptation just to enjoy the ambience here and lose yourself in the attractive surroundings. It is an excellent site for those who do not want the brashness of the larger sites.

Facilities

The sanitary unit for tourers is very high grade, bright and airy. British style toilets and very clean showers, plus an excellent unit for disabled visitors. Hot water throughout. Washing machine. Excellent new restaurant. Bar (all season). Swimming pool (May-Sept). Water aerobics. Small play area. Entertainment for adults (weekends). Lake beach. Off site: Village with shops, bars and restaurants 300 m. Riding and golf 20 km.

At a glance

Welcome & Ambience	✓✓✓✓	Location	✓✓✓✓
Quality of Pitches	✓✓✓✓	Range of Facilities	✓✓✓

Directions

From Perugia - Bettolle road, take Torrecella exit and follow lakeside road south to San Feliciano. Site is well signed off this road.

Charges 2003

Per person	€ 5.50 - € 6.50
pitch	€ 5.50 - € 7.00

Reservations

Made with 30% deposit. Tel: 0584 76270. Email: parcodeipini@tiscalet.it

Open

1 April - 15 October.

IT6657 Camping Villa Ortoguidone

S.S. 298 km 13,5, 06024 Ortoguidone (Umbria)

This is a site with a difference, just three kilometres from the walls of the fabulous old city of Gubbio. It has been constructed on an old farm surrounded by fields of sunflowers and corn. The family have owned the farm for over 135 years and the old villa is now used for guest accommodation. Dominated by the Pre Appennino and Appennino mountains, and enjoying views of the city, the site can be hot by day but is cool at night. It has a pleasant and peaceful open feel. There are 14 excellent large pitches in the grounds of this old villa (book ahead for these) and 100 serviced pitches in a new, flat area where young trees are just beginning to provide some shade. There is a solar heated pool and a snack bar (a restaurant is planned). For now there are discounts arranged at the super Fabiani restaurant in the city. This is an environmentally aware site where campers are encouraged to use free solar heated water. Campers can take a 'maxi package' (four star) where everything is included, or a 'mini package' (three star) which is ideal for using the site as a base to explore the city.

€Two cane covered prefabricated units (in sympathy with the surroundings) provide excellent sanitary facilities with British and Turkish style toilets and facilities for disabled campers. Solar heating is used throughout. Hot water at the sinks. Washing machines. Motorcaravan service point. Snack bar (all season). Swimming pools, paddling pool, spa (July-Sept). Fitness area by the pool. Basic play area. Volleyball. 5-side football. Tennis. Off site: Restaurants, bars and shops 3 km. River fishing 500 m. Riding 5 km. Golf 30 km.

At a glance

Welcome & Ambience	✓✓✓✓✓	Location	✓✓✓✓
Quality of Pitches	✓✓✓	Range of Facilities	✓✓✓

Directions

From autostrada A1 take Orte exit and the E45 towards Perugia - Cesena, and then Bosco Gubbio exit. Take SS298 to Gubbio and follow camping signs (site signs change from brown to white with 'Agriclub Villa Ortoguidon' in black on a white background.

Charges 2003

Per person	€ 6.50 - € 9.00
child (2-7 yrs)	€ 5.50 - € 6.50
pitch	€ 7.00- € 10.50
electricity	€ 2.50
animal	€ 2.50

Reservations

Made with deposit. Tel: 075 9272037. Email: info@gubbiocamping

Open

1 April - 30 September.

IT6658 Camping Paradis d'Été

Str. Fontana 29/h, Colle della Trinità, 06074 Perugia (Umbria)

A small, unassuming site high above Perugia in cool green hills, Paradis d'Ete is on a slope, although most of the 45 unusually large, heavily shaded pitches are well terraced to be reasonably flat. Two old villas have been converted to provide amenities for the campsite and a large swimming pool sits between them offering dreamy bathing after a day touring the sights. There is a charming snack bar with terrace and pizzas are served on the large open terrace from a separate building and breakfast is available if required. Rustic but friendly, this is a 'get away from it all' site with good prices, even if it lacks the luxuries of the sites around Trasimeno lake. English is spoken on site which is ideal for those who enjoy the simple life.

Facilities

The sanitary units are small but neat and clean with British and Turkish style toilets, hot showers and a unit for disabled campers. Hot water at sinks. Washing machine. Bar (all season). Small pizzeria. Swimming pool (June-Sept). Small play area. Off site: Very good restaurant 500 m. Bars and shops. Riding and golf 20 km.

At a glance

Welcome & Ambience	✓✓✓✓	Location	✓✓✓✓
Quality of Pitches	✓✓✓✓	Range of Facilities	✓✓✓

Directions

Site is 8 km. west of Perugia and a little tricky to find. From Perugia - Foligno road take exit for Ferro di Cavallo, then road for Fontana (look for huge green faced PAMS store at turn for Fontana). Pick up signs for Trinita and camping signs (these are few and far between). Site is right at the top of the hill to Trinita - do not be put off by 'cul de sac' signs - keep climbing! Site is on the right.

Charges 2003

Per person	€ 5.20 - € 6.20
child (under 5 yrs)	€ 3.20 - € 3.70
pitch	€ 4.20 - € 7.75
electricity	€ 1.00

Reservations

Made with 30% deposit. Tel: 0755 173121. Email: jnlagu@tin.it

Open

1 April - 15 October.

Lying between the Adriatic Sea and the Apennine mountains, Marche boasts a pretty mixture of woods and remote hills, medieval towns and seaside resorts, sandy beaches and sleepy coves, plus the snow-capped peaks of the Monti Sibillini.

There are four provinces in Marche: Ancona, Ascoli Piceno, Macerata and Pesaro e Urbino

Marche is not as well known or publicised as other regions but despite that it has plenty to offer. The medieval town of Urbino with its spectacular Renaissance palace is one of the highlights, as is Ascoli Piceno, which also boasts a medieval heritage, various churches and an enchanting town square. The dramatic fortress at San Leo is considered to be one of the best, while nearby San Marino is Europe's oldest republic. A tiny area with no customs regulations, its borders are just seven miles apart at its widest point. The republic has its own mint, an army and produces its own postage stamps. South of Ancona, the regional capital, and overlooked by the dramatic white cliffs of Monte Cónero is the Cónero Riviera, an impressive stretch of coast with small beaches, coves and picturesque little resorts, including Portonovo, Sirolo and Numana. Along the coast is Loreto, one of Italy's most popular pilgrimage destinations, and more beaches can be found at San Benedetto del Tronto. Further inland near the Verdicchio wine-producing hilltop villages around Jesi, is the Grotte di Frasassi, one of Europe's largest accessible cave networks. And the mountainous region of Monti Sibillini in the south offers good walking trails and skiing plus stunning views.

Cuisine of the region

The food is a mix of seafood along the coastline and country cooking inland, involving locally grown produce – tomatoes, fennel and mushrooms. Typical seafood dishes include *zuppa di pesce* (fish soup with saffron) and *brodetto* (fish broths). Rabbit and lamb is popular plus *porchetta* (roast suckling pig). The region is best known for its Verdicchio wine although it does produce a variety of others.

Coniglio in porchetta: rabbit cooked with fennel

Cicerchiata: balls of pasta fried and covered in honey

Olive ascolane: olives stuffed with meat and herbs, served with *crema fritta*, little squares of fried cream

Vincisgrassi: baked pasta dish with ham and truffles

Places of interest

Ancona: regional capital and Adriatic's largest port

Fano: beach resort with old centre and historic monuments

Jesi: medieval town walls, Renaissance and Baroque palaces

Macerata: university town surrounded by lovely countryside, famous for its annual outdoor opera and ballet festival

Numana: seaside resort on Córnero peninsula, boat trips to the offshore islets of Due Sorelle

Sarnano: spa town

Urbania: palace with art gallery and museum

Ússita: winter sports resort

tip

REGULAR FERRIES DEPEAT FROM ANCONA TO GREECE AND CROATIA. CHARGES DEPEND ON THE SPEED OF THE CROSSING ALTHOUGH PRICES DROP OUTSIDE HIGH SEASON.

IT6618 Camping Stella Maris

Via A Cappellini 5, 61032 Torrette di Fano (Marche)

This clean, modern Adriatic coast site is, in our opinion, the best in the area. The owner Francesco Mantoni is friendly, enthusiastic and proud of his site. For swimming and relaxing there is the choice of an excellent long fine soft sand beach or an excellent pool complex with loungers, umbrellas, jacuzzi and paddling pool. Alongside the pool is a most attractive restaurant (white linen tablecloths) with table service, a varied menu and good selection of wine. The nearby paved terrace area has its own separate bar and snack service. Cleverly incorporated in this area is the entertainment stage, its attractive striped canvas hood matching the nearby pool umbrellas. The pitches are of a good size with some touring pitches. Beach access is gained through a security gate. In this informal setting touring pitches, permanent sites and cabins are blended together but the mixture works. The beach is excellent and unlike many hereabouts is not packed with umbrellas and sun-loungers. English is spoken and the site has a crisp efficient feel about it. A site for holidays and for touring, a high standard of service is provided in all areas.

Facilities

Clean, modern sanitary blocks are nicely decorated with a separate ladies room including hair dryers. Children's facilities are locked for security and parents are given keys. Facilities for disabled campers. Washing machines, dryers and ironing boards. Motorcaravan services. Excellent large supermarket. Restaurant/bar. Snacks. Large swimming pool. Games room, billiards,TV room. Hard court with arena style seating used for organized games (volleyball and five a-side soccer). Animation in season. Dogs or other animals are not accepted.

Directions

Site is between Fano and Falconara. From autostrada take Pesaro exit and follow signs on the SS16 for Ancona, site is approx 3 km. past Fano on waters edge.

Charges 2003

Per pitch	€ 11.88 - € 12.91
person	€ 6.20 - € 7.23
child (2-6 yrs)	€ 4.13 - € 5.42
Electricity (6A) included.	

Reservations

Advised in high season. Tel: 0721 884231.
Email: stellamaris@camping.it

Open

April - September.

At a glance

Welcome & Ambience	✓✓✓✓	Location	✓✓✓✓
Quality of Pitches	✓✓✓✓	Range of Facilities	✓✓✓✓

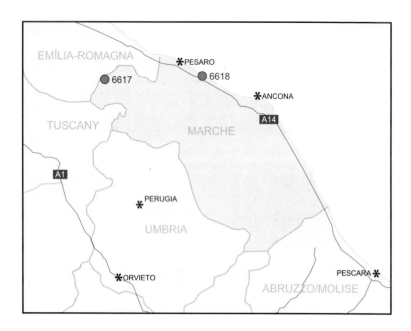

IT6617 Camping Perticara

Via Serra Masini 10/d, 61017 Novafeltria (Marche)

High in the Marche hills, Camping Perticara is a brand new, purpose built camping site with glorious views across a valley to the mountains and the nearby traditional village of Perticara. Its 75 pitches have water and drainage and are very large, all arranged on terraces to take advantage of the fabulous scenery. Good sized trees have been planted to provide shade in the future. The shop, bar and restaurant area is attractively presented, with a terrace overlooking the swimming pool which shares the incredible vistas. Dutch owners, Bert and Nell, have thoughtfully designed the campsite, which has everything a traditional camper could desire. This is a quiet country location with family activities, a place to relax and unwind. The facilities here are of the highest standard, although the steep slopes make this a difficult sitee for the infirm.

Facilities

Two immaculate modern units provide really excellent facilities with all the extras. Unusually the facilites are all in large luxury cabins with shower, toilet and basin. Units for disabled campers are of the same extremely high standard. Washing machine and dryers. Gas. Small shop. Restaurant (limited menu but good value) with very pleasant views. Snack bar. Swimming and paddling pools in upper site area. (water polo). Small play areas. Animation (mini-club) in high season. Torches useful. Off site: Bicycle hire 500 m. Fishing 10 km. Golf 25 km. Restaurants, bars. Shop in small local village.

At a glance

Welcome & Ambience	✓✓✓✓✓	Location	✓✓✓✓✓
Quality of Pitches	✓✓✓✓✓	Range of Facilities	✓✓✓✓

Directions

Leave E14 near Rimini and take SS258 for Novafeltria. In the town is a small blue camping sign to Perticara with the direction signs. Travel uphill to the northwest for 7 km. and site is well signed. Leave your unit on the lower level and go to reception on the upper level on foot.

Charges 2003

Per person	€ 5.00 - € 8.00
child (4-12 yrs)	€ 3.00 - € 5.00
pitch	€ 10.00 - € 13.00

Reservations

Contact site. Tel: 0541 927602.
Email: info@campingperticara.com

Open

15 April - 15 October.

Lazio lies between the Apennines and the Tyrrhenian Sea, with the Pontine marshes in the south and wooded hills in the north. Home to the historic city of Rome it also has numerous lakes and coastal resorts which provide the perfect antidote to the heat of the city and its crowds.

Lazio has five provinces:
Frosinone, Latina, Rieti, Roma and Viterbo

Rome, the capital city of Italy, is crammed full of history, boasting a dazzling array of architectural and artistic masterpieces of the ancient world. Within Rome lies the Vatican City, the world capital of Catholicism, ruled by the Pope, Europe's only absolute monarch. It's also the world's smallest state, occupying 43 hectares within high walls watched over by guards. More historical sites can be found just outside Rome, including the ruins of Villa Adriana, just outside the hilltown of Tivoli. Once a favoured resort of the ancient Romans, the town is also home to the 16th century Villa d'Este, renowned for its beautiful gardens. Nearby Ostia Antica boasts one of the finest of Roman sites. For 600 years it was the busy, main port of Rome, and the site is well preserved, while Viterbo, in the north, is a medieval town with grand palaces, medieval churches enclosed by a preserved set of medieval walls. For recreation, there are numerous lakes including Lakes Bolsena, Bracciano, Vico and Albano. Ideal for swimming and sailing, these lakes were created by volanic activity which also left Lazio with hot springs, most notably those around Tivoli and Fiuggi. Popular coastal resorts include Sperlonga, Anzio and Nettuno, with some of the best beaches lying between Gaeta and Sabaudia.

Cuisine of the region

Pasta is eaten with a variety of sauces including *aglio e olio* (oil and garlic), *cacio e pepe* (percorino cheese and black pepper) and *alle vongole* (with baby clams). The well known dish *spaghetti alla carbonara* was first devised in Rome. Fish and offal is popular. Mushrooms and, in particular, artichokes (*carciofi*) are used in a variety of dishes, and rosemary, sage and garlic is used a lot for seasoning. Local wines include Frascati and Torre Ercolana, one of the few red wines produced in Lazio. Fresh drinking water is freely available in the numerous fountains scattered around Rome.

Risotto all Romana: rice with sauce of liver, sweetbreads and Marsala

Saltimbocca: veal with ham and sage

Torta di Ricotta: cheesecake made with ricotta, Marsala and lemon

Places of interest

Anguillara: pretty medieval lake town on the shore of Lake Bracciano

Bolsena: lakeside beach resort on Lake Bolsena with medieval castle

Caprarola: medieval village 4 km. from Lake Vico, with grandiose Renaissance villa

Fiuggi: spa town

Rome: Colosseum, Forum, Palatine Hill, Pantheon, Trevi Fountain, the list is endless

Sermoneta: pretty hilltown overlooking the Pontine Plains, with medieval houses, palaces and churches

Tarquinia: archeology museum, frescoed tombs of the necropolis

Vatican City: St Peter's church, Sistine Chapel with famous painted ceiling by Michelangelo, museums

 tip

IF YOU FANCY A TRIP TO ROME CONSIDER LEAVING THE CAR BEHIND AND USE PUBLIC TRANSPORT INSTEAD. THE CITY IS RENOWNED FOR ITS MAD TRAFFIC CONGESTION.

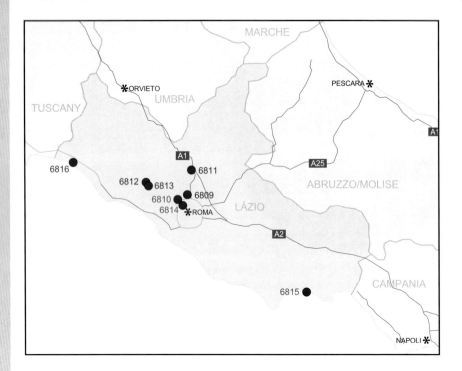

IT6815 Holiday Village Fondi

Via Flacca km 6,800, 04020 Salto di Fondi (Lazio)

Fondi is a picturesque seaside site with unusual cultural activity, midway between Rome and Naples. Set in a pinewood area, the carefully tended flowers and trees and the white painted buildings make it a very pleasant location. The facilities are on a natural raised area between the beach and the tourers area. There are open-air theatres on both sides of the highest point which also has the restaurant/ bar, huge TV room and breakfast room. Damask linen and fine glasses in the Girasole restaurant present an elegant spectacle completed by a fine menu and cellar. During high season there are cultural and sporting activities, and plays, shows and films staged on one of the open-air stages. There is a wardrobe of over 400 costumes for children to use. As well as the Mediterranean beach, there are two swimming pools by the second stage. The 100 large pitches for tourists are at the rear of the site under effective, but sombre, green shading, but close to the amenities. They are on flat grass, all with 3/5A electricity. The large beach is of fine sand (with lifeguard) and there is a pleasant grass promenade between the beach and the restaurant complex. Below this complex is a further layer with an excellent boutique and a large supermarket. Signora Banotti, the lady owner speaks good English. All in all, it is an excellent site.

Facilities

One large and five smaller toilet blocks are of modern construction and have some British type WCs. Showers have hot water on payment, with cold water in washbasins and dishwashing sinks. Two family washrooms have hot water. Facilities for disabled visitors. Washing machines and dryers. Gas supplies. Bar/restaurant, pizzeria and snack bar (all June-Sept). Supermarket. Greengrocer. Boutique. Hairdresser. Main and children's swimming pools (instructor). Tennis. Table tennis. Handball. Disco. TV. Live theatre and ballet. Organised excursions to Rome, Capri, Naples, Pompei, Monte Cassino (with local agency). Doctor on site daily. Dogs and pets are not accepted. Torches required in some areas.

Directions

Site signed on coast road SS213 between Gaeta and Terracina, 7 km. south of Terracina. It is reached from the Rome - Naples autostrada, depending on approach, from several exits between Frosinone and Ceprana. The site is well signed.

Charges 2003

Per pitch incl. 2 adults	€ 15.00 - € 46.00
extra person	€ 5.00 - € 14.00

No credit cards.

Reservations

Contact site. Tel: 0771 555009.
Email: holidayvillage@tiscalinet.it

Open

All year.

At a glance

Welcome & Ambience	✓✓✓✓	Location	✓✓✓✓
Quality of Pitches	✓✓✓✓	Range of Facilities	✓✓✓✓

IT6816 California International Camping Village

01014 Marina di Montalto (Lazio)

The first vision of California Camping is the excellent pool complex with its large fountain surrounded by palms. A smart bar, pizzeria and restaurant complex overlook the pool and the sporting areas are also of a high standard. The smart restaurant with gay yellow décor boasts a fine menu at very good prices. The 450 pitches are a little small, arranged in close level rows under tall pines, which give excellent shade. Pitches are a little dusty from the combination of the pine needles and fine dark sand. Electricity (4A) is provided and cars are parked separately in high season. A great effort has been made to maintain large areas of cool green grass, giving a pleasing appearance and it is ideal to relax on, especially near the pools and beach. The long grey sand/shingle beach, is virtually private and easily accessed through gates on one side of the site. There is a very pleasant feel to the site and everyone was enjoying themselves when we visited. This is certainly due to the fact that it is a professionally run site where the staff are keen to please.

Facilities

Nine blocks contain different sanitary facilities. They were tired when we saw them but we are assured that they will all will be totally rebuilt in 2004. Facilities for disabled campers. Hot water for the showers but otherwise it is cold only at sinks. Large supermarket. Restaurant, bar and takeaway (1/5-20/9). Large swimming pool and paddling pool. (June-Sept). Minigolf. Volleyball. Basketball. Archery. Play area and large open building with shaded area for children to play. Animation. Mini-club. Boat hire. Dogs and other animals are not accepted. Off site: Fishing. Riding 2 km. Bicycle hire 3 km. Golf 10 km.

At a glance

| Welcome & Ambience | ✓✓✓✓✓ | Location | ✓✓✓✓ |
| Quality of Pitches | ✓✓✓ | Range of Facilities | ✓✓✓✓ |

Directions

Site is off the SS1 at the 150 km. mark, signed Porto S. Stefano. Site is on the right, clearly marked.

Charges 2003

Per person	€ 6.50 - € 10.00
child (1-6 yrs)	€ 4.50 - € 6.00
pitch	€ 6.50 - € 10.00
Camping Cheques accepted.	

Reservations

Made with no deposit (min. 2 weeks in high season). Tel: 0766 802848.
Email: info@californiacampingvillage.com

Open

1 May - 20 September.

IT6811 Ipini Camping

Via Delle Sassete-1/A, Fiano Romano, 00065 Roma (Lazio)

The many years Roberto and his Australian born wife Judy have spent in the camping industry are reflected in this site built only a few years ago. The 115 pitches are set on shaded grassy terraces with views of the nearby hills, access is easy for all units via tarmac roads, and everything is here including a supermarket. The beautifully designed restaurant with its high ceilings and wooden beams are typical of the thought that has gone into making Ipini a place where you can relax. Simone, Roberto's daughter is responsible for the restaurant. This is a family business with son Robbie sharing in the task of making your stay enjoyable. Thought has gone into the location of the bungalow village which is separated from the camping, and in the new soundproof pub where one can enjoy a drink and dance the hours away without unsettling the peace and calm of the site.

Facilities

The one excellent sanitary block is of hotel standard down to the decorative fittings in all cubicles. All facilities are spotless and hot water is free in showers, washbasins and dishwashing sinks. Two very large and well equipped units for disabled visitors. New washing machines. Motorcaravan services. Bar. Restaurant. Snack bar. Separate market. Boule. Swimming pool with spa and children's lagoon. Tennis. Play area. Table tennis. Torches required in some areas. Air conditioned bus to Rome daily. Night tours of Rome. Off site: Free initial pick-up from the local station.

At a glance

| Welcome & Ambience | ✓✓✓✓✓ | Location | ✓✓✓✓ |
| Quality of Pitches | ✓✓✓✓ | Range of Facilities | ✓✓✓✓ |

Directions

From Rome ring road (GRA) take A1 exit to Fiano Romano. As you enter the town turn right along via Belvedere opposite an IP petrol station. and follow the camping signs – there is only the one site.

Charges 2003

Per person	€ 8.00 - € 9.20
child (3-12 yrs)	€ 5.50 - € 6.00
caravan	€ 5.80 - € 6.80
tent	€ 3.30 - € 4.20
car	€ 3.30 - € 4.20
motorcaravan	€ 7.90 - € 9.20
Electricity included.	

Reservations

Contact site. Tel: 0765 453349.
Email: ipini@camping.it

Open

15 March - 15 November.

IT6810 Camping Seven Hills

Via Cassia 1216, 00191 Roma (Lazio)

If you are looking for a very lively site with many young people, which tends towards the impersonal then Seven Hills may be for you. It is situated in a delightful valley, flanked by two of the seven hills of Rome (four kilometres from the city centre – the site runs a bus shuttle service with a frequency dictated by demand; extra charge). Arranged in two sections, the top half, near the entrance, restaurant and shop, consists of small, flat, grass terraces with two to four pitches on each, with smaller terraces for tents. Access to some pitches may be tricky. The flat section at the lower part of the site is reserved mainly for ready erected tents used by British, Dutch and international tour operators who bring guests by coach. These tend to be younger people and the site, along with its very busy pool, has a distinctly youthful feel. Consequently there may be a little extra noise. The site is a profusion of colour with flowering trees, plants and shrubs and a good covering of trees provide shade. The 80 pitches for tourers (3A electricity to some) are not marked, but the management supervise in busy periods. English is spoken and many notices are in English. All cash transactions on the site are made with a metal tag on a necklace from reception and there is a tight regime of passes and indelible ink wrist stamping at the pool (disco music, no paddling pool and an extra charge). This is an extremely busy and bustling site with up to 15 touring buses with their occupants on the site during high season, in addition to a very busy camping routine. There are bungalows, chalets and cabins to hire, all of varying standards adding to the large number of people and the feeling of constant changeover, also some may find the pools a little crowded in summer.

Facilities

Three soundly constructed sanitary blocks are well situated around the site, with open plan washbasins, and hot water in the average sized showers. Dishwashing under cover with cold water. Facilities for disabled campers. Washing machines and irons. Well stocked shop. Bar/restaurant and terrace. Money exchange. Table tennis. Volleyball. Swimming pool at the bottom of the site with bar/snack bar and a room where the younger element tends to gather. Disco. Off site: Golf (good course) 4 km. Bus service to Rome. Excursions and cruises arranged. Internet. Torches required in some areas.

At a glance

Welcome & Ambience	√√√	Location	√√√√
Quality of Pitches	√√√	Range of Facilities	√√√√

Directions

Take exit 3 from the autostrada ring-road on to Via Cassia (signed SS2 Viterbo - NOT Via Cassia Bis) and look for camp signs. Turn right after 1 km (13 km. stone) and follow small road for about 1 km. to site.

Latest charges

Per person (over 4 yrs)	€ 7.23
caravan	€ 7.75
tent	€ 4.39
car	€ 3.62
motorcaravan	€ 7.75
motorcycle	€ 2.07

No credit cards.

Reservations

Write to site. Tel: 0630 310826.
Email: seven_hills@camping.it

Open

All year.

IT6809 Camping Tiber

Via Tiberina Km 1,400, 00188 Roma (Lazio)

An excellent city site which is unusually peaceful, Camping Tiber is ideally located for visiting Rome with an easy train service (20 minutes to Rome), a free shuttle bus every 30 minutes and trams for later at night. The 350 tourist pitches are mostly shaded under very tall trees (with 3/6A electricity) and many have very pleasant views over the river Tiber. This mighty river winds around two sides of the site boundary (safely fenced) providing a cooling effect for campers. There is a new section with little shade as yet and bungalows to rent are in another, separate area of the campsite. A small but pleasant outdoor pool with a bar awaits after a busy day in the city and the main bar, restaurant with terrace and takeaway are attractive and give good value. The site is extremely well run and especially good for campers with disabilities.

Facilities

Fully equipped sanitary facilities include modern British toilets, hot water and good facilities for disabled campers. Washing machines and dryers. Market. Internet. Drive-over motorcaravan service point. Car wash. Bar, restaurant, pizzeria and takeaway. Free shuttle bus to underground. Trams. Night bus. Tourist information. Torches useful. Off site: Local bars, restaurants and shops. Golf and riding 20 km. River fishing.

At a glance

Welcome & Ambience	✓✓✓✓	Location	✓✓✓✓✓
Quality of Pitches	✓✓✓✓	Range of Facilities	✓✓✓✓

Directions

From Florence, exit at Rome Nord Fiano on A1 and immediately turn south onto Via Tibernia and site is signed. From other directions on Rome ring road (known and signed as the GRA – like the M25 but less crowded) take exit 6 northbound on S3 Via Flaminia and the site is very well signed.

Charges 2003

Per person	€ 8.50 - € 9.60
child (3-12 yrs)	€ 6.00 - € 7.00
car	€ 4.20 - € 4.60
caravan	€ 4.20 - € 7.10
tent	€ 4.20 - € 4.70
motorcaravan	€ 9.70 - € 10.70

Reservations

Advised and possible on-line, or by phone/fax. Tel: 06 3361 0733. Email: info@campingtiber.com

Open

15 March - 31 October.

IT6812 Roma Flash Sporting

Via Settevene Palo km 19,800, 00062 Bracciano (Lazio)

The dynamic Monni family greet you with a smile at this clean and pleasant site on the western side of Lake Bracciano, which supplies Rome's drinking water. Mature trees provide cover for the 200 pitches, some of which have fine lake side views. Elide and Edoardo, who both speak English, have built their site on flat ground with the bar/restaurant facilities to the southern side, again with lake views. The rustic restaurant shares a building with the very small shop. There is one covered and one terraced area where you can sample the pizzas or the daily dish on offer. The lake panorama is very pleasant. You can swim in the pool or from the two 'beaches' on the lake which both have grass areas for sunbathing. Boats and windsurfers can be launched (no powered vessels are allowed). You are 40 km. from Rome and the site provides a bus (extra charge) to travel to Piazzale Flaminio in the centre of the city. There are regular excursions from the site to local areas of interest.

Facilities

Two toilet blocks of traditional construction have some British type WCs. Showers, washbasins and dishwashing sinks have free hot and cold water (two new luxury units planned for 2002). Facilities for disabled visitors. Washing machine. Gas supplies. Bar/pizzeria (all season). Small shop. Swimming pool and small paddling pool (bathing caps compulsory). Table tennis. Beach handball. Play area. Watersports. Canoes-kayaks. Games room. Boule. Animation for children in high season. Excursions possible. Torches required in some areas. Dogs are accepted but not allowed on beach areas.

At a glance

Welcome & Ambience	✓✓✓✓	Location	✓✓✓✓
Quality of Pitches	✓✓✓✓	Range of Facilities	✓✓✓✓

Directions

From E35/E45 north of Rome, take Settebagni exit. Follow GRA (Rome's equivalent of the M25) west to Cassia exit. Follow sign for Lago Bracciano to town of Bracciano. Site is well signed from town.

Charges 2003

Per person	€ 4.13 - € 6.19
child (3-10 yrs)	€ 3.10 - € 4.64
small tent	€ 4.13 - € 5.16
large tent	€ 5.16 - € 6.71
caravan	€ 5.16 - € 6.71
car	€ 2.06 - € 3.10
motorcaravan	€ 5.16 - € 6.71
dog	€ 2.60 - € 3.60

Camping Cheques accepted.

Reservations

Contact site. Tel: 0699 805458.
Email: info@romaflash.it

Open

1 April - 30 September.

Visiting Rome

It is easy to fall in love with Rome, but invariably one will depart with guilty feelings because only a fraction of the sights have been seen and the history of this ancient city has been barely scratched. Rome is breathtaking: magnificent ancient remains abound, and the splendour of the Vatican City – complete with its colourful Swiss guard – is totally fascinating.

The easiest and cheapest way to travel around Rome by public transport is to buy the Birg ticket, which allows you to use the metro and the buses within the city and outskirts, all for a low daily rate. The choice of campsite is yours. It is possible to use the sites close to the city centre if you do not mind the noise and bustle normally associated with city sites. These sites include no. 6810 Camping Seven Hills. The other option is to

select a site further afield which provides direct transport to the city, for example, no. 6811 Ipini Camping, thus allowing one to relax in peaceful, cool and pleasant surroundings between forays into the extremely busy city, which can prove tiring.

If you wish to see St Peter's Square and the Basilica in all their glory, we recommend arriving there at 7am, before the day-trippers pour into the city. At this time you will have the Square and the Vatican virtually to yourself, albeit temporarily. Remember to cover bare knees and shoulders (a thin shawl will suffice). It is possible to arrange a Papal audience, which usually take place on Wednesdays, by sending a fax to the *Prefettura della Casa Pontificia* (fax no. 0669 88 58 63). There is a post office within the Vatican should you wish to send postcards bearing their unique postmark.

Another useful tip is to take full advantage of the free hour-long tour (conducted in English) of the Colosseum; after buying your ticket, look for the guides in blue uniforms inside the gates on the right.

And above all, allow as much time as you can to take in the sights of this amazing city.

Colin Sams

IT6814 Flaminio Village

Via Flaminia 821, 00191 Roma (Lazio)

We were impressed with Camping Flaminio. An attractive, quite large campsite with some shade, it is on ground which is sloping in parts. It is located about 400 metres up a lane leading off the main road, which results in its being surprisingly quiet. There is a regular bus/underground service into the centre of Rome from outside the site entrance, which operates until late evening. There is limited space allocated to touring units, but the majority of these pitches are of average size, have electrical connections (6A) and are approached by 'environmentally approved' brick access roads. There are also some 80 well-equipped bungalows, quite attractively arranged in a 'village' setting.

Facilities

The sanitary facilities are currently housed in somewhat ancient blocks, but a new block is planned for the 2003 season. Bar-pizzeria and restaurant. Shop. Swimming pool and solarium (15/6-5/9 charged for in peak season). Fitness centre. Play area. Off site: The Vatican City, shops, supermarket, service station, bank and access to cycle route alongside river into the City. Buses and trains outside the gate.

At a glance

Welcome & Ambience	✓✓✓✓	Location	✓✓✓✓✓
Quality of Pitches	✓✓✓	Range of Facilities	✓✓✓✓

Directions

From the ring road due north of the city take the Via Flaminia exit (6) south towards the city centre, and after 3 km. bear left to avoid tunnel – site is 150 m. on the right after passing tunnel entrance.

Charges 2004

Per adult	€ 8.90 - € 10.00
child (under 12 yrs)	€ 6.20 - € 7.20
caravan or motorcaravan	€ 10.90 - € 12.50
tent	€ 4.90 - € 6.40

Reservations

Contact site. Tel: 06 333 2604.
Email: info@villageflaminio.com

Open

All year.

IT6813 Camping Porticciolo

Via Porticciolo, 00062 Bracciano (Lazio)

This small family run site, useful for visiting Rome, has its own private beach on the southwest side of Lake Bracciano. Alessandro and his wife Alessandra, who have worked hard to build up this site since 1982, are charming and speak English. Alessandro is a Roman classical history expert and provides free documentary information on the local area and Rome. A pleasant feature is that the site is overlooked by the impressive castle in the village of Bracciano. There are 170 pitches (150 for tourers) split into two sections, some with lake views and 120 having electricity. Pitches are large and shaded by very green trees which are continuously watered in summer by a neat overhead watering system. The friendly bar has two large terraces, shared by the trattoria which opens lunch-times and the pizzeria with its wood fired oven in the evenings. A small amount of entertainment is offered during the season and the lake is clean for swimming with powerboats banned. Small boats and windsurfers may be launched from the site. As an uncomplicated, lakeside site away from the heat and hassle of the city, it is ideal.

Facilities

Three somewhat rustic, but clean, sanitary units. Hot showers (by token), laundry facilities and washing machines. Motorcaravan services. Shop (basics). Bar. Trattoria/pizzeria (15/5-5/9). Tennis. Five-a-side soccer. Play area. Table tennis. Volleyball. Fishing. Gas supplies. Tourist information (from computer terminal by reception). Internet point. Torches required in some areas. Bicycle hire. Excursions 'Rome By Night' and nearby Nature Park's. Off site: Riding 2 km. Bus service from outside the gate runs to central Rome (approx. 1 hour – all day ticket known as a 'Birg' is very good value). Air conditioned train service from Bracciano (1.5 km) into the city and the site runs a morning connecting bus

At a glance

Welcome & Ambience	✓✓✓✓	Location	✓✓✓✓
Quality of Pitches	✓✓✓✓	Range of Facilities	✓✓✓✓

Directions

From Rome ring road (GRA) northwest side take Cassia exit to Bracciano S493 (be careful not to confuse this exit with 'Cassia bis' which is further northeast). Follow signs to village of Bracciano on southwest shore of Lago di Bracciano and site is clearly signed.

Charges 2004

Per person	€ 4.10 - € 5.50
child (3-10 yrs)	€ 3.30 - € 4.50
tent, caravan or motorcaravan	
less than 5 m.	€ 4.10 - € 5.70
over 5 m.	€ 4.65 - € 6.40
small tent	€ 3.30 - € 4.50
car	€ 1.60 - € 3.00
electricity (6/15A)	€ 1.50 - € 3.60
dog	€ 2.60 - € 3.50

Special low season offers.

Reservations

Write to site. Tel: 06 99803060.
Email: info@porticciolo.it

Open

1 April - 30 September.

Abruzzo & Molise

Until 1963 Abruzzo and Molise was just one combined region known as Abruzzi. With some of the wildest terrain in Italy, Abruzzo is bordered by the Apennine mountain range with vast tracts of forest while Molise has a gentler countryside with high plains, soft peaks and valleys.

The regions are divided into the following provinces:
Abruzzo: Chieti, L'Aquila, Pescara and Teramo
Molise: Campobasse and Isemia

A popular attraction in Abruzzo is the medieval hilltown of Scanno. Surrounded by high peaks looming above, the town hosts a range of activities in the summer including riding, boating and a classical music festival. Close by is Italy's third largest national park. With mountains, rivers, lakes and forests it is an important wildlife refuge, home to bears, wolves and the golden eagle. It also offers good walking, with an extensive network of paths, plus riding, skiing and canoeing. Around Scanno are the historic mountain towns of L'Aquila and Sulmona, and the village of Cocullo, where the bizarre festival of snakes takes place in May; a statue of a local saint is draped with live snakes and paraded through the streets. Along the Abruzzo coast is Pescara, the main resort, which has a 16 km. long beach. Ferries to Croatia and the Dalmatian islands depart from here. Nearby are the small hilltowns of Atri, Penne, and Loreto Apruntino, one of the regions most important market towns. In Molise, the city of Isernia is where traces of a million-year-old village were unearthed in 1979, the most ancient signs of human life ever found in Europe. And the quiet resort and fishing port of Térmoli, from where Italian and Central European time is set, is a good place to relax.

Cuisine of the region

As sheep-farming dominates the regions, lamb is popular: *abbacchio* (roasted baby lamb), and *castratro* (castrated lamb) is used to make *intingolo di castrato*, a casserole prepared with tomatoes, wine, onion and celery. Chilli is another favourite ingredient, known locally as *pepdinie* (*peperoncino* elsewhere in Italy). Abruzzo is famous for *maccheroni all chitarra*, pasta made by pressing sheets over a wooden frame, and other local pastas include *stengozze* and *maltagliati*, usually served with a lamb sauce.

Ceci e Castagne: chickpeas and chestnuts

Coniglio all zafferano: rabbit with saffron

Linguine d'Ovidio: pasta with pancetta and truffles

Places of interest

Alba Adriatica: most northern of Abruzzo's coastal resorts

Atri: 13th century cathedral, archaeology and ethnography museums

Celano: pretty village with turreted castle

Lanciano: historic town

Larino: medieval town centre, cathedral, amphitheatre

Pineto: coastal resort

Saepinum: ruined Roman town

Téramo: remains of Roman amphitheatre, theatre and baths

Alan Rogers tip

IN LORETO APRUNTINO THERE ARE NUMEROUS ARTISANS' WORKSHOPS MAKING A VARIETY OF TERRACOTTA ITEMS, COPPER POTS, KNIVES AND GLASSWARE, WHICH ARE OPEN TO THE PUBLIC.

IT6800 Europe Garden

Via Belvedere 11, 64028 Silvi (Abruzzo)

This site is 13 kilometres northwest of Pescara and, lying just back from the coast (two kilometres) up a very steep hill with pleasant views over the sea. The 204 pitches, all with 10A electricity, are mainly on good terraces – access may be difficult on some pitches. However, if installation of caravans is a problem a tractor is available to help. When we visited the site was dry but we suspect life might become difficult on some pitches after heavy rain. Cars stand by units on over half of the pitches or in nearby parking spaces for the remainder, most pitches are shaded. There is a good swimming pool at the bottom of the site, with a small bar and an entertainment programme in season on a small stage and associated area within the pool boundary. The restaurant has large olive trees penetrating the floor and ceilings of the eating area and good views but the terrace views are fabulous. The site has very steep slopes and is not suitable for disabled or infirm campers.

Facilities

Two good toilet blocks are well cleaned and provide mixed British and Turkish style WCs. Washing machines. Restaurant. Bar. Tennis. Playground. Swimming pool (300 sq.m; swimming caps compulsory), small paddling pool and jacuzzi. Free bus service (18/5-7/9) to beach. Entertainment programme. Free weekly excursions (15/6-8/9) organised to different parts of the Province. Electronic money is used throughout the site (credit is bought on the site's swipe cards). Dogs are not accepted.

At a glance

| Welcome & Ambience | ✓✓✓✓ | Location | ✓✓✓✓ |
| Quality of Pitches | ✓✓✓✓ | Range of Facilities | ✓✓✓✓ |

Directions

Turn inland off S16 coast road at km. 433 stone for Silvi Alta and follow camp signs. From autostrada A14 take Pineto exit from north or Pescara Nord exit from the south. Signing is very good.

Charges 2003

Per person	€ 4.10 - € 5.10
child (0-3 yrs)	€ 3.60 - € 4.20
pitch	€ 9.30 - € 11.30
electricity	€ 1.80

No credit cards.

Reservations

Made with € 103 deposit for first 2 weeks of August (min 2 weeks), at other times without deposit. Tel: 085 930137. Email: egarden@camping.it

Open

27 April - 20 September.

IT6805 Camping Heliopolis

Contrada Villa Fumosa 1, 64025 Pineto (Abruzzo)

Heliopolis is an attractive, well run site with a charming English speaking lady owner named Gigliola who is delighted to receive British customers in her site which is very popular with Italians. This is an unusual site for the Adriatic as most of the pitches have their own neat, clean and covered private units with shower/WC and washing facilities. The pitches are of average size arranged in rows at right angles to the beach and most have artificial shade provided. All have electrical connections (4A). Cars may be parked off the pitch. The site opens directly onto a wide pleasant sand and shingle beach that shelves gently in most conditions. Like many Adriatic sites, it is close to the railway and there is some noise from passing trains especially on the western side of the site. An attractive covered restaurant will make you local dishes or pizzas and the house wine is very good. A separate bar operates all the time and overlooks the clean pools. From the terraces you can enjoy the entertainment which the Italians love. The shop is amazingly reasonable and offers attractive souvenirs of the Abruzzo region. If you would like to experience what we consider to be a 'real' Italian campsite then this may be for you.

Facilities

Two excellent toilet blocks, one for men and one for women, also have facilities for disabled campers. Laundry facilities. Individual units for 120 of the 160 pitches. Bar/coffee shop. Restaurant (weekends only until 1/6). Shops (from 1/6). Swimming pool and children's pool (from 15/6). Volleyball. Tennis. Playground. Games room and electronic games. Entertainment in high season. Hairdresser and massage on site in season. Doctor attends daily. Torches required near beach areas. Off site: Trips to Rome, Napoli, Capri, San Marino and other local attractions organized.

At a glance

| Welcome & Ambience | ✓✓✓✓ | Location | ✓✓✓ |
| Quality of Pitches | ✓✓✓✓ | Range of Facilities | ✓✓✓ |

Directions

Site is to the north of the town sharing an approach with Camping Pineto Beach; both sites are clearly signed from A14 road (exit Pineto) and SS16 (in town).

Charges 2003

Per person	€ 4.00 - € 8.00
child (3-12 yrs)	€ 3.50 - € 7.00
standard pitch	€ 9.50 - € 23.00
pitch with private facilities	€ 16.50 - € 29.50

Reservations

Write to site for details. Tel: 085 9492720. Email: info@heliopolis.it

Open

1 April - 30 September.

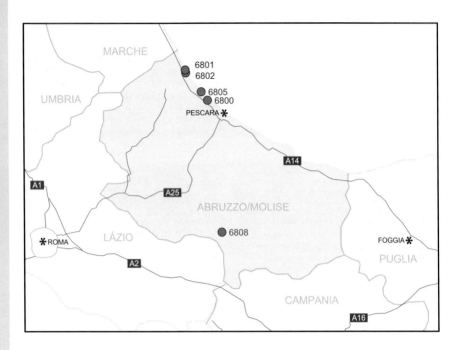

IT6801 Camping Holiday

Lungomare Zara, 64022 Giulianova Lido (Abruzzo)

A site for Italian families on the Adriatic coast, this site has a tropical atmosphere. It appears that some families have been coming here for years and have developed imaginative 'homes away from home' using all the available space for their comforts. The 320 pitches are flat, reasonably sized and many are with shade, water and drainage. There is lively entertainment at night and music during the day and the site is generally buzzing with activity, the centre being under the tall palms near the huge pool, sun deck and bar. About a quarter of the area is devoted to mainly older style cabins and mobile homes. There is easy access to the long inviting sandy beach at the front of the site, which is brimming with happy Italians enjoying their holiday. Many of the site's facilities are shared by the smaller sister site (IT6802) which is very close by.

Facilities

Three sanitary blocks have a mixture of adequate facilities although it will be busy at peak periods for showering. The units for disabled campers are in one block so choose your place carefully. Washing machines and dryers. Gas. Bar. Self service restaurant with large terraces. Snack bar. Pizzeria. Large supermarket. Fresh fruit stall. Very good, large swimming pool and paddling pool (built 2002 and shared with IT6802). Large play area. Electronic games. Tennis. Mini soccer. Volleyball. Canoeing. Table tennis. Electronic games. Sitting room. Ambitious animation with themed nights. Disco. Beach club and bar. Fun club on beach. Dogs and other animals anot accepted in July/Aug. In high season cars are parked in separate secure area. Off site: Sea fishing. Watersports. Bars, restaurants, discos and entertainment of a typical resort. Local council offers free excursions in local area.

Directions

Leave autostrada E14 north of Pescara and take SS80 to Giulianova Lido. Follow camp signs – there are many of them. Providing you follow the signs and end up at the north town you will find the bridge with a 3.6 m. clearance. All other bridges have 'car only' clearances. Site is 400 m. on left after the bridge.

Latest charges

Per pitch	€ 8.90 - € 16.16
adult	€ 4.83 - € 7.23
child	€ 2.97 - € 4.98

Reservations

Contact site. Tel: 0858 00 00 53.
Email: holiday@camping.it

Open

1 June - 15 September.

At a glance

Welcome & Ambience	✓✓✓	Location	✓✓✓✓
Quality of Pitches	✓✓✓✓	Range of Facilities	✓✓✓

IT6802 Camping Baviera

Lungomare Zara 127, 64022 Giulianova Lido (Abruzzo)

Set alongside the beautiful Adriatic coast with its sandy beaches, Baviera is a small site with basic, older style facilities. However, there is access to the facilities of its larger sister site Camping Holiday (IT6801) with its tempting pool, restaurant, games and supermarket. Many of the campers also pop 'next door' to join in and enjoy the organised entertainment. This quiet site may be subject to some noise during the evening and music in the daytime from the other camp sites in the immediate area. A lovely simple café and gelateria is at the front of the site near the beach where there is also a beach bar. The friendly staff speak a little English and make a great cappachino. A simple no frills site, but one where the many Italian families appear to be enjoying themselves.

Facilities

Four traditional units provide a mixture of sanitary facilities which are clean but a litle tired. The new units for disabled campers are of a high standard. Washing machine. Snack bar. Beach bar. Torches useful. Dogs and other animals are not accepted in July/Aug. Off site: Beach fishing. Bicycle hire 1 km. Golf 35 km. All resort facilities in town.

At a glance

Welcome & Ambience	✓✓✓✓	Location	✓✓✓✓
Quality of Pitches	✓✓✓✓	Range of Facilities	✓✓✓

Directions

Leave autostrada E14 north of Pescara and take SS80 to Giulianova Lido. Follow camp signs - there are many, many signs so travel slowly! Providing you follow the signs and end up at the north town you will find the bridge with a 3.6 m. clearance. All other bridges have 'car only' clearances. The site is 400 m. on left after the bridge.

Latest charges

Per pitch	€ 7.28 - € 15.38
adult	€ 3.31 - € 6.66
child	€ 2.35 - € 4.75

Reservations

Contact site. Tel: 0858 00 89 28.
Email: baviera@camping.it

Open

1 June - 15 September.

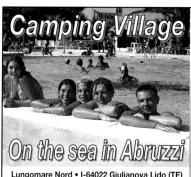

IT6808 Camping La Genziana

SS 83 Contrada Tre Croci, Parco Nazionale D'Abruzzo, 67030 Barrea (Abruzzo)

This is the place to get away from it all – situated in the middle of Italy, high in the Abruzzi mountains with views over Barrea lakes. It is an hour from Rome or Pescara, but the village of Barrea with the usual supplies is just 500 m away. The ebullient owner Tommaso Pasetta and his family make everyone welcome to his site where he attempts to retain a 'natural' feel; this means that you should not expect any luxuries. The facilities are adequate and the 110 informal pitches (100 have electricity 3A) and 50 more for tents are embraced by wild flowers and grasses. Tommasso is an expert in Alpine walking and a great raconteur. If mountain walking is for you he will give sound advice and many tracks start from the site. The site has limited facilities but swimming, riding and fishing are all possible nearby. The site is not suitable for disabled people.

Facilities

Single, basic but clean sanitary block with free hot showers. British and Turkish syle toilets. Washing facilities. Motorcaravan services. Bar coffee bar and small shop. Off site: Tourist information. Trekking and walking information. Torches required.

At a glance

Welcome & Ambience	✓✓✓✓	Location	✓✓✓
Quality of Pitches	✓✓✓	Range of Facilities	✓✓✓

Directions

From autostrada A25, either take route 83 from Celano and site is signed 4 km. before Barrea, or take route 17 from Pratola/Sulmona through Castel di Sangro. Then turn right to route 83 and site is 1 km. before Barrea.

Charges 2004

Per person	€ 5.20
child (under 9 yrs)	€ 3.00
caravan	€ 8.00
tent	€ 8.00
motorcaravan	€ 8.00
car	€ 4.00
pet	€ 3.00
electricity	€ 1.60

No credit cards.

Reservations

Contact site. Tel: 0864 88101.
Email: pasettanet@tiscalinet.it

Open

All year.

Tales of Abruzzo

Pasetta racconta by T. D. Pasetta

In August 2003 we received a package from Camping La Genziana in the region of Abruzzo in Italy. In it was a guide book about the National Park of Abruzzi partly written in English by the site owner. In reality, it provides fascinating insights into the character of Tommaso D'Amico, the owner also known as Pasetta, whilst bringing the area to life and making one want to visit and understand this unique area of Italy.

His roots are to be found in the history of the people of Abruzzo and their struggle to survive in the harsh conditions of this mountainous region. Even in the latter part of the twentieth century, the people lived in small fortified villages with the gates closed at night to protect against bandits, robbers, gypsies and, last but not least, wolves. Pasetta's grandfather was a *lupari* or wolf-man. He earned his meagre living by killing the wolves and bears which reeked such havoc with the flocks of sheep, the principle income for the region. From these roots Pasetta developed a passionate love of nature and a tremendous talent in finding and interpreting the foot marks and other traces of wild animals which he uses to take groups on guided tours of the mountains.

Pasetta followed his girlfriend to America, spending seven and a half difficult years there before returning to his native village of Barrea with his wife and two little boys where life was still difficult. He started a restaurant in a nearby village sensing that tourism would eventual develop in the Abruzzi mountains. Barrea is 1,060 m above sea level, surrounded by the Apennine mountains in the centre of the National Park with a lake at the foot of the village. To Pasetta it was a little paradise in the centre of the world and he started to build a campsite. Despite problems with the locals not understanding tourism and the army using the site, it slowly developed and in 1992 the site was opened all year instead of just for the holiday season.

The activities of the campsite now give Pasetta a satisfaction he never thought he would have. His love of the mountains and his knowledge of English has enabled him to make acquaintance with people from every corner of the world and from every profession and sport. Today about 90% of visitors come from abroad. Pasetta has many stories to tell, advice to give and suggestions for hiking and other activies in the mountains. A visit to his campsite would be a memorable experience but perhaps not for the faint hearted.

Campania boasts one of the finest coastlines in Italy, incorporating the dramatic Amalfi coast, the beautiful Bay of Naples, and the enchanting islands of Capri, Ischia and Prócida. It is also home to some of the best preserved ancient sites, most notably Pompeii, plus the historic city of Naples.

The region has five provinces:
Avellino, Benevento, Caserta, Napoli and Salerno

Filled with palaces, churches and convents, the regional capital of Naples also boasts an archaeology museum housing artifacts excavated from the nearby Roman sites of Pompeii and Herculaneum. Situated on the Bay of Naples, these sites were buried after Mount Vesuvius erupted in 79 AD, leaving them frozen in time. Although still active (the only one on mainland Europe) it is possible to scale up the volcano. Not far from Pompeii, is the popular holiday destination of Sorrento and off the coast of the bay are the islands of Ishchia, Capri and Prócida. The largest is Ischia, which along with Capri, attracts vast numbers of tourists; Prócida is the smallest and least visited. All three can be explored on day trips from the mainland. Further south is the Amalfi coast, a spectacular stretch of coastline littered with superb beaches and resorts, including Positano, Amalfi and Ravello. The busy port of Salerno is near to the ancient Greek site of Paestum, with temples dating back to the 6th century BC, and the area known as the Cilento, a mountainous region with a quiet coastline. It has a number of seaside resorts including Agropoli, Acciaroli and Palinuro plus the inland villages of Castelcivita and Pertosa, both of which have caves systems open to the public.

Cuisine of the region

Naples is the home of pizza, pasta and tomato sauce. Aubergines and courgettes are frequently used in pasta sauces. Seafood is widely available along the coast including fresh squid, octopus, clams and mussels. Cilento produces strawberries, artichokes and mozzarella cheese. Made with buffalo milk, mozzerella is usually accompanied with tomatoes.

Calzone: stuffed fried pizza with ham and cheese

Marinara: pizza topped with tomato, garlic and basil, no cheese

Sfogliatella: flaky pastry case stuffed with ricotta and candied peel

Zuppa di cozze: mussels with a hot pepper sauce

Zuppa Inglese: dessert made with sponge fingers, peaches, custard, brandy and egg whites

Places of interest

Benevento: once an important Roman settlement, monuments include the Arch of Trajan and the Roman theatre

Campi Flegri: area known as the Fiery Fields, with volanic craters and hots springs

Caserta: opulent royal palace with gardens open to the public

Ravello: offers best view of the Amalfi coast

Salerno: medieval old quarter, 11th century cathedral, annual fair in May

San Marco: picturesque fishing village

Santa Maria Capua Vetere: ruined Roman amphitheatre with series of tunnels beneath it

Alan Rogers tip

FERRIES AND HYDROFOILS DEPART FROM SEVERAL PLACES ALONG THE COAST, OPERATING BETWEEN THE ISLANDS AND MAIN RESORTS. ASK THE TOURIST OFFICE FOR DETAILS.

IT6830 Camping Zeus

Via Villa dei Misteri, 80045 Pompei (Campania)

The naming of this site is obvious once you discover it is just 50 m. from the entrance to the fantastic ruins at Pompei. It is a reasonably priced, city type site with no frills but it is perfect for visiting the famous Roman archaeological sites here. The site's 80 pitches, all for tourers, are under mature trees which give shade. Pitching is informal with lines of trees dictating where large units park – ensure you liaise with other units so that you can get out in the morning! All are on flat grass, with 5A electricity and an energetic watering programme keeps the trees and grass green. It is worth noting that the ruins have limited disabled access so a telephone call is recommended. This site provides a safe central location, albeit with none of the holidaying trimmings, for visiting the wealth of Roman historical sites and wonderful places hereabouts.

Facilities

The single sanitary block is clean and modernised, with British and Turkish type WCs. Showers have hot water, with cold water in washbasins and dishwashing sinks. Facilities for disabled campers. Washing machines Gas supplies. Bar/restaurant with good value daily menu at lunch times (evening in high season) with waiter service. Shop.

At a glance

Welcome & Ambience	✓✓✓✓	Location	✓✓✓✓
Quality of Pitches	✓✓✓	Range of Facilities	✓✓✓

Directions

Leave Napoli -Salerno autostrada at Scavi di Pompei exit. After the pay booth turn hard left at sign for Gran Camping Zeus. It is an uphill approach for approximately 200 m.

Latest charges

Per adult	€ 4.65
child (under 8 yrs)	€ 3.10
tent	€ 3.10 - € 4.13
car	€ 3.62
motorcycle	€ 2.58
caravan or motorcaravan	€ 5.68

Reservations

Not taken. Tel: 081 8655320.
Email: campingzeus@libero.it

Open

All year.

IT6835 Camping Riposo

Via Cassano 12-14, 80063 Piano di Sorrento (Campania)

Just 500 m. from the picturesque port of Piano di Sorrento is the tiny site of Camping Riposo. Simple, pretty and clean, this is only for those who just want a secluded place to park their unit whilst they explore this famous area. The Scalici family offer a courteous and helpful service. The site is shaded by citrus trees, there are electrical connections available and hot water is is free. Like most Italian sites, Riposo is very crowded in August.

Facilities

There are no entertainments and no pool – just a tiny bar and shop. Three excellent food shops nearby

At a glance

Welcome & Ambience	✓✓✓✓	Location	✓✓✓✓
Quality of Pitches	✓✓✓	Range of Facilities	✓✓

Directions

From Meta follow plentiful directions off main road SS145 (to Sorrento from autostrada at Castellamare). Access could be tricky for large units but gates can be opened wide.

Latest charges

Per person	€ 4.65
child (1-6 yrs)	€ 3.10
tent acc. to size	€ 3.87 - € 5.16
caravan	€ 5.68
car	€ 3.62
motorcycle	€ 2.07
motorcaravan	€ 6.46

Electricity and tax included. Less 10% for AR readers.

Reservations

Write to site. Tel: 081 8787374.

Open

1 June - 30 September.

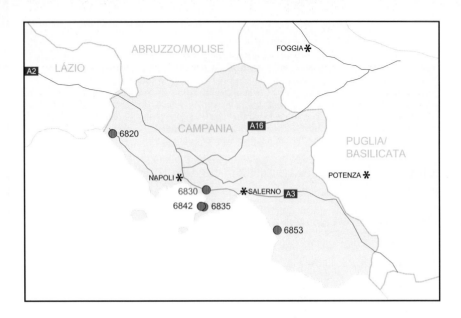

IT6820 Camping Villaggio Baia Domizia

81030 Baia Domizia (Campania)

This large well kept, seaside site is about 70 km. north west of Naples, and is within a pinewood, cleverly left in a natural state. There are 1,200 touring pitches in clearings, either of grass and sand, or on hardstanding, all with electricity (5A). Finding a pitch may take time, but staff help in season. The entire site is beautifully kept with shrubs, flowers and huge green areas. Most pitches are well shaded, but others near the beach are not. The site is well run with particular regulations (eg. no dogs or radios) and the general atmosphere is peaceful. Although the site is big, there is never very far to walk to the beach, though it may be some 300 m. to the central shops and restaurant from the site boundaries. The central complex is superb with well designed buildings containing all your needs. Restaurants, bars and a gelaterie enjoy live entertainment and attractive water lily ponds surround the area. Near the entrance are two excellent pools, which are a pleasant alternative to the sea on windier days. The supervised beach is 1.5 km. of soft sand and a great attraction. A wide range of sports and other amenities is provided. Charges are undeniably high, but this site is well above average and most suitable for families with children.

Facilities

Seven good toilet blocks have hot water in washbasins (many cabins) and showers, and facilities for disabled people. Washing machines, spin dryers. Motorcaravan services. Gas supplies. Huge supermarket and general shop. Large bar and restaurants with pizzeria and takeaway. Ice cream parlour. Sports ground. TV. Playground. Bicycle hire. Windsurfing hire and school. Disco. Church. Bureau de change. Doctor on site daily. Tennis. Excursions to major attractions in the area. Torches required in some areas. Barrier closed 2 pm-4pm; no entry. Dogs are not accepted. Off site: Fishing and riding 3 km.

At a glance

| Welcome & Ambience | √√√ | Location | √√√√ |
| Quality of Pitches | √√√√ | Range of Facilities | √√√√ |

Directions

The turning to Baia Domizia leads off the Formia - Naples road 23 km. from Formia. From Rome-Naples autostrada, take Cassino exit to Formia. Site is to the north of Baia Domizia and well signed.

Latest charges

Per person (12 yrs and over)	€ 4.10 - € 9.30
car	€ 2.60 - € 5.20
motorcycle	€ 2.10 - € 4.10
tent or caravan	€ 7.20 - € 13.90
motorcaravan	€ 9.80 - € 17.80
Electricity included.	

Reservations

Not taken, but min. 1 week stay in high season (July/Aug). Tel: 0823 930164. Email: baiadomizia@iol.it

Open

1 May - 21 September.

Baia Domizia

★★★★ Camping Village

I-81030 Baia Domizia (CASERTA)
Tel. +39 0823.930.164 - 930.126 • Fax +39 0823.930.375

www.baiadomizia.it e-mail: info@baiadomizia.it

IT6842 Camping Sant' Antonio

Via Marina d'Equa 21, Seiano, 80069 Vico Equense (Campania)

A base from which to explore Pompei, Herculaneum and Sorrento, this pretty little site, just across the road from Seiano beach, would suit caravanners who like a peaceful (for Italy) location. There are only 150 pitches which are in shade offered by orange, lemon and walnut trees. All pitches have electricity (5A) and access is easy on the flat ground. In summer (mid-June- end Sept) there is a regular 15 minute bus service to the Circumvesuviana railway which runs frequently to Sorrento, Pompei, Herculaneum and Naples. English is spoken by the Maresca family who run the site.

Facilities

The single sanitary block provides hot and cold showers, washbasins and British style WCs. Hot water is on payment. Small shop, bar and restaurant. Dogs are not accepted in August. Off site: Fishing and boat slipway 100 m.

At a glance

Welcome & Ambience	✓✓✓	Location	✓✓✓✓
Quality of Pitches	✓✓✓✓	Range of Facilities	✓✓✓

Directions

Take route SS163 from Castellamare to Sorrento. Just 50 m. after tunnel by-pass around Vico Equense, watch for very hard right turn for Seiano beach and follow signs down the narrow road.

Latest charges

Per person	€ 6.20 - € 7.23
child (up to 8 yrs)	€ 4.13 - € 5.68
car	€ 2.58 - € 3.10
caravan	€ 6.20 - € 7.23
motorcaravan	€ 6.71 - € 8.26

Reservations

Contact site. Tel: 081 8028570.

Open

15 March - 30 October.

IT6853 Camping Villagio Athena

Via Ponte di Ferro, 84063 Paestum (Campania)

This level site, which has direct access to the beach, has most facilities to hand. Much of the site is in woodland, but sun worshippers will have no problem here. The access is easy and the staff are friendly. There are 150 pitches, of which only 20 are used for static units and these are unobtrusive. There is no disco, although cabaret shows are staged in July/Aug. The management, the Prearo brothers, aim for a pleasant and happy environment.

Facilities

Toilet facilities in three blocks have mixed British and Turkish style WCs, washbasins and showers (cold water only) and hot showers on payment. Dishwashing and laundry sinks. Toilets for disabled people. Shop. Bar and restaurant (1/5-30/9). Riding. Watersports. Dogs and barbecues are not permitted. Off site: Tennis 1 km. Hourly bus service. Greek temples nearby.

At a glance

Welcome & Ambience	✓✓✓✓	Location	✓✓✓✓
Quality of Pitches	✓✓✓✓	Range of Facilities	✓✓✓✓

Directions

Take SS18 through Paestum and, at southern end of town before the antiquities, turn right as signed and follow road straight down to sea. Site is well signed.

Charges 2003

Per person	€ 4.65 - € 6.50
pitch incl. electricity	€ 8.50 - € 13.00

Reservations

Facilities/directions textContact site. Tel: 0828 851105. Email: vathena@tiscalinet.it

Open

1 March - 30 October.

Puglia is the long strip of land that forms the "heel" of the Italian boot, with the Gargano Peninsula as its 'spur'. A popular destination, holidaymakers are attracted to its sandy beaches and clean seas. Lying next to it is Basilicata, a remote and wild region that has remained largely unspoilt.

Puglia has five provinces:
Bari, Brindisi, Foggia, Lecce and Taranto

Basilicata has two:
Matera and Potenza

Made into a national park in 1991, the Gargano peninsula in Puglia boasts a diverse landscape of beaches, lagoons, forests and mountains. Up in the hills is the town of Monte Sant'Angelo. Home to one of the earliest Christian shrines in Europe, it attracts pilgrimages from all over the country. Further inland is the Forest of Shadows, an area covering 11,000 hectares with a variety of wildlife, ideal for walking. The seaside towns of Vieste, Rodi Garganico, Péshici and Manfredonia are popular with tourists, as are the Trémiti Islands – including San Nicola, San Domino and Capraia – off the Gargano coast. Heading south is Trani, one of the most important medieval ports with an ornate cathedral, and Bari. Ferries to Greece depart from Bari, as well as from Bríndisi. At the southern tip of Puglia is Lecce, renowned for its Baroque architecture, and the Salentine peninsula. Good beaches can be found along the western coast of the peninsula around Gallipoli. To the west Basilicata is mostly upland country, scattered with ruins. The brooding town of Melfi has a formidable Norman castle, while nearby Venosa was once the largest Roman colony. The town has an archaeology park with remains of Roman baths, plus an amphitheatre and a ruined abbey complex.

Cuisine of the region

Puglia is the main source of the Italy's fish. It also produces some of the country's best olives and is famous for its almonds, tomatoes, figs, melons and grapes. Lamb is commonly eaten, often roasted with rosemary and thyme, and as there is little poultry, beef or pork in the region, horsemeat is popular, particularly in the Salento area. Peppers and *zenzero* (ginger) are widely used in dishes throughout Basilicata. Local cheeses include *ricotta*, *mozzarella*, *scamorza*, *burrata* (soft and creamy, made with cow's milk), and *caprini* (small fresh goat's cheese preserved in olive oil).

Braciole di cavallo: horsemeat steaks cooked in a rich tomato sauce

Latte di mandorla: almond milk

Panzarotti alla barese: pasta stuffed with meat sauce, egg and cheese, deep-fried in olive oil

Places of interest

Alberobello: home to whitewashed circular buildings with conical roofs known as *truilli*, there are truilli restaurants, shops plus a cathedral

Galatina: important wine-producing town, famous for its tarantella dance performed on the feast day of Saints Peter and Paul in June.

Lucera: ruins of Roman amphitheatre, 13th century castle with fortified walls and towers

Matera: town perched on edge of a ravine

Mattinata: popular, small resort in Gargona

Metaponto: Roman ruins, museums

Vieste: holiday capital of Puglia with excellent beaches

THE TARANTELLA DANCE DATES BACK TO A TIME WHEN ALLEGED VICTIMS OF THE TARANTULA'S BITE PERFORMED A FRENZIED DANCE IN A BID TO 'SWEAT OUT' THE POISON.

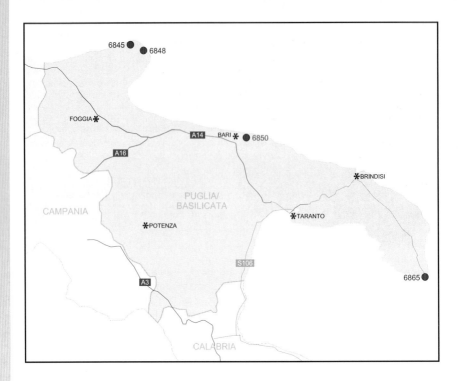

IT6845 Centro Turistico San Nicola

71010 Peschici (Puglia)

This is a really splendid site occupying a hill-side position, sloping down to a cove with a 500 metre beach of fine sand. Surrounded by tree clad mountains, it is generally a quiet, well regulated site which is part of, but separate from, a tourist holiday complex in the same area. Hard access roads lead to spacious well constructed, grassy pitches, under shade from mature trees. Scores of pitches are on the beach fringes (no extra charge) and there is a separate area for campers with animals. There are 750 pitches of varying size, all with 5A electricity. Cars may have to be parked away from the pitches in high season. There are no static caravans, but some bungalows are on site. With a neat, tidy appearance, many flowerbeds provide a garden atmosphere. The site is popular with German campers (tannoy announcements and most notices in German only) although English is spoken. It is fairly remote with some interesting hairpins in the last 14 km. of the 75 km. journey from the autostrada. However, we think it is well worth the drive if you enjoy high quality beach sites and wish to explore the Gargano National Park.

Facilities

Six excellent, modern toilet blocks, two in the beach part, the others around the site, are excellent with British and Turkish style toilets, hot water in the washbasins (some with toilets in private cabins), showers and dishwashing facilities. Washing machines and dryers. Supermarket, fruit shop and bazaar. Two beach bars (from 1/5; some evening noise until 22.30 hrs). Large bar/restaurant with terraces and separate pizzeria (all season). Electronic games. Tennis. Watersports. Playground. Organised activities and entertainment for young and old (July/Aug). Off site: Coach and boat excursions. Gargano National Park.

At a glance

Welcome & Ambience	✓✓✓✓	Location	✓✓✓✓
Quality of Pitches	✓✓✓✓	Range of Facilities	✓✓✓✓✓

Directions

Leave autostrada A14 at exit for Poggio Imperiale, and proceed towards Peschici and Vieste. When signs for Peschici and Vieste diverge, follow Vieste signs keeping a sharp lookout for San Nicola and Camping Baia San Nicola signs. Then follow large pink campsite signs. It will take at least 1.5 hrs from the motorway.

Charges 2003

Per adult	€ 6.00 - € 9.50
child (1-8 yrs)	€ 3.50 - € 5.50
tent	€ 5.00 - € 8.00
caravan or trailer tent	€ 7.50 - € 12.00
car	€ 3.00 - € 5.00
motorcaravan	€ 9.00 - € 13.50

Reservations

Only made for site's own accommodation (min one week). Tel: 0884 964024. Email: sanicola@sannicola.it

Open

1 April - 15 October.

IT6850 Sea World Village

San Giorgio - Padiglione Nauti, ss Adriatica 78, 70126 Bari (Puglia)

The sites in this southern part of Italy vary enormously, but Sea World Village (formerly Camping San Giorgio) is acceptable as a transit stop or for a short stay. The owners have put much effort into improving the site. Bari is a busy city, but Sea World Village is on the southern edge and avoids much of the bustle. There are only 20 tourist pitches, all with electricity, well separated from the static pitches. Access to the sea is over rocks and concrete platforms, with a small swimming pool in the rock at the water's edge, plus a separate, man-made, sandy beach which is cleaned daily. The large car park and many public changing cabins means the site is crowded at weekends with day visitors. There are many bungalows on site built in the attractive local 'Trulli' style. Facilities here are basic, but with some unusual features which may appeal to campers who wish to explore Bari for a short time.

Facilities

The sanitary blocks are acceptable and of modern construction with mainly British style toilets and free hot showers. Restaurant, pizzeria and market (all year). Bar (15/6-15/9). Swimming pool (15/6-15/9; all shared with the public). Roller skating, hockey, football and tennis areas. Bowling. Disco. Watersports. Writing room. Doctor calls. Torches useful. Off site: Fishing 5 km. Riding and golf 10 km.

At a glance

Welcome & Ambience	√√√	Location	√√√
Quality of Pitches	√√√	Range of Facilities	√√√

Directions

Take Bari exit from autostrada A14 and follow signs for Brindisi on the dual carriageway ring road (Tangenziole). After exit 15 watch carefully for the San Giorgio exit. Follow brown campsite signs and at first traffic lights site is directly across the road.

Charges 2003

Per person	€ 6.00 - € 8.00
pitch	€ 7.50 - € 12.00
small tent with car	€ 6.00 - € 10.00
electricity	€ 1.50

Reservations

Only made for site bungalows. Tel: 0805 491175. Email: sworld@tin.it

Open

All year.

IT6848 Punta Lunga Camping Village

C.P. 339, Loc. Defensola, 71019 Vieste (Puglia)

Punta Lunga is located in the spectacularly beautiful Gargano region, a huge National Park. This site nestles into a bay with easy access to a second beach in the next cove. Pitches are flat on a mixture of sand and grass and of a reasonable size. Some are shaded by trees, others by a mixture of shade cloth and trees, and most are on steep terraces. Camping along the shore is less formal and in some cases less shaded, but some pitches have spectacular views. A small shop and large bazaar are on site and there is a shuttle bus to the town of Vieste. The friendly staff arrange daily and weekly excursions to local attractions. This is a delightful place to relax by the sea and to explore the dramatic wilderness of the Gargano peninsula with its coves, cliffs and coastal towns.

Facilities

Two unusual units consist of a mixture of unisex showers and dedicated toilets. The facilities are clean and fresh. A single central unit for disabled campers is of a high standard. Washing machines and dryer. Small shop. Gas. Excellent restaurant with pleasant views. Beach bar with snacks and electronic games. Animation (children's clubs) in high season. Small play area. Bicycle hire. Weight training room. Very good windsurfing school on site. Dogs and other animals not accepted. Off site: Restaurants, bars and shops. Boat launching 3 km. Riding 10 km.

At a glance

Welcome & Ambience ✓✓✓✓ Location ✓✓✓✓
Quality of Pitches ✓✓✓✓ Range of Facilities ✓✓✓

Directions

From north take A14 exit for Poggio Imperiale, then to Vico Gargano and Vieste. From south take A14 exit Foggia, then towards Manfredonia, Mattinata and Vieste.

Charges 2003

Per person	€ 3.50- € 9.25
child (2-12 yrs)	€ 2.45 - € 6.18
pitch	€ 3.70 - € 11.00
electricity	€ 1.80 - € 2.20

Camping Cheques accepted.

Reservations

Not made. Tel: 0884 706031.
Email: puntalunga@puntalunga.com

Open

1 week before Easter - October.

IT6865 Camping Riva di Ugento

Litoranea Gallipoli, S. Maria di Leuca, 73059 Ugento (Puglia)

There are some campsites where you can be comfortable, have all the amenities at hand and still feel you are connecting with nature. Under the pine and eucalyptus trees of the Bay of Taranto foreshore is Camping Riva di Urgento. Its 950 pitches are nestled in and around the sand dunes and the foreshore area. They have space and trees around them and the sizes differ, as the environment dictates the shape of most. The sea is only a short walk from most pitches and some are at the waters edge. The area is sandy but well shaded. This site has an isolated, natural feel which defies its size. There are adults and children's pools, although these are expensive to use in high season. A free cinema also shows special events via satellite TV near the main bar and restaurant area. The site buildings resemble huge wooden umbrellas and are in sympathy with the environment.

Facilities

Twenty toilet blocks are in two different styles, of which 10 have complete amenities. Bar. Restaurant and takeaway. Swimming and paddling pools. Tennis. Basketball. Volleyball. Watersports incl. windsurfing school. Cinema. TV in bar. Entertainment for children. Bicycle hire. Off site: Fishing. Riding 0.5 km. Boat launching 4 km. Golf 40 km.

At a glance

Welcome & Ambience ✓✓✓✓ Location ✓✓✓✓✓
Quality of Pitches ✓✓✓✓✓ Range of Facilities ✓✓✓✓

Directions

From Bari take the Brindisi road to Lecce, then SS101 to Gallipoli, followed by the SR274 towards S. Maria di Leuca, and exit at Ugento. Site is very well signed and has a long bumpy approach road. Night parking area available if late or between 13.00-15.00 hrs.

Charges 2003

Per pitch incl. 3 persons	€ 16.00 - € 34.00
extra person	€ 5.00 - € 9.00

Camping Cheques accepted.

Reservations

Contact site. Tel: 0648 72823.
Email: rivadiugento@rivadiugento.it

Open

15 May - 30 September.

The 'toe' of the Italian boot, Calabria, like its neighbouring region, is a sparsely populated region with unspoilt countryside. The coastline boasts fine, sandy beaches, while the interior features the rugged Aspromonte and Sila mountains, which dominate the landscape.

There are five provinces in Calabria: Catanzaro, Cosenza, Crotone, Reggio di Calabria and Vibo Valentia

One of the main towns in the region is Cosenza, which is completely enclosed by mountains – the Sila to the east, the Catena Costiera to the west separating it from the sea. The Sila massif is divided into three parts: the Sila Greca, Sila Grande and the Sila Piccola. Lying in the Sila Greca are the villages of Santa Sofia, San Sosmo and Vaccarizzo, which come alive during the annual festivals, held throughout the year. There are ski slopes in the Sila Granda plus numerous lakes, ideal for fishing. Camigliatello is one of the best-known resorts here offering winter-sports, riding and hiking. Lastly, Sila Piccola is the region's most densely forested section, which has been designated national park status. South of Cosenza along the Tyrrhenian coast is the picturesque town of Tropea, whose old town clings to the cliffside, offering superb views of the sea and beaches. There are more sandy beaches nearby at Capo Vaticano, while across on the Ionian coast is the popular resort of Rossano Scalo. Just inland from here is the attractive hilltown of Rossano while further south are the vineyards of Cirò. To the north of Rossano is Sibari, home to the world's largest archaeological site, covering 1000 hectares; excavations have revealed evidence of ancient Greek and Roman civilisations.

Cuisine of the region

Food is largely influenced by Greek cuisine – aubergines, swordfish and sweets, using figs, almonds and honey. Many biscuits and cakes are made in honour of a religious festival or saint's day, which can be deep-fried in oil, soaked in honey or encrusted with almonds. Pasta is popular plus pork and cheeses such as mozzarella and perorino. Locally produced wines include the Greco di Bianco, a sweet white wine, and those from Cirò.

Places of interest

Aspromonte: scenic mountainous region in the southernmost tip of Italy's boot

Capo Colanna: Greek ruins, nearby beaches

Gerace: impressive cathedral, ruined castle

Locri: Greek ruins

Pizzo: picturesque town with small castle and beaches

Reggio di Calabria: national museum

Soverato: popular resort with good beaches

Stilo: home to the 10th century five-domed Cattolica

 tip

ALTHOUGH THERE ARE GOOD TRANSPORT SERVICES THROUGHOUT THE REGION, A CAR IS USEFUL IN THE HILLY AND COASTAL AREAS.

153

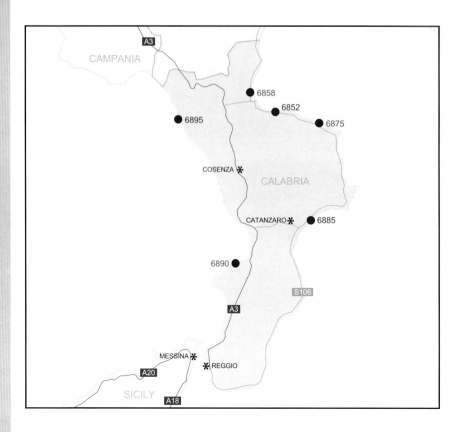

IT6852 Village Camping Marina di Rossano

C. da Leuca, CP 363, 87068 Rossano (Calabria)

This is a traditional site with a good pool. There are about 250 pitches, all under tall, shady poplar and eucalyptus trees, cars are parked in a secure area away from the pitches. It is a secluded site and a stretch of private beach is reached directly via a tunnel under the road (some road noise). A large power station is visible from the beach and this is fairly close to the site. Some staff in reception, the shop, bar and restaurant speak English. This is a very modest site which may suit some campers as an overnight stop. There are many apartments and bungalows on site but in a separate area. We do not consider this site as suitable for disabled campers. Torches are essential.

Facilities

When we inspected many of the sanitary facilities were out of use meaning there were only 10 showers working for 250 pitches. Disabled campers should make contact to confirm availablity. Five toilet blocks, some with free hot water but most were not functioning when we visited. The central block includes facilities for disabled visitors but the ground is difficult. Shop. Bars. Restaurant. Pizzeria. Swimming pools. Most facilities open from July. Private beach. Tennis. Small football pitch. Basketball. Volleyball. Bicycle hire. Weight training (on beach). Off site: Fishing. Riding 10 km.

At a glance

Welcome & Ambience	✓✓✓	Location	✓✓✓
Quality of Pitches	✓✓✓✓	Range of Facilities	✓✓

Directions

From north take the east coast highway (route 106). Leave at Rossano exit. A football stadium is across the road on the right. Look carefully for Marina di Rossano sign (small camping note at bottom) and drive across road and through gates. Follow a very long narrow road without turn offs, and eventually site signs come up. Site can be reached by either west or east autostrada. Care must be taken along the final approach (possible difficulties for larger units).

Charges 2003

Per pitch	€ 15.49 - € 23.24
adult	€ 3.62 - € 6.46
child (3-4 yrs)	€ 2.32 - € 5.16
dog	free - € 4.65

Reservations

Contact site. Tel: 0983 516054.
Email: marina.club@tiscalinet.it

Open

1 April - 30 September.

IT6858 Camping Il Salice

Contrada Ricota Grande, 87060 Corigliano Cálabro (Calabria)

This is a campsite with attitude! Starting with the huge elegant, air-conditioned reception with welcoming coffees, there are attractive landscaped gardens, fountains and the most enormous pool in the shape of Calabria. There are many choices here – to visit the hairdresser, have a massage, enjoy the warm Ionian sea or have a relaxing drink by the pool. The large flat pitches are under tall pines and eucalyptus, many with views of the beach, some right alongside the sand. In the distance the mountains of Pollino National Park can be seen. This is the place to catch up on your reading whilst being fanned by the cool sea breezes as the children play under expert supervision in the children's club. It is a real treat to stay here and enjoy the excellent facilities and we think it well worth the drive.

Facilities

One large heated and two small unheated toilet blocks provide high quality facilities including excellent units for disabled campers. Laundry. Restaurant, pizzeria, takeaway and bar. Shop. Hairdresser. Massage. Very large outdoor pool (fairly hefty family charge in high season € 36 - € 62). Solarium. Tennis courts. Soccer. Volleyball. Basketball. Bicycle hire. Electronic games room. Internet (€ 5/hour). Amphitheatre and entertainment. Pedaloes. Windsurfing. Off site: Excursions to historic sites of Sybaris (3 km) away and Park National of Calabria. Fishing. Boat launching 4 km. Golf 20 km.

At a glance

Welcome & Ambience	✓✓✓✓✓	Location		✓✓✓✓✓
Quality of Pitches	✓✓✓✓✓	Range of Facilities		✓✓✓✓✓

Directions

From A3 Salerno-Reggio Calabria autostrada take Sibari exit, followed by the SS106 road towards Crotone. At the km. 19 marker look for the campsite sign and turn for Centro Vacanze Il Salice towards the beach. Site is well signed through small 'estate'.

Charges 2004

Per adult	€ 2.00 - € 10.00
child (3-6 yrs)	free - € 8.00
pitch	€ 3.00 - € 14.00
small tent	€ 1.50 - € 13.00
electricity (3-6A)	€ 2.00 - € 3.00

Camping Cheques accepted.

Reservations

Contact site. Tel: 09 83 85 11 69.
Email: info@salicevacanze.it

Open

All year.

IT6875 Vascellero Villagio Camping

87063 Cariati Marina (Calabria)

The superb, irregularly shaped pool with its bar and gelateria are the hub of Vascellero Village Camping. Alongside is the air conditioned restaurant which is bedecked with tasteful artefacts. The pool area is a delightful place to while away the day and the beach is equally tempting. Here, through a secure gate, you will find a sophisticated beach bar serving food on terraces overlooking the sea. Aerobics are conducted here by the animation team, and later you can enjoy discos without disturbing the campers some 250 m. away. The camping area is just inside the gate and is modest, but there are 100 generous pitches of gravel and sand under artificial shade and giant poplars. An ambitious programme for children runs during the day, and evening entertainment for adults is held in an arena with a spacious building is set aside for games, movies and special events on satellite TV. Senora Franca and her family aim to please their guests, whether it is for summer holidays or ski-ing in the winter.

Facilities

The single toilet block, kept clean at all times, provides mixed Turkish and British style toilets, six fully equipped cabins and facilities for disabled campers. Washing machines. Motorcaravan service point. Excellent restaurant. Pizzeria. Good swimming pool with pool bar. Two good play areas. Hairdresser. Table tennis. Billiards. Electronic games. Tennis. Bicycle hire. Mini-club, entertainment and aerobics. Beach 250 m. Beach volleyball. Beach restaurant serving takeaway and casual food with stage and disco. Watersports. Excursion service. Dogs and other animals not accepted in Aug. Off site: Riding 0.5 km. Sailing. Go karting 3 km. Fishing Boat launching 3.5 km. Aqua park 30 km.

At a glance

Welcome & Ambience	✓✓✓✓	Location		✓✓✓✓
Quality of Pitches	✓✓✓	Range of Facilities		✓✓✓✓

Directions

Take SS106 Taranto - Reggio road. At km. 299.2 marker in village of Carati turn towards beach at campsite signs. Site is well signed over the railway line.

Charges 2003

Per person	€ 4.00 - € 10.00
child (2-5 yrs)	€ 3.00 - € 7.00
pitch	€ 4.00 - € 12.00
dog	€ 1.50 - € 4.00
electricity	€ 1.50 - € 3.00

Reservations

Made with € 150 deposit. Tel: 0983 91127.
Email: vilagio@vascelloro.it

Open

All year.

IT6885 Camping Costa Blu

Loc. Finocchiaro, 88050 Sellia Marina (Calabria)

This tiny campsite of just 50 clean flat pitches has remarkable features for its size plus an attractive Italian ambience. The generously sized pitches (with electricity) are shaded by pines and eucalyptus. The very attractive pool has a slide and separate paddling pool and close by there is a small, smart amphitheatre for children and adult entertainment, which again is unusual in a site this size. First class tennis and 'bocce' courts (artificial surfaces) are near the beach access. The clean beach is just 30 m. through a secure gate and it is excellent for relaxing and enjoying the tranquil atmosphere, to soak up the sun or swim in the cool Ionian sea. A small restaurant serves the menu of the day and the friendly owners and staff are very keen that you enjoy your stay, although little English is spoken. This is a great site if you think small is beautiful and is a cut above the other sites in this area and the prices in low season are very favourable.

Facilities

One block of sanitary facilities has mixed Turkish and British style toilets and unisex coin operated showers (20c). Washing machine. Motorcaravan service point. Small restaurant with dish of the day. Snack bar. Small shop. Very nice small pool complex with a slide. Paddling pool. Play area. Beach volleyball. Small amphitheatre. Animation and mini-club. Off site: Watersports. Fishing. Restaurants, bars and shops.

At a glance

Welcome & Ambience	✓✓✓✓	Location	✓✓✓✓
Quality of Pitches	✓✓✓✓	Range of Facilities	✓✓✓

Directions

Take SS106 Crotone - Reggio road. At km. 199.7 marker in village of Carati take turn towards the beach indicated by the campsite signs. Site is well signed over the railway line through a small estate. The entrance is a sharp turn off the village road.

Charges 2003

Apply to site.

Reservations

Contact site. Tel: 044 960232.

Open

15 June - 3 September.

IT6890 Villaggio Camping Dolomiti sul Mare

SS522 per Tropea km 16,5, 89817 Briatico (Calabria)

Set high above the gulf of Eufemia, 300 metres from the beach, Dolomiti is a large sprawling site where the focus is on bungalows. It is popular with Italians and the village area within the resort is growing fast resulting in a little chaos at times, especially at reception and the restaurant where it is advisable to book well ahead and then confirm on the day. The pitches are informally laid out in a large, somewhat dusty olive grove where the ground slopes to the sea (chocks useful). Campers share the pool, bar, restaurant and entertainment with the other residents, but the high standards of the main complex make a stay worthwhile. The view from the attractive traditional house which forms the restaurant, bar and terraces has stunning views to the sea. This is an excellent stop-over point when in the area and compares favourably with other local sites.

Facilities

One unit with mixed British and Turkish style toilets and hot showers provides adequate, clean facilities. Site is unsuitable for disabled campers (rough terrain). Washing machines and dryers. Motorcaravan service point. Shop. Bar and terrace with views. Self service restaurant and snack bar. Swimming pool plus spa and paddling pool. Aerobics. Play area. Bicycle hire. Amphitheatre with entertainment and mini-club. Dogs and other animals not accepted. Torches useful. Off site: Beach and riding 500 m.

At a glance

Welcome & Ambience	✓✓✓	Location	✓✓✓✓
Quality of Pitches	✓✓✓	Range of Facilities	✓✓✓

Directions

Take E45 Cosenza - Reggio road and leave at Serre exit. Head for Vibo Valentia, then take the coast road and Briatico; the site is well signed.

Charges 2003

Per person	€ 6.00 - € 12.00
pitch	€ 4.00 - € 17.00
dog	€ 3.00 - € 6.00

Reservations

Contact site. Tel: 0963 391355. Email: dolmar@tin.it

Open

All year.

IT6895 Villaggio Turistico Mare Blu

Cirella di Diamante, 87020 Diamante (Calabria)

Mare Blu is a large site with lots of watersports activities and an open feel to the site, and is aimed at Italian families spending their holidays by the sea. The 160 pitches are flat with some grass, all have electricity and most enjoy shade from trees. There is a beach access under the railway line and the fine sand provides a safe area for children to play. Here you will find the many watersports and a beach bar. The friendly staff speak a little English and are keen to please. A self-service restaurant has a very large covered terrace, as does the pizzeria and is popular with the families who linger to enjoy the professional entertainment provided in high season. The performance area becomes a disco later in the evening. This is a good site for a short stay to get a taste of the Italian way of camping, or a transit site whilst passing as it is one of the best in the area with many supporting amenities.

Facilities

Two units provide mixed British and Turkish style toilets. Facilities are in separate blocks – showers from toilets but are clean with hot water. Unit for disabled campers. Washing machines and dryers. Motorcaravan service point. Shop. Self service restaurant. Bar and terrace with views. Snack bar. Play area. Minigolf. Tennis. Table tennis. Animation on the beach. Boat, mountain bike and bicycle hire. Full evening animation programme. Disco. Mini-club. Beach (300 m). Canoes. Windsurfing. Off site: Riding 0.5 km. Golf 40 km.

At a glance

Welcome & Ambience	✓✓✓✓	Location	✓✓✓✓
Quality of Pitches	✓✓✓✓	Range of Facilities	✓✓✓✓

Directions

From E45 Salerno - Cosenza road take Cosenza Nord and SS107 to Paola. Then SS585 coast road north to Diamante. Site is well signed before reaching the village of Cirella.

Charges 2003

Per person	€ 7.00 - € 13.00

Reservations

Made for low season only; contact site. Tel: 0985 86097. Email: info@villagiomareblu.com

Open

May - September.

The largest island in the Mediterranean, Sicily has seen a range of settlers come and go, from the early Greeks and Romans to the Arabs and Normans, French and Spanish. With its beach resorts, volcanic islands, ancient sites and varied cuisine, Siciliy is also home to Mount Etna.

Sicily is comprised of the following provinces: Agrigento, Caltanissetta, Catania, Enna, Messina, Palermo, Ragusa, Siracusa and Trapani

The capital of Sicily is the bustling city of Palermo. With its medieval streets and markets, it has the island's greatest concentration of sights, and architecture that boasts a range of styles from Arabic to Norman, Baroque and Art Nouveau. Boats depart from here to the tiny volcanic island of Ústica, renowned for its marine life and popular among divers. Along with Milazzo and Messina, the capital also provides connections to the Aeolian Islands, of which Lípari is the most popular. Outside the capital is Monte Pellegrino, which offers superb views of the city, plus the seaside resort of Mondello. Europe's highest volcano, Mount Etna is situated in the east. Still active, its lower reaches can be reached on foot or by public transport. The closest town to the summit is Randazzo, built entirely of lava, as is Catania, situated further down the Ionian coast. Engulfed by lava in 1669 followed by an earthquake in 1693, Catania has been rebuilt on a grand scale. The coastline also bears traces of ancient Greek cities, most notably at Megara Hyblaea and Siracusa. More Greek ruins can be found near Agrigento, on the south-west coast, while around to the west is Marsala, famous for its fortified wine, and the harbour town of Trápani, a jumping off point for the Egadi Islands.

Cuisine of the region

Given its location, Sicily has attracted an endless list of invaders which has impacted on its food, resulting in one of Italy's most varied cuisines. Fish is abundant, including anchovies, sardines, tuna and swordfish, often teamed with pasta, as in *spaghetti con le sarde*. Sicily is famous for its sweets, in particular *cannoli*, fried pastries stuffed with sweet ricotta. Made from sheep's milk, ricotta is used in a variety of desserts, with percorino and provolone cheeses also widely available. Wines include Marsala, Corvo and Regaleali.

Maccheroni con le sarde: sardines cooked with fennel, raisins, pine nuts, breadcrumbs and saffron

Pesce spada: swordfish steak, grilled or pan-fried with lemon and oregano

Sicilin cassata: ice-cream made with ricotta, nuts, candied fruit and chocolate in a sponge cake

Places of interest

Acireale: spa centre, hosts one of Sicily's best festivals in February

Agrigento: nearby archaeological area known as the Valley of the Temples

Enna: Sicily's highest town

Erice: medieval town, cathedral

Marsala: home of the famous wine, in production since the 18th century

Segesta: ancient temple, nearby ruins of an ancient theatre where summer concerts are held

Taormina: lively resort with sandy beaches, ancient Greek theatre and 13th century cathedral

Vulcano: Aeolian Island, with hot mud baths and fine black beaches

TO VIEW MOUNT ETNA IN COMFORT, THE CIRCUMETNEA RAILWAY RUNS AROUND THE BASE FROM GIARRE-RIPOSTO TO CATANIA. THE TRIPS LASTS 5 HOURS; TICKETS COST € 5-10.

IT6880 Camping Biscione

Via Biscione, 91020 Petrosino (Sicily)

This is a relatively new, peaceful site on flat ground with walls surrounding most of the spacious area. The sliding security gate has an inconspicuous communications box on the left portal for late arrivals and ensures instant communications through the modern reception room. There are some exotic palms and fruit trees offering a little shade but some pitches are available with artificial shade on frames. The 383 average sized pitches are clean, well marked and unusually for Sicily, have a lush covering of grass. All have electricity (3A) and some pitches have pleasant views of neat rows of vines alongside the site. The restaurant is a really strong feature here, with a wood fired oven produces tasty succulent pizzas and a great atmosphere abounds. Some singing and dancing entertainment is provided in high season along with a school for English and Italian. There is much to do in the local area, ask for help at reception. English is spoken.

Facilities

Fully equipped, clean, central heated sanitary building. It could be under pressure in peak periods. Washing machines, dishwashing (H&C) and laundry sinks under cover. Facilities for disabled campers. Shop with essentials only. Other items can be ordered and will be brought from town (15/6 - 31/8). Restaurant/bar all year (night time only in low season). Club and TV room. Baby football and electronic games. Barbeques not allowed on pitch. Floodlit football, boules and tennis courts. Standby generator as electricity supplies can be unreliable. Municipal bus service to town and beach. Motorcaravan service point (under-vehicle spray incorporated). Torches useful. Off site: Biscione beach 500 m. Boat launching 500 m.Sailing 4 km. Torrazza beach 5 km. Bars, restaurants and shops in local village 1.5 km. Tours of vineyards. Tastings. Excursions.

At a glance

Welcome & Ambience	✓✓✓✓	Location	✓✓✓
Quality of Pitches	✓✓✓✓	Range of Facilities	✓✓✓

Directions

Petrosino is between Marsala and Mazara del Vallo in the south west corner of Sicily. Take the E90 then the E931 and exit at Petrosini. Take the beach road out of town and follow camping signs.

Charges 2003

Per person	€ 4.60 - € 5.20
child (7-14 yrs)	€ 2.60 - € 3.60
pitch	€ 7.20 - € 8.30
tent	€ 4.10 - € 6.70
car	€ 2.10

Reductions in low season. Credit cards not accepted.

Reservations

Write to site. Tel: 0923 73 14 44.

Open

All year.

IT6910 Camping Lu Baruni

C/da Barone 27, 91014 Castellammare del Golfo (Sicily)

Recommended by a reader, we hope to include this distant campsite in a future visit programme. Camping La Baruni (the Baron's campsite) is one kilometre from the beach and is arranged around a traditional villa (where there are rooms to rent). In addition to caravans and bungalows (also available for rent), there are 50 pitches on sandy grass shaded by many trees. Electricity connections are available. Any further comments from readers are welcome.

Facilities

Sanitary facilities include warm showers and facilities for disabled visitors. Bar. Shop. Gas. Play area. Tennis court. Table tennis. Boules. Off site: Restaurant 1 km. Swimming pools 1 km. Fishing 2 km. Riding 5 km. Town 8 km.

Direction

Castellammare del Golfo is on the coast to the west of Palermo, exit A29 onto S187.

Reservations

Contact site. Tel: 0924 39133.

Open

15 March - 15 October.

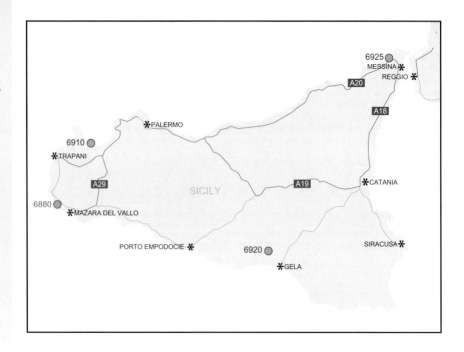

IT6920 Camping Due Rocche

Loc. Falconara s.s. 115 km 241,8, 93011 Butera (CL) (Sicily)

Covering 2.8 hectares, Due Rocche is in a peaceful situation by the sea. There are 100 marked but small touring pitches (40-75 sq.m) which are obviously best suited for tents, although caravans and motor-caravans are also accepted. Most pitches have shade and 3/6A electricity is available in all areas. In addition, the site provides 100 seasonal or permanent places in a separate area. The site is right beside the sea with a sandy beach.

Facilities

Sanitary facilities are fairly basic, with cold washbasins, hot showers and both British and Turkish style WCs. Washing machines and ironing. Play area. Games room. Table tennis. Boules. Mini-club and entertainment programme with disco in high season.

At a glance

Welcome & Ambience	✓✓✓	Location	✓✓✓✓
Quality of Pitches	✓✓✓	Range of Facilities	✓✓

Directions

Site is 9 km. east of Ortes. At km. 241.8 turn onto SS115 road to site (signed).

Charges 2003

Per person	€ 4.20 - € 5.20
child (0-3 yrs.)	free
pitch	€ 7.80 - € 10.40
tent pitch	€ 3.70 - € 7.30
car	€ 2.70 - € 3.10

Reservations

Contact site. Tel: 0934 349006.
Email: 2rocche@camping.it

Open

All year.

IT6925 Camping Il Peloritano

C'trada Tarantonio s. 113d., Rodia, 98161 Messina (Sicily)

Recommended by our agent, this site will be inspected in 2004. Rodia is situated on the S113d on the northeast tip of Sicily on the opposite side to Messina. Il Peloritano is just 200 metres from the sea, with a sandy beach and is well placed for excursions from Messina or Milazzo to the volcanic islands such as Stromboli. It is a peaceful, friendly site where most pitches are shady, set under old olive trees and with electrical connections (6A).

Facilities

As well as the normal sanitary facilities, there are washing machines and hot water for dishwashing. Small shop. Snack bar in high season. Takeaway.

Reservations

Contact site. Tel: 090 348496.
Email: info@peloritanocamping.it

Open

1 March - 30 October.

Directions

From Messina take the A20 exiting at Villafranca, where you turn right for the S113d to Rodia, where the site is signed.

Charges 2003

Per person	€ 4.80 - € 6.00
child (3-7 yrs)	€ 2.80
caravan	€ 4.80 - € 6.00
motorcaravan	€ 5.80 - € 7.00
tent	€ 3.80 - € 6.20
car	€ 2.40
electricity	€ 2.30

Sardinia

With dramatic, rolling uplands covered with grassland, and a beautiful coastline boasting isolated coves, long sandy beaches and hidden caves, Sardinia offers more than just sunshine and clear waters: littered around the island are thousands of prehistoric nuraghic remains.

Sardinia has four provinces:
Cagliari, Nuoro, Oristano and Sassari

The busy port of Cágliari is the island's capital. Main attractions include the city walls, archaeology museum and cathedral plus an impressive Roman amphitheatre. More ruins can be found just outside the city at Nora, while some 7,000 or so *nuraghi* are dotted all around the island. Unique to Sardinia, these stone-built constructions are remnants of Sardinia's only significant native culture. The most famous of them is at Su Nuraxi, the oldest and largest nuraghic complex, dating from around 1500 BC. The island's second city, Sássari, is known for its spectacular *Cavalcata* festival on Ascension Day; festivities include traditional singing and dancing plus a horseback parade and race. Not far from Sássari is Alghero, a major fishing port and the island's oldest resort. Surrounded by walls and defensive towers the old town is full of narrow, cobbled streets with flamboyant churches and brightly-coloured houses. Boat or car trips can also be made to Neptune's Grotto, a spectacular, deep marine cave, around the point of Capo Caccia. Sardinia's best known resort is the Costa Smeralda, one of the Mediterranean's loveliest stretches of coast, a 10 km. strip between the gulfs of Cugnana and Arzachena. Beaches can be found at Capriccioli, Rena Bianca and Liscia Ruia.

Cuisine of the region

Fresh ingredients are widely used to create simple dishes: seafood, especially lobster, is grilled over open fires, as is suckling pig. Fish stews and pasta is popular. The island also produces a variety of breads. Cheeses tend to be made from ewe's milk, including percorino Sardo. Nougat is a sweet Sardinian speciality and pastries are often flavoured with almonds, lemons or orange. Vernaccia is the island's most famous wine.

Agnello arrosto: roast lamb, roasted on a spit or in casseroles with rosemary and thyme.

Bottarga: a version of caviar made with mullet eggs

Culigiones: massive ravioli stuffed with cheese and egg

Maloreddus: saffron flavoured pasta

Places of interest

Bosa: small, picturesque seaside town

Cala Gonone: bustling seaside resort and fishing port, with good beaches, isolated coves and natural caves including the famous Grotta del Bue Marino

Carloforte: an attractive town on the island of San Pietro

Dorgali: in wine-growing region of Cannonau

Maddalena Islands: popular tourist attraction, sandy and rocky beaches

Oristano: nearby lagoon is home to one of the island's largest populations of flamingo

REGULAR FERRIES RUN FROM THE MAINLAND OF ITALY TO SARDINIA. THEY ALSO OPERATE BETWEEN SICILY, TUNIS, CORSICA AND FRANCE.

IT6950 Camping La Foce

Via Ampurias, 1 c.s, 07039 Valledoria (Sardinia)

English speaking Stefano Lamparti is the enthusiastic owner of La Foce which is a large sprawling site in the Golfo del Asinara. A river flows through the site into the sea and Stefano has a motorised punt to ferry campers to a secluded area of the coast on the other side of the river where they can enjoy the golden sand dunes and have a refreshing swim away from other beachgoers. The 300 sandy pitches vary in size and are informally arranged under tall shady eucalyptus trees stretching along the length of the site, some close to the river. This unpretentious site has a family atmosphere and there appears to be something for everyone here in a distinctly old style way, communing with nature. A pleasant surprise was the Gulliver Centre in a remote are of the campsite. This is a place for children from all over Italy and other parts of Europe to learn about the challenges of nature.

Facilities
Four mature toilet blocks house good facilities with British and Turkish style toilets but no facilities for disabled campers. Hot water is available 24 hours. Washing machine. Motorcaravan service point. Supermarket. Restaurant and snack bar. Play areas. Tennis. Bocce. Excursion service. Beaches – some by free punt. Boat launching. Windsurfing. Canoeing. Sub-aqua diving.
Off site: Fishing. Sailing 1.5 km. Riding 2 km.

At a glance
Welcome & Ambience	√√√√	Location	√√√√
Quality of Pitches	√√√√	Range of Facilities	√√√√

Directions
From Sassari take coast road go east to Castelsardo and Valledoria. As you arrive at the village watch for campsite signs towards beach.

Charges 2003
Per person	€ 5.50 - € 14.00
child (3-8 yrs)	free - € 8.00
Camping Cheques accepted.	

Reservations
Made for min 7 days – with deposit. Tel: 079 582 109. Email: lafoceuno@libero.it

Open
15 May - 30 September.

IT6955 Camping Baia Blu La Tortuga

Pineta di Vignola Mare, 07020 Aglientu (Sardinia)

In the northeast of Sardinia near the Costa Smeralda and well situated for the Corsica ferry, Baia Blu is a large, professionally run campsite. The beach with its golden sand, brilliant blue sea and pretty rocky outcrops is warm and inviting. The site's 550 touring pitches are of fine sand and shaded by tall pines with banks of colourful olleanders and wide boulevards providing good access for units. This is a busy bustling site with lots to do and attractive restaurants. It is under the same ownership as Marepineta (IT6000) and is very popular with Italian families who enjoy the wide range of amenities here.

Facilities
Four blocks provide an exceptionally good ratio of facilities to pitches including combined private shower/washbasin cabins (for rent), free hot showers and mixed British and Turkish toilets. Numerous footbaths, basins for children, sinks for dishes and laundry. Facilities for disabled people. Washing machines and dryers. Motorcaravan services. Supermarket. Gas. Bazaar. Bar. Restaurant, pizzeria, snack bar and takeaway (May-Sept). Supermarket. Playground. Tennis. Volleyball. Football. Table tennis. Games and TV rooms. Windsurfing and diving schools. Entertainment and sports activities organised in season. Excursions. Barbecue area (not permitted on pitches). First aid. Torches useful. Used by tour operators. Off site: Disco 50 m. Riding 5 km.

At a glance
Welcome & Ambience	√√√√	Location	√√√√
Quality of Pitches	√√√√	Range of Facilities	√√√√

Directions
Site is on the north coast between towns of Costa Paradiso and S. Teresa di Gallura (18 km) at Pineta di Vignola Mare and is well signed.

Charges 2003
Per person	€ 4.30 - € 9.80
junior (4-10 yrs) or senior (over 60 yrs)	€ 3..20 - € 7.50
pitch incl. electricity	€ 8.30 - € 21.20
tent pitch incl. electricity	€ 6.70 - € 13.00
dog	€ 1.00 - € 4.65

Reservations
Facilities/directions textMade with 30% deposit and € 15,50 fee. Tel: 079 602060. Email: info@baiablu.com

Open
12 April - 28 September.

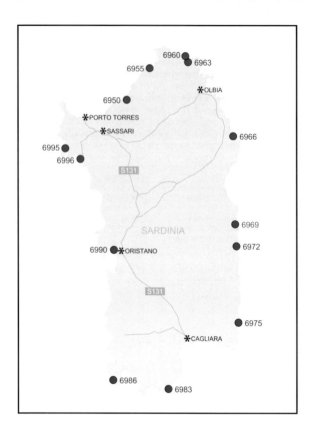

IT6960 Camping Capo d'Orso

Loc Saline, 07020 Palau (Sardinia)

Capo d'Orso is some 4.5 km. from the village of Palau in northern Sardinia. It is an attractive terraced site with views of the Maddalena Arcipelago. Set into a hillside that slopes down to the sea, the 450 terraced pitches (40-80 sq.m) are of gravel, grass and sand, some with views over the sea and some others set alongside the beach. Access to the pitches is quite good despite the rocky terrain. Cars are parked away from the pitches in high season (July/Aug). The very Italian (self service) restaurant serves delicious meals which can be eaten on a small terrace with sea views. Some English is spoken and the staff are friendly and helpful. Capo d'Orso is in the Costa Smeralda region, traditionally one of the most popular camping areas in Sardinia.

Facilities

Three toilet blocks provide adequate facilities, including hot showers (on payment in season, free at other times), washbasins, dishwashing and laundry sinks (cold water) and mainly Turkish, but with some British, type WCs. When seen in early June facilities were well maintained although not all the blocks are open then. Shop. Bar/restaurant. Pizzeria. Takeaway (all from 1/6). Scuba diving, windsurfing, sailing school, boat excursions, boat hire and moorings (all main season). Tennis. Underground disco. Entertainment programmes for children and adults. Excursions arranged in high season. Off site: Scuba diving.

At a glance

| Welcome & Ambience | ✓✓✓ | Location | ✓✓✓✓ |
| Quality of Pitches | ✓✓✓ | Range of Facilities | ✓✓✓✓ |

Directions

Site is 5 km. from Palau, in the northeast of Sardinia. On the SS133 Porto Pozzo - Cannigione road, the site is well signed to the beach.

Charges 2003

Per adult	€ 4.00 - € 7.00
child (6-12 yrs)	€ 3.00 - € 5.00
small tent (max 2 persons)	€ 4.00 - € 15.00
large tent or caravan	€ 5.00 - € 20.00
car or motorcycle	free - € 3.00
motorcaravan	€ 5.00 - € 23.00
electricity	€ 3.00

Reservations

Contact site. Tel: 0789 702007.
Email: info@capodorso.it

Open

1 May - 30 September.

IT6963 Camping Villaggio Isuledda

Cannigione di Arzachena, 07020 Sardegna (Sardinia)

Located in the centre of the Arzachena Gulf, Isuleda has access to three kilometres of beaches. These include a small bay with a marina, a more rugged long, open beach and a small bay with some attractive coves. This high quality resort style operation has something for everyone, with an amazing choice of restaurants, activities and entertainment. The staff are professional and vibrant, campers appeared relaxed and happy. The central area buzzes with activity, although it is possible to find a quiet area to relax. There is a balance of activities for all age groups and a large range of pitch choice. Most of the 650 good sized, gravel pitches are shaded by eucalyptus trees and flat; some are on the water's edge and others enjoy sea views (book early for high season). This site takes camping in Sardinia a step further and can be considered at the cutting edge for the area.

Facilities

Four modern and two older blocks provide the sanitary facilities with mainly British style toilets and good facilities for disabled campers (we recommend the smaller blocks). Showers are on payment (€ 0,50). Washing machines. Motorcaravan service point. Large supermarket. Tabac and paper shops. Restaurants (à la carte and self service), pizzeria and snack bar. Aerobics. Play areas. Doctor. Bicycle and motor scooter hire. Small boat launching. Windsurfing. Sailing. Sub Aqua diving school. Beach volleyball. Marina. Mini-club, animation and entertainment. Excursion service. Disco and beer bar – both isolated for noise management. Dogs and other animals not accepted. Off site: Golf and riding 2 km.

At a glance

Welcome & Ambience	✓✓✓✓	Location	✓✓✓✓✓
Quality of Pitches	✓✓✓✓	Range of Facilities	✓✓✓✓✓

Directions

Site is on the Costa Smeralda in the northeast of Sardinia. From SS125 Olbia - Cannigione road, south of Arzachena, take road north to Baia Sardinia. Site is well signed off this road in about 12 km. Be sure to travel up the west side of the inlet.

Charges 2003

Per person	€ 5.00 - € 10.00
child (2-12 yrrs)	€ 3.00 - € 6.00
pitch	€ 4.50 - € 23.00
electricity	€ 3.00

Reservations

Contact site. Tel: 0789 86003. Email: informazioni@isuledda.it

Open

18 April - 17 October.

IT6966 Camping Selema

08029 Santa Lucia di Siniscola (Sardinia)

Selema is a pretty site with a tropical feel. There is considerable shade from pine and eucalyptus, flowers and cacti have been used to provide landscaping features and unusually there are grassy areas. Located in a quiet rural area near the fishing village of Sant' Lucia di Siniscola on the more rugged coast of Sardinia, this is a comfortable and well managed site. This is the place to discover Sardinia away from the crowds. Staff speak some English and are very helpful. The bar, market and restaurant buildings are of traditional design and there is a shaded terrace. There are 180 large pitches of grass and sand, well shaded with shallow terracing. The site runs along the Pineta coast with its long white sandy beaches and vibrant blue water and has a wide river flowing along the other side. Some pitches are on the beach and many have views of the distant mountains.

Facilities

Two sanitary blocks have good facilities with a mixture of British and Turkish toilets. Facilities for disabled campers. Washing machine. Motorcaravan service point. Pleasant shop. Restaurant and snack bar. Play areas. Tennis. Football. Bocce. Table tennis. Large screen TV. Electronic games. Bicycle hire. Windsurfing. Beach volleyball. Small boat launching. Excursion service. Off site: Fishing. Riding 500 m. Sailing 4 km. Golf 40 km.

At a glance

Welcome & Ambience	✓✓✓✓	Location	✓✓✓✓
Quality of Pitches	✓✓✓✓✓	Range of Facilities	✓✓✓

Directions

From SS131 Olbia - Nuoro road take exit to Siniscola then SS125 south towards Orosei. Turn left at 245 km. marker to S. Lucia. Site is well signed.

Charges 2003

Per adult	€ 5.50 - € 10.00
child 3-6 yrs	€ 3.00 - € 5.00
child 7-12 yrs	€ 4.50 - € 7.00
pitch	€ 4.00 - € 15.00
electricity	€ 2.00 - € 2.50

Reservations

Made by telephone. Tel: 0784 819068. Email: info@selemacamping.com

Open

1 May - 15 October.

IT6996 Camping Mariposa

Via Lido 22, 07041 Alghero (Sardinia)

Mariposa is situated right by the sea with its own beach and the range of sports available here probably makes it best suited for active young visitors. Kite surfing, diving, windsurfing, sailing, surfing and paragliding courses are all available here on payment, whilst evening entertainment is provided free. Pitch sizes range from 50 to 90 sq.m. so are also better suited for tents, although they do all have 6A electrical connections and caravans and motorcaravans are welcome. Cars must be parked away from the pitches. Dogs are not accepted in August.

Facilities

The sanitary facilities are fairly basic, partly open plan, with cold washbasins and troughs, dishwashing and laundry sinks and an equal amount of warm (token needed) and cold showers. The shop, self service restaurant and bar are open all season. Bicycle hire. Washing machines and dryer. Motorcaravan service point. Off site: Alghero is 1.5 km away and still has a strong 'catalan' flavour from its 400 year occupation by the Spanish. There are many small coves and the Neptune caves are well worth a visit.

At a glance

Welcome & Ambience	✓✓✓	Location	✓✓✓✓
Quality of Pitches	✓✓✓✓	Range of Facilities	✓✓✓

Directions

Alghero is on the northwe st coast, about 35 km southwest of Sassari. Mariposa is at the north of the town.

Charges 2003

Per person	€ 7.50 - € 10.50
child (3-12 yrs)	€ 4.00 - € 8.50
tent	free - € 10.00
caravan	free - € 10.00
motorcaravan	€ 3.50 - € 11.00
electricity	€ 2.50
car	free - € 4.00

Reservations

Contact site. Tel: 079 950 360. Email: info@lamariposa.it

Open

1 April - 31 October.

I-07041 ALGHERO (SS)
Tel. +39 079950360
+39 0799504800

e-mail: info@lamariposa.it
www.lamariposa.it

la Mariposa
★★★ camping con bungalows
il gioco, ritrovarsi

IT6972 Camping L'Ultima Spiaggia

Localita Planargia, 08042 Bari Sardo (Sardinia)

A great name for this campsite, 'the ultimate beach', and the beach really is extremely good, along with the bright colourful décor and amenities. Tastefully laid out with a rather tropical feel, this is a very pleasant place to spend time. The 350 pitches are terraced on sand, some enjoying sea views, and large stone barbecues are provided. The good entertainment programme can be enjoyed from the terrace of the friendly restaurant which offers a reasonably priced menu which includes the local seafood specialities. Access to the fine beach (with lifeguard – unusual in these parts) with its water-sports is gained through a security gate. Sub-aqua diving is extremely good hereabouts. Much thought has been put into the décor of the campsite and the effect is very relaxing. We think you will enjoy this clean and pleasant site where some English is spoken.

Facilities

Two toilet units include mainly Turkish style toilets and good facilities for disabled campers. Washing machines. Motorcaravan service point. Small supermarket. Restaurant and snack bar. Play areas. Football. Beach volleyball. Windsurfing. Aerobics. Riding. Tennis. Minigolf. Canoeing. Bicycle hire. Mini-club. Entertainment. Excursion service. Torches useful. Off site: Restaurants, bars and shops. Fishing. Boat launching.

At a glance

Welcome & Ambience	✓✓✓✓	Location	✓✓✓✓✓
Quality of Pitches	✓✓✓✓	Range of Facilities	✓✓✓✓

Directions

Site is on east coast of Sardinia and is well signed from SS125 in village of Bari Sardo. Note that the roads are very winding from the north – allow lots of time for transit.

Charges 2003

Per person	€ 5.50 - € 12.00
child (1-6 yrs)	€ 3.50 - € 4.50
pitch	€ 5.50 - € 11.50
dog	€ 1.50 - € 3.50

Reservations

Made without charge. Tel: 0782 29363. Email: info@campingultimaspiaggia.it

Open

20 April - 30 September.

IT6975 Camping Villaggio Porto Pirastu

Capo Ferrato, 09043 Muravera (Sardinia)

This delightful site situated at Capo Ferrato has a wide range of facilities in a tranquil area alongside the beautiful Mar Tirreno with its warm turquoise water, rocky outcrops and long stretches of sandy beach. This is a resort style venture with a professional approach. The attractive traditional buildings lend atmosphere to the main square and the restaurant has a charming ambience with its arched ceilings. There are shaded terraces and sitting out areas where you can relax and enjoy the sea breezes whilst enjoying an aperitif or ice-cream. The large staff provides excellent activities for adults and children including water aerobics at the beach. Tennis lessons are available, a cinema and lively entertainment. The 260 shaded, reasonably sized pitches are attractively spaced on gravel and sand, some having views of the water. Porto Piratsu is a quality site with innovative management who aim to provide an enjoyable holiday.

Facilities

Two very pleasant blocks of sanitary facilities with mainly style British toilets, facilities for disabled campers and some children's washbasins. Washing machine. Motorcaravan service point. Shop. Restaurant and snack bar. Play areas. Mini-club and entertainment all day in high season. Cinema. Tennis. Excursion service. Beach volleyball. Water aerobics. Sub-aqua diving. Windsurfing school. Torches useful. Off site: Sailing 1.5 km. Bicycle hire 4 km. Golf and riding 5 km.

At a glance

Welcome & Ambience	✓✓✓✓	Location	✓✓✓✓✓
Quality of Pitches	✓✓✓✓	Range of Facilities	✓✓✓✓✓

Directions

Site is in southeast corner of Sardinia in the north of the Costa Rei. From coast road SS125 at S. Priamo travel south to Villagio Capo Ferrato. Site is well signed from here.

Charges 2003

Per person	€ 4.00 - € 11.50
child (3-9 yrs)	€ 3.00 - € 7.90
pitch	€ 7.20 - € 12.50

Reservations

Made with 50% deposit. Tel: 070 991 437. Email: info@portopirastu.net.

Open

1 April - 30 September.

IT6986 Camping Tonnara

09017 Sant'Antioco (Sardinia)

A small and simple campsite, Tonnara is situated on the west side of Sant Antico island in the south-west corner of Sardinia. Access to the island is via a narrow isthmus in the less attractive industrial end of the island. Don't be put off by this introduction as Tonnara is located 12 km. away in the pretty Cala Sapone inlet with its delightful sandy beach and rocky outcrops. The local seafood is good and cooked to perfection in the small restaurant where you can sit out on the terrace and watch the sun set into the sea. The 60 sandy pitches are on terraces with small trees and some artificial shade. Some are very close to the beach and most enjoy views of the inlet. Bore water is used on the site so watch for drinking water signs.

Facilities

One stucco unit houses mixed Turkish and British style toilet facilities with hot showers but no facilities for disabled campers. Washing machine. Motorcaravan service point. Neat little shop. Restaurant and snack bar. Small play area. Volleyball. Bicycle hire. Tennis. Table tennis. Bocce. Sub aqua diving arranged. Excursion service. Off site: Sailing 1 km. Nearest town 12 km. Riding 20 km.

At a glance

| Welcome & Ambience | ✓✓✓✓ | Location | ✓✓✓✓✓ |
| Quality of Pitches | ✓✓✓✓ | Range of Facilities | ✓✓✓ |

Directions

Site is on island of Di S' Antioco on southwest coast of Sardinia. Go over the causeway and turn left towards Cala Sapone (site signed). When road forks, look carefully for yellow campsite sign (straight ahead) to cross to western side for site.

Charges 2003

Per adult	€ 6.50 - € 9.20
child (3-10 yrs)	€ 2.40 - € 4.40
pitch	€ 5.60 - € 15.10
electricity	€ 1.90 - € 2.40
dog	€ 1.80 - € 4.30

Reservations

Made with 50% deposit (min. 15 days in August). Tel: 0781 809058. Email: tonnaracamping@tiscalinet.it

Open

1 April - 30 September.

IT6983 Camping Torre Chia

Chia, 09010 Domus de Maria (Sardinia)

Torre Chia is set on a beautiful sandy beach in the Golfo di Cagliari – you have an hour's drive over good roads from Cagliari port or airport. There are stylish Italian buildings including a large restaurant with a huge terrace area to enjoy the cool breezes. The modern amenable bar is part of the same building. Good sized sandy pitches are mostly level (some are quite close together)and they are shaded by tall eucalyptus and pine trees. Access to the beach is via a 60 m. walk through tall pines where families enjoy picnics in the shade. A family oriented site, Torre Chia has a modest range of facilities, ideal for independent campers who like a simple site with good amenities. A torch is very useful here.

Facilities

A single modern block has excellent, clean sanitary facilities with mainly British style toilets and locked facilities for disabled campers. Showers are coin operated. Motorcaravan service point. Shop. Restaurant and snack bar. Play area. Football. Tennis court. Bicycle hire. Washing machine. Fishing. Windsurfing. Canoeing. Beach volleyball. Small boat launching. Excursion service. Off site: Golf and riding 2 km. Sailing, sub-aqua diving and canoeing.

At a glance

| Welcome & Ambience | ✓✓✓✓ | Location | ✓✓✓✓ |
| Quality of Pitches | ✓✓✓✓ | Range of Facilities | ✓✓✓ |

Directions

Site is south of Cagliari near S. Margherita di Pula. Go to the village and the site is brightly signed towards the beach.

Charges 2003

Per person	€ 6.50 - € 7.50
child (1-10 yrs)	€ 5.50 - € 6.00
pitch	€ 4.50 - € 9.00
electricity	€ 1.75

Reservations

Contact site. Tel: 0709 230054.

Open

15 April - 30 September.

IT6969 Camping La Cernie

08040 Lotzorai (Sardinia)

Le Cernie is situated in a remote area on the east coast of Sardinia. You arrive at the site after a long drive through spectacular mountain ranges, but this means hard driving. Originally a diving enterprise, Le Cernie has grown into a very modest campsite which is suprisingly expensive. It is somewhat chaotic in nature, although most amenities are here, including a popular restaurant. Life at Le Cernie seems to meander along at its own pace – it is somewhat rugged and would not suit campers without a sense of humour and patience. The attractive beach is alongside the site and the diving here is very good. The 70 small pitches are flat, sandy and informally arranged under tall pines and eucalyptus. Access to the pitches throught the trees is rather tight in places (chocks useful, torches essential). This site is more suited to single adults/couples than families.

Facilities

A single modern unit has a rather confusing mixture of clean sanitary facilities with mainly British toilets and very good facilities for disabled campers and babies. Washing machines. Motorcaravan service point. Small shop. Restaurant and snack bar. Bicycle hire. Play area. Beach volleyball. Small boat launching. Sub-aqua diving. Off site: Riding 10 km.

At a glance

Welcome & Ambience	✓✓✓	Location	✓✓✓✓
Quality of Pitches	✓✓✓	Range of Facilities	✓✓✓

Directions

Site is off the eastern coast road SS125. At Lotzorai village the site is well signed - it is a long winding drive from the SS131!

Charges 2003

Per person	€ 9.00 - € 12.90
child 3-7 yrs	€ 4.50 - € 8.50
child under 3 yrs	free - € 6.00
pitch	free - € 7.00

Reservations

Made for low season only with deposit.
Tel: 0782 669472. Email: info@campinglecernie.it

Open

All year.

IT6990 Campeggio-Villaggio Spinnaker

Strada Provinciale, Oristano, 09170 Torre Grande (Sardinia)

Set on the undulating foreshore under tall pines, with beach frontage to the camping area, Spinnaker Village is a purpose built modern beach site. The restaurant (rather expensive with limited menu but also offering pizzas), a café and a pool are set around a large unshaded square where activities for families take place. Children must be kept under close supervision as the pool is unfenced and alongside the play area. The 100 pitches are sandy and sloping (chocks are required). This site will prove difficult for anything with wheels. Views of the sea are possible and the water is a 60 m. walk. The white sandy beach shelves teeply into big rolling waves and again you will need to keep an eye on your children. When we visited reception was being operated from the rear of the restaurant rather than at the entrance. We see this as a site for adults rather than for families.

Facilities

The single sanitary block has British style toilets and facilities for disabled campers. Showers are coin operated (€ 0.50) and there are few for the number of pitches so expect to wait in busy periods. Washing machine. Motorcaravan service point (extra charge € 15). Shop. Restaurant and small snack bar. Swimming pool (unfenced and near the play area - supervision required). Bicycle hire. Small boat launching. Volleyball. Mini-club and animation in high season. Excursion service. Torches essential. Off site: Riding 2 km. Golf 23 km.

At a glance

Welcome & Ambience	✓✓✓✓	Location	✓✓✓✓
Quality of Pitches	✓✓✓	Range of Facilities	✓✓✓

Directions

Take SS131 Cagliari - Oristano road then minor road to Cabras and Torre Grande. Just before Torre Grande village by large water tower on right take angled left turn back on yourself to site (signed). Access to the site is down the side of the site as the main entrance is not in use - ask directions for reception.

Charges 2003

Per person	€ 7.50 - € 13.00
child (3-12 yrs)	€ 5.00 - € 8.50
pitch	free - € 3.00
electricity	€ 2.00 - € 2.50

Reservations

Contact site. Tel: 0783 22074.
Email: info@spinnakervacanze.com

Open

1 April - 15 October.

IT6995 Camping Torre del Porticciolo

C.P.n. 83, Sede lagale via G. Ferret 17, 07041 Alghero (Sardinia)

Set high on a peninsula with fabulous views over the sea and old fortifications, is Torre del Porticciolo. It is a friendly, family owned site with striking traditional old buildings, attractive landscaping and large pools. The owner Marisa Carboni and her friendly staff speak a little English and are very helpful. A wonderfully decorated restaurant is close to the large bar and terrace. Nearby is the equally attractive pizzeria with its own terrace. It is in this area that the evening entertainment takes place. It is a 300 m. walk out of the site down a steep slope with stunning views to the attractive beach and warm waters. The 333 pitches are sandy and shaded and average 100 sq.m. in size. There are some with views, although most are tucked in under the pine trees.

Facilities

Four good toilet blocks have mainly Turkish style toilets plus facilities for disabled campers. Washing machines. Motorcaravan service point. Big supermarket. Excellent restaurant. Snack bar. Good pool complex with paddling pool. Aerobics. Fitness centre. Play areas. Bicycle hire. Mini-club. Animation. Excursion service. Beach 100 m. down steepish slope. Excellent diving. Off site: Fishing. Riding 1 km. Sailing.

At a glance

Welcome & Ambience	✓✓✓✓	Location	✓✓✓✓✓
Quality of Pitches	✓✓✓✓	Range of Facilities	✓✓✓✓✓

Directions

Take SS291 Sassari - Alghero road east, then SS55 to Capo Caccia. Turn to Porticciolo town where site is well signed.

Charges 2003

Per person	€ 7.00 - € 12.50
junior or senior (under 12 and over 60 yrs)	€ 6.00 - € 10.00
pitch	€ 2.00 - € 5.00
dog	€ 3.00 - € 5.00

Reservations

Made with 30% deposit by bank draft.
Tel: 079 919007. Email: info@torredelporticciolo.it

Open

1 June - 10 October.

Ferries to the islands of Elba, Sardinia and Sicily

Elba

Italy's third largest island.

Main departure port: PIOMBINO, Tuscany (approx 90 km. south of Pisa).

It is also possible to use the larger port of LIVORNO (about 15 km. from Pisa).

Three companies offer services:
Toremar, Moby, and Etruria Shipping ferries.

Destination port:	Portoferraio, Elba
Departures:	every 30 minutes in summer, winter every hour.*
Crossing time:	one hour.
To book:	phone or visit office at port where there are ticket outlets for all ferries.

* Ferries run every day of the year, the first around 6am and the last around 9pm.

Ferry Companies:
Toremar Nuova Stazione Marittima   Tel. 0565 31 100
Moby Nuova Stazione Marittima   Tel. 0565 225 211
Etruria Shipping, Porto Medicco   Tel. 0565 263 319

Sardinia

It is essential to book ahead in the summer months and this can be done from travel agents in other parts of Italy or at the port.

Ferry Companies operating from Livorno:
Lloyd Sardegna/Linea dei Golfi   Tel. 0565 222 300 to Olbia and Caglira
Moby Lines   Tel. 0586 826 823 to Olbia
Sardinia Ferries   Tel. 019 215 511 to Golfo Aranci

Ferry Companies also operate from Civitavécchia (north of Rome), Genoa and Naples The tourist office sells tickets but you can book ahead from many travel agents both in the town or in other parts of Italy.

The Tirrenia Line operates from both Genoa and Civitavécchia to Arbatax, Cagliari and Olbia.

Sicily

Getting to Sicily by road involves crossing the Straits of Messina. Ferries leave Villa San Giovanni every 20 minutes in the summer and take 40 minutes to get to Messina.

There are other longer crossings from Naples, Livorno and Cágliari.

Driving in Europe

If you are planning to take your caravan, tent, trailer tent or motorcaravan to the continent you will need to be familiar with the rules, regulations and customs that pertain to driving abroad.

A recent survey looked at why many Britons would not entertain a holiday abroad and why many foreigners would not contemplate coming here. According to the findings, the biggest single put-off was driving on the 'wrong' side of the road. However, statistics clearly show that you are less at risk of being involved in accidents – and that includes minor shunts – when driving in another country. The theory is that motorists of that country recognise that the nationality plate on your vehicle means that you might be slightly hesitant and give you that extra few inches which makes the difference between a minor ding and a trouble free journey. Of course it could also be that when driving in another country we take things a bit easier, so we are less at risk of being involved in an accident.

With European harmonisation eliminating most of the differences between driving in your home country and another, there has never been a better time to consider driving abroad. Where there are differences, they are in the detail.

For example all European countries require you to carry your driving documents whenever you are behind the wheel; there's no three day's grace to get to your local police station. Amongst the documents you are required to carry is your vehicle registration document, the V5 (what used to be called the log book). If yours is a hire or company vehicle you may have difficulties getting your hands on the V5. However the police will accept a photocopy of the V5 provided it is accompanied by a brief letter – signed by the vehicle owner – saying you have their permission to take the vehicle abroad.

European harmonisation also means that most common road signs are the same in all countries. Where mainland Europe differs from the UK is in the use of direction signs. If you are following signs through a town and arrive at a junction without signage – don't panic. The logic is that if all major routes are straight on, you don't need another sign to tell you the obvious.

As to language difficulties, you will find that most continental road signs are similar in style to those in the UK, although what is written on them will be in the language of the country concerned (for example Barcelona is spelt Barcelone in French), so it's worthwhile mugging up some of the more important and/or more usual ones. See articles on individual countries – the main signs have been translated for you.

When it comes to traffic regulations around school entrances, the Europeans are also ahead of us. In mainland Europe the law, or common practice, is that you should not pass a parked school bus unless it is absolutely safe to do so. If you can pass, you must keep your speed to a walking pace. It is the same when you drive past a school when the children are outside. The law, or best practice, says you should reduce your speed to a crawl.

We would never dream of suggesting that you would ever break the speed limit, but if you are tempted it is worth remembering that European police seem to have as many speed cameras as British police. The difference between speeding in the UK and mainland Europe is in the way fines can be levied. If you are caught in a manned speed trap you may be expected to pay an on-the-spot fine, so it's no good arguing that you haven't got enough money to pay the fine. Most manned speed traps will take cash, traveller's cheques, debit and credit cards.

Checklist

Before you set off for a holiday abroad it's worth making yourself a checklist of things to do, and what to pack – we've been travelling abroad several times a year for more than thirty years and we still don't rely on our memory for this, so it's best to consult a checklist; here's the one we use:

- ☐ Passports
- ☐ Tickets
- ☐ Motor Insurance Certificate, including Green Card or Continental Cover clause
- ☐ V5 Registration Document and/or (if not your own vehicle) the owners authority
- ☐ Breakdown Insurance Certificate
- ☐ Driving Licence (The new PHOTO style licence is now MANDATORY in most European countries)
- ☐ Form E1-11 (to extend NHS Insurance to European destinations)
- ☐ Foreign Currency (Euros and Swiss Francs, if appropriate) and/or Travellers Cheques
- ☐ Credit Card(s)
- ☐ Campsite Guide(s) and Tourist Guide(s)
- ☐ Maps/Road Atlas
- ☐ GB Stickers on car and caravan/trailer
- ☐ Beam deflectors to ensure that your headlights dip towards the right hand side
- ☐ Red Warning Triangle
- ☐ Spare vehicle/caravan driving light bulbs
- ☐ Torch
- ☐ First-Aid Kit, including mosquito repellent
- ☐ Fire extinguisher
- ☐ Basic tool kit (e.g screwdriver, pliers, etc)
- ☐ Continental mains connector/adaptor, and a long cable – for continental sites
- ☐ Polarity tester
- ☐ Spare fuses for car and caravan
- ☐ Spare fan/alternator belt

Finally bear in mind it's well worth having your car and caravan serviced before you go, and do check that your outfit is properly 'trimmed' before you set off.

Be sensible at all times and do not leave valuables in your vehicle or leave anything visible which could tempt a petty thief. Take care if waved down by anyone; in the past tactics like this have been used to get you to leave your car so an accomplice can have a field day rummaging through your belongings.

Driving in France, Germany & Switzerland

France

The most likely thing to catch out the unwary first time motorist in France is their *Prioite a Droite* rule whereby you are required to give way to traffic entering from the right, even when they are joining a main road from a minor one. In recent years this rule has been abandoned on the approach to most main roads where there are now *Passage Protégé* signs (a yellow diamond, indicating you have priority) or by a sign saying *Vous n'avez pas Priorite* (ie. it's NOT your right of way).

French drivers have a reputation for driving fast, but recently the laws have been tightened up, the fines for speeding increased, and generally they probably don't drive any faster than we do in Britain, although the maximum speed limit on Autoroutes (motorways) in dry weather is 130 kph which is about 83 mph (110 kph in the wet, about 68 mph). Unlike Britain there are no lower limits for towing caravans.

Within towns, there are no speed limit signs as such, but usually the 'town sign' as you enter a town or village has a red reflective border around it and these signs serve as a 50 kph (30 mph) speed limit sign. It is actually a clever idea as it saves cluttering up the environment with loads of separate speed limit signs – the end of the speed-limited area is indicated by a similar sign on leaving the town or village, but this time the sign has a diagonal black line across it.

With regards to drinking and driving – don't! The limit is actually LOWER in France than it is in the UK (50 mg of alcohol per 100 ml of blood, as opposed to 80 mg in the UK).

The most important essential equipment which must be carried at all times is a warning triangle and a spare set of light bulbs. The minimum driving age in France is 18 years, and children under ten years of age must occupy a rearward facing child seat, with a belt. Driver and passengers are all required to wear seat belts, and motor-cyclists are required to wear crash hats, and to ride with their headlights on at all times.

The following are particularly common road signs:

Allumez vos phares	switch on headlights
Peage	Toll booth ahead
Ralentissez	slow down
Rappel	continue to hold your speed down
Attention travaux	road works ahead
Deviation	diversion
Cedez le Passage	Give Way
Toutes Directions	means 'all directions' so keep following this route
Autres Directions	means all directions EXCEPT for places individually signed
Sens Interdit	no entry
Risque de Verglas	risk of black ice
Serrez a droite/gauche	keep to the right/left
Sortie	exit (from Autoroute)

Germany

At one time Germany didn't have any speed limits on their motorways (Autobahns) but that is no longer the case, except on some sections of their extensive network. In general there is a limit of 130 kph (83 mph) on Autobahns, and a lower limit of 80 kph for towing. The limits on other main roads are 100 kph and 80 kph respectively. Don't run out of fuel on an Autobahn – it is an offence carrying a hefty on the spot fine. Generally speaking, German drivers are skilful and law-abiding.

Essential equipment includes a warning triangle, spare bulbs, and seat belts all round; children under 12 are not allowed in the front seats unless wearing a special child restraint, and motorcyclists must wear crash hats and keep their headlights on at all times.

The following road signs are among the more important:

Achtung	Attention
Gefahr	Danger
Vorfahrt	Right of way
Licht einschalten	Turn on headlights
Bei Nasse	In wet weather
Ausfahrt	Exit (from Autobahn)

Switzerland

Switzerland's mountain roads provide an opportunity to see some of the most spectacular scenery in Europe, but care is needed, especially in winter. The country has an excellent motorway network, but unlike most European countries the motorway toll system requires you to buy a special motorway pass (a *vignette*) valid for a whole year, which makes using the motorways for a short time when merely passing through the country a fairly expensive proposition. You can buy a vignette at border crossings, and at some service areas or toll booths. Do not be tempted to risk driving without one, the fines are large and payable on the spot.

You must carry a warning triangle and have seat belts fitted all round; motorcyclists are required to wear crash hats and keep their headlights on all the time.

The maximum speed limits are 120 kph (75 mph) on motorways, and between 80 kph and 100 kph on other main roads. There is a lower limit (80 kph) if you're towing, and an even lower limit of 60 kph if your towed caravan or trailer exceeds 1000 kgs.

Road signs in Switzerland may be in French, German or even Italian!

Driving in Italy

Driving in Italy is really little different from driving in France, or elsewhere in Europe, but the Italian driver does seem to have a somewhat different temperament. For some strange reason young Italian drivers in small cars seem to love nothing better than to stay behind you on those stretches of roads where it is quite safe to overtake, and to wait until you've reached a really twisty stretch before trying to pass! Even better and more exciting if there are hairpin bends and sheer drops at the side of the road!

Apart from that, and a tendency in Rome to treat all traffic lights as if they are the start of a Formula 1 Grand Prix, Italian drivers are generally pretty skilful, but do beware of moped riders in cities such as Rome and Naples, some of whom are accomplished bag-snatchers and will take belongings from your car while you are stopped at those traffic lights listening to the other car drivers gunning their engines in preparation for a tyre-burning take off when the lights go green (the traffic lights go straight from red to green in most European countries, without going through orange first).

The overall speed limits are the same as those in France, but there are LOWER LIMITS for towing – 70 kph on main roads, and 80 kph on motorways (Autostradas).

The only mandatory essential equipment which must be carried is a warning triangle, seat belts are compulsory, and children must be at least 12 years of age to occupy a front seat, unless using a proper child seat and belt. Motorcyclists must wear crash hats, and the drink-drive limit is 80 mg (the same as in the UK).

The following are a few of the more common, and important, Italian road signs:

Destra	Right
Sinistra	Left
Incrocio	Crossroads
Rallentare	Slow Down!
Senso Vietato	No Entry
Svolta	Sharp bend or turning
Uscita	Exit (from Autostrada)

Driving routes to Italy

There are quite a few different routes one could use to drive from the Channel Ports to Italy and to a large extent the choice of which one will be determined by your final Italian destination. For example, the quickest route to Venice would be substantially different to the quickest route to Florence or Rome. The following outlines a couple of suggestions, but there are many alternatives depending on your own preferences in terms of time available and places you would like to visit en-route, etc.

If you are intending to travel via the south of France and the Côte d'Azur, the route can involve driving round Paris on the crowded inner ring road (the *Peripherique*) or via the slightly less crowded outer ring road (the *Francilienne*). The alternative to these busy routes around Paris is to use the A26 and head for Reims, avoiding Paris completely.

We suggest the following campsites for overnight stops (full details can be found in the Alan Rogers guides to France and Europe or on www. alanrogers.com):

A1 (south)

FR80030 Camping du Port de Plaisance

Route de Paris, 80200 Péronne (Somme)

Run by a non-profit making association under the auspices of the Chamber of Commerce, this is a good quality site. Formerly a municipal site, it is informally laid out beside the Canal du Nord on the outskirts of the small town of Peronne, on the river Somme. Only some two or three hours drive from the Channel ports and Tunnel, Peronne is convenient for overnight stops. The site itself is attractive, being surrounded by trees, with 90 marked pitches (87 have electricity) of varying shapes and sizes on mainly level grass, some being seasonal. A heated swimming pool is open when the weather is suitable.

Directions

From north and the ferries, on the A1 autoroute, take exit 14 and follow N17 south to Peronne; head towards town centre. Pass over river and Canal du Nord; site is on right just past garage at Porte du Plaisance (2 km. from town centre). From south use exit 13 and follow RN29 to Villers Carbonnel to pick up the N17 going north; signs on left.

Reservations

May be necessary in main season; contact site. Tel: 03 22 84 19 31.

Open

17 May - 8 September.

A26 (south)

FR02000 Camping Caravaning du Vivier aux Carpes

10 Rue Charles Voyeux, 02790 Seraucourt-le-Grand (Aisne)

Vivier aux Carpes is a small quiet site, close to the A26, two hours from Calais, so it is ideal for an overnight stop but is also worthy of a longer stay. The 60 well spaced pitches, are at least 100 sq.m. on flat grass with dividing hedges. The 45 for touring units all have electricity, some also with water points, and there are special pitches for motorcaravans. This peaceful site has a comfortable feel and is close to the village centre. The enthusiastic owners and the manager speak excellent English and are keen to welcome British visitors. Although there is no restaurant on site, good and reasonable hotels are close.

Directions

Leave A26 (Calais - Reims) road at exit 11 and take D1 left towards Soissons for 4 km. Take D8 and on entering Essigny-la-Grand (4 km.) turn sharp right on D72 signed Seraucourt-le-Grand (5 km). Site is clearly signed - it is in the centre of the village.

Reservations

Advised for peak season. Tel: 03 23 60 50 10. Email: camping.du.vivier@wanadoo.fr

Open

1 March - 30 October.

Driving Routes to Italy

From Reims continue on the A26 southbound to Troyes to join the A5 to Langres.

Our suggested campsite:

A5 (south)

FR52030 Camping Lac de la Liez

Peigney, 52200 Langres (Haute-Marne)

Managed by the enthusiastic Baude family, this newly renovated lakeside site is near the city of Langres, which has been elected one of the 50 most historic cities in France. Situated only ten minutes from the A5, Camping Lac de la Liez provides an ideal spot for an overnight stop en-route to the south of France. There is also a lot on offer for a longer stay, including the lake and an impressive indoor pool complex, with a sauna. The site provides 135 fully serviced, terraced pitches with panoramic views of the 500 acre lake. There is easy access to the lake for swimming with a sandy beach and a harbour where boats and pedaloes may be hired.

Directions
From Langres take the N19 towards Vesoul. After approximately 3 km. turn right, straight after the large river bridge, then follow site signs.
Reservations
Contact site. Tel: 03 25 90 27 79. Email: campingliez@free.fr
Open
17 May - 8 September.

At Langres join the A31 which by-passes Dijon to join up with the A7 near Beaune (the *Autoroute du Soleil*, the busiest autoroute in France during the summer) where you continue south past Lyon to Orange.

Our suggested overnight campsites:

A6 (south towards Mediterranean)

FR21020M	Municipal Les Cents Vignes (at Beaune)
FR21300M	Municipal Savigny-les-Beaune
FR71070	Castel Château de l'Eperviere (at Gigny-sur-Saone)

or:

FR21060 Camping Les Bouleaux

21200 Vignolles (Côte d'Or)

Camping Les Bouleaux is an excellent little campsite located at Vignolles, northeast of Beaune. There are just 40 pitches, all with an electrical connection (long leads may be required on some pitches). The large flat pitches are attractively laid out and most are separated by hedges and trees giving some shade. Monsieur Rossignal takes great pride in his campsite, keeping the grounds and facilities exceptionally clean and tidy. Les Bouleaux makes a perfect overnight stop, especially as it's open throughout the year (including Christmas Day). The nearest shops and restaurants are three kilometres from the site – there are none on-site.

Directions
Leave A6 autoroute at junction 24.1 south of Beaune. Turn right at roundabout, straight on at traffic lights, then turn right at next roundabout. Cross the autoroute, turn left at sign for Vignolle and the follow campsite signs.
Reservations
Not usually required, but phone during July and August to confirm availability. Tel: 03 80 22 26 88.
Open
All year.

A7 (south towards Mediterreanean)
FR26110 Les 4 Saison Camping de Grane (at Grane)
FR26120 Gervanne Camping (at Mirabel et Blacons)
or:

FR26020 Castel Camping du Château de Senaud

26140 Albon (Drôme)

Château du Sénaud, near the N7 south of Vienne, makes a useful stopover on the way south, but one could enjoy a longer stay to explore the surrounding villages and mountains. It is one of the original sites in the Castel chain and is still run with character and hands-on attention by Mme. Comtesse d'Armagnac. There are a fair number of permanent caravans used at weekends, but it also has some 85 pitches in tourist areas. Some have shade, some have views across the Rhône valley, and electricity and water connections are available on all pitches. There may be some noise from the autoroute.

Directions
Leave autoroute at Chanas exit, proceed south on N7 for 8 km. then east on D301 from Le Creux de la Thine to site. From south, exit autoroute for Tain-Tournon and proceed north, approaching the site on D122 through St Vallier then D132 towards Anneyron to site.

Reservations
Made with deposit for min. 3 nights. Tel: 04 75 03 11 31. Email: camping.de.senaud@libertysurf.fr

Open
15 March - 31 October.

From Orange pick up the A8 eastbound at Aix-en-Provence.

Our suggested overnight site:

A8 (eastward)

FR83160 Parc Camping Les Cigales

721, chemin du Jas de la Paro, 83490 Le Muy (Var)

Parc Les Cigales has been developed over the last 30 years by the same family to become a pleasant site. It has now undergone major rejuvenation. The entrance is wide and smart with a new reception, shop and all facilities. A riding school, a vegetable garden and a small animal farm complete this unusual but environmentally thought out development. The pitches are of a good size, terraced where necessary and nestling amongst the trees. There are 163 pitches in total with 35 mobile homes to rent, nicely landscaped. There is an attractive pool complex including a children's pool with sloping beach effect. Convenient for the autoroute, this is a spacious family site away.

Directions
Site is signed off approach to autoroute péage on A8 at Le Muy exit and is 2 km. west of Le Muy on N7. It is necessary to cross the dual-carriageway as you approach the toll booth from Le Muy. Site entrance is well signed.

Reservations
Advised for July/Aug. Tel: 04 94 45 12 08. Email: contact@les-cigales.com

Open
28 March - 1 November.

Continue on the A8 past Frejus where the autoroute starts to follow the coast very closely, providing some spectacular views of the Cote d'Azur, Cannes, Nice and Monte Carlo, interspersed by numerous tunnels. The tunnels are mainly all well lit, but do be careful (especially if you're wearing 'reactalight' sunglasses) as entering even a well-lit tunnel from bright sunlight can leave you in what seems like the dark by comparison.

The A8 continues past Menton to the Italian border near San Remo, where it becomes the (Italian) A10 through to Genoa. At Genoa you have the option of continuing eastward on the A12 past La Spezia to the once hugely popular and rather elegant resort of Viareggio, or you might want to turn northward at Genoa on to the A7 for Milan, and perhaps on to Venice on the A4. If you continue to head east at Genoa along the A12 to Viareggio you then have a choice of continuing south east to Pisa, Livorno, Grosseto and Rome via the coast, or of turning due east on to the A11 for Florence and then on to Rome via the inland A1 Autoroute.

Another of the more popular routes to Venice is via eastern France and Switzerland, starting from Calais where you join the A26 Autoroute feeder road immediately on leaving the port, and head down the A26 for Reims. Once you have gone through the *péage* (toll booth) on the outskirts of Reims and paid your toll for the A26 section you've just driven down do be careful – the road surfaces on those parts of the Autoroute where you pay are excellent, but the surfaces on the 'free' parts around cities are often pretty rough, and Reims is certainly no exception.

Our suggested overnight campsites:

A26 (south)

FR02060M Camping Municipal Guignicourt

14 Bis Rue Godins, 02190 Guignicourt (Aisne)

This very pleasant little municipal site has 100 pitches, 50 for long stay units and 50 for tourists. These two sections are separated by the main facilities on a higher terrace. Pitches are generally large and level, although you might need an extra long electric lead for some, but there are few dividing hedges. Pitches along the river bank have most shade, with a few specimen trees providing a little shade to some of the more open pitches. There is a bar, children's playground, tennis and boules courts, and even fishing on site. The town is quite attractive, with all services including a supermarket and bank, and is worthy of an evening stroll.

Directions

Guignicourt is about 20 km. north of Reims, just east of the A26, junction 14. The site is well signed from D925 in the village.

Reservations

Contact site for details. Tel: 03 23 79 74 58. Email: mitche02@aol.com

Open

1 April - 30 September.

---

or:

FR02000   Camping-Caravaning du Vivier aux Carpes (at Seraucourt-le-Grand)

On the Reims by-pass you should join the A4 (The Autoroute de l'Est) heading towards Metz. En-route to Metz you pass close to Verdun, scene of one of the bloodiest battles of the First World War, a shrine etched deeply into the French psyche even today, more than 80 years later.

Our suggested overnight campsite:

A4 (east)

FR57050M   Camping Metz Plage (at Metz)

There is another free section of autoroute around Metz, before you re-join the A4 proper heading for Strasbourg. At Strasbourg turn south onto the A35, via Colmar until reaching the autoroute interchange north of Mulhouse where you turn east onto the A36 into Germany before heading south on the A5 to Basel in Switzerland. At the Swiss border take the lane indicated by the overhead gantry – left hand if you already have a Swiss Motorway pass (*vignette*) or the right hand lane if you don't have such a pass. You can buy one here; the fines for travelling on Swiss motorways without one are by no means cheap.

Suggested overnight campsites:

N83/A35 (east/south to German border/ Switzerland)

FR68040   Les Trois Chateaux (at Eguisheim)

FR69080   Camping Clair Vacances (at Ste. Croix-en-Plaine

or:

FR68060M Camping Intercommunal Riquewihr

Route des Vins, 68340 Riquewihr (Haut-Rhin)

Surrounded by vineyards and minutes from the delightful village of Riquewihr, this is a well run site which has earned its good reputation. Situated in the heart of the Alsace wine region the site covers three hectares with views across the open countryside. Immediately to the right of the security barrier stands a modern, part-timbered building housing reception and information area. Close by is a small summer house and both are heavily garlanded with flowers. The 161 spacious individual grass pitches, many with shade and divided by hedging, have electrical connections. Wine caves are just 200 m. walk from reception and you might just see a stork or two on site.

Directions

From N83 north of Colmar take D4 westwards to Bennwihr. Turn north on D18 for 2 km. towards Ribeauvillé. Site is signed off roundabout at southern end of Riquewihr bypass. Do not enter village.

Reservations

Not accepted. Tel: 03 89 47 90 08. Email: camping.riquewihr@tiscah.fr

Open

Easter - 31 October.

Driving Routes to Italy

Continue along the autoroute past Basle where you pick up the A2 to Luzern. The autoroute takes you under the town via tunnels, and follow signs for Gotthard. The autoroute now skirts the lake before entering the Seelesberg Tunnel. Continue south through the 17 km long St Gotthard Tunnel to enter Italy at Como. Continue on the A2 southbound heading towards Milan, where several motorways merge, and where you need to keep in the left lane to join the A4 eastbound for Venice.

Our suggested campsite

Switzerland

CH9120 Camping Lido Luzern

Lidostr. 8, CH-6006 Luzern

Luzern is a traditional holiday resort, which attracts many British visitors. It lies near the shores of Lake Luzern, just outside the town itself. Next to the site (but not associated with it so you have to pay for entrance) is the Lido proper, which has a large sandy beach and sports field, and you can also swim in the lake. Camping Lido Luzern is divided into separate sections for caravans, motorcaravans and tents; the first two have hardstandings which, in effect, provide formal and small individual pitches with shade in parts. There are about 100 electrical connections (10A). Quiet in early season, from late June to late August, it usually becomes full and can at times seem rather crowded, especially in the tent section. Good English is spoken.

Directions

Follow camping signs out of Luzern; there is a large sign to Lido on the right just outside the town, past the casino.

Reservations

Advised for mid-June - mid-Sept. Write to site.

Open

15 March - 31 October.

Although these routes to Italy are probably the quickest, especially if you are towing, they are not the most scenic or interesting, and by virtue of using autoroutes with toll they are not the cheapest either (although bear in mind they can save you the cost of night stops).

The roughly triangular area of France and Italy bounded by Lyon, Turin and Nice could well be described as 'Monte Carlo Rally territory' and in both the Ardeche and the Alps there are literally hundreds of small roads affording spectacular views, but in many cases they are unguarded with sheer drops of several thousand feet. We would only contemplate driving many of these roads in a well set-up car without anything substantial in tow and with the car shod with studded snow tyres during the winter or early spring. That said, there are several towns and villages which are accessible for most of the year via fairly main (ie. wide) roads which are generally kept reasonably clear of snow and ice.

The following are a few suggestions of places where you might be tempted to venture en-route to Italy during the spring, summer or autumn, depending of course on the prevailing weather.

In the Ardeche, starting at Montelimar, the roads to the west around Aubenas, La Souche, the Col de la Croix de Bauzon, and the Col de Meyrand, Val-les-Bains, Burzet, Mezilhac, Antraigues and Le Moulinon.

In the Vercours, an area southwest of Grenoble which seems to attract large numbers of foreign visitors but few British for some reason, there are places such as St Barthelemy, St Andeol, Gresse-en-Vercours, the Col des Deux and the Col de l'Allimas.

In the Chartreuse the D192 through Bellecombette thence over the Col de Granier, the Col de Cucheron and the Col de Porte to Le Sappey-en-Chartreuse takes you though some of the most glorious countryside in France.

Driving Routes to Italy

In the Maritime Alps the most famous places are Gap, Digne-les-Bains, Sisteron, Sospel (from where in good weather you can drive the most famous Monte Stage of all, over the Col de Turini – stopping at the café at the top for a well-earned drink). If you can make your way back to coast to arrive in Monte Carlo via the small roads through the villages of L'Escarine and La Turbie, you will get some great views on the descent into Monaco that you certainly won't get via the Autoroute.

Obviously detours or excursions such as we have described are not recommended when towing a caravan or in the winter and they will occupy quite a bit of time. However if you are looking for a scenic route through the Alps which just happens to take in some of the Monte territory but without having to resort to anything other than an N road (Route National, roughly equivalent to a British A road) then you could do worse than consider the Route Napoleon.

This route involves your turning off the Autoroute A6 at Lyon, and making for Grenoble, either via the N6 and N85 via Bourgoin-Jallieu or via the A43 and A48 Autoroutes.

From Grenoble take the N75 just as far as Pont de Claix, where you turn onto the N85 (the Route Napoleon) and simply follow this all the way through La Mure, Gap, Sisteron, Digne-les-Bains, Castellane and Grasse, famous for its perfumes, to join the A8 Autoroute above Cannes. A spectacular route, on a good fairly wide main road, but with some pretty steep climbs and numerous hairpin bends.

Suggested campsites for overnight stops:

N85 (Route Napoleon)

FR04010 Sunêlia Hippocampe

or:

FR04100 Camping International

Route Napoleon, 04120 Castellane (Alpes-de Haute-Provence)

Camping International has very friendly, English speaking owners and is a reasonably priced, less commercialised site situated in some of the most dramatic scenery in France. The 250 pitches, 130 good sized ones for touring, are clearly marked, separated by trees and small hedges, and all have electricity and water. The bar/restaurant overlooks the swimming pool with its sunbathing area set in a sunny location, and all have fantastic views. In high season English speaking young people entertain children (3-8 years) and teenagers. There are twice weekly guided walks into the surrounding hills in the near-by Gorges du Verdon – a very popular excursion. Access is good for larger units.

Directions

Site is 1 km. north of Castellane on the N85 'Route Napoleon'.

Reservations

Necessary for July/Aug. and made with deposit (€ 45), no booking fee. Tel: 04 92 83 66 67. Email: info@campinginternational.fr

Open

1 April - 30 September.

Driving Routes to Italy

The table below gives brief details of some of the better known of the passes through the Alps which you might want to use en-route to Italy. It is by no means a complete list as there are literally dozens of passes in the Alps, and these are just a few:

Area	Name	From-to Road number	Height (metres) Gradient %	Comments
France/ Switzerland	Faucille	Morez/Geneva N5	1323 (10%)	Usually open
France/Italy	Mt.Cenis	Chambery/Turin N6	2083 (12.5%)	Closed Nov-May
France	Croix-Haute	Grenoble/Sisteron N75	1180 (7%)	Usually open
France	Bayard	Grenoble/ Gap N85	1248 (14%)	Usually open
France/Italy	Petit St.Bernard	Bourg St.Maurice/Aosta N90/SS26	2188 (8,5%)	Closed mid Oct-Mar
France/Italy	Montgenevre	Briancon/Vizille N91	1850 (9%)	Often closed Dec-Mar
France/Italy	Col de Tende	Borgo S.Dalmazzo/La Giandola N204	1321 (9%)	No caravans in winter
Italy	Great St. Bernard	Aosta/Martigny SS27/A21	2473 (11%)	Closed Oct-Jun Caravans restricted
Italy	Stelvio	Bormio/Spondigna SS38	2757 (12.5%)	Closed Oct-Jun Unsuitable caravans
Switzerland	St.Gotthard	Andermatt/Belinzona N2	2108 (10%)	Closed Oct-Jun
Switzerland/ Italy	Simplon	Domodossola/Brig N9	2005 (11%)	Often closed Nov-Apr
Austria/Italy	Brenner	Innsbruck/Bolzano B182/SS12	1374 (14%)	Usually open Easy but v.busy

Pets Abroad

The Pet Travel Scheme allowing pets (dogs and cats) travelling from certain European countries to enter the UK without having to go into quarantine was first introduced in 2000. It has proved very popular, to such an extent that the scheme has been extended in the past year or so to include more ferry routes. These include those direct to Spain, but given the longer crossing times on those routes and the fact that pets have to remain in your vehicle (or in kennels) on the car deck, where in both cases access is restricted, our advice would be to check with your own vet and with the ferry operator when booking regarding the need for access to your pets during these long crossings.

Essentially the Pet Travel Scheme requires that you obtain a 'Pet's Passport' which involves your pet having a microchip implant to enable it to be correctly identified and for it to be vaccinated against rabies, and blood-tested to ensure that this vaccination has 'taken'. There are various other requirements and documentation, particularly in respect of treatment against parasites and tapeworm necessary immediately prior to your return journey to the UK. We would advise anyone thinking about taking their dog or cat abroad to contact their local vet, and/or the PETS Helpline (tel. 0970 241 1710, email pets.helpline@defra.gsi.gov.uk) well in advance of their intended date of travel – bear in mind paticularly that the rabies/vaccination/blood testing procedure is quite a long-drawn-out process.

For further information visit their website: www.defra.gov.uk

Insurance

In theory European law means that a vehicle insured for use in the UK is still insured in any other European country. But some insurers know that doesn't really mean what you think it means. Somewhere in the fine print on page 37 of your policy you could find that if you take your vehicle abroad your insurance coverage is reduced to third party only. So two weeks before you venture abroad contact your vehicle insurer and find out if you need additional coverage.

Most vehicle breakdown insurance schemes claim to offer pan-European cover. But again it is worth asking just how good that cover is. If you car expires beside the road in a cloud of steam you don't want to have to try explaining the problem to a telephone receptionist who is fluent in every language – except yours.

The travel insurers Alan Rogers work with (see advert on page 188) operate language-specific call centres. If anything goes wrong you'll speak to somebody totally fluent in your language. What all insurers will insist on is that your vehicle must be in good condition before you set off on holiday. A full service a few weeks before your departure date will take care of that.

There is probably no subject which causes campers, caravanners and motor-caravanners venturing abroad more worries than insurance, so notwithstanding the notes above, if you're in any doubt about insurance it may be worthwhile you giving the subject some further thought, and the following will hopefully help to clarify things:

The problem with insurance is that there is often an 'overlap', so that sometimes one aspect is apparently covered on two insurance policies. To avoid confusion let's cut through the hype and take a clear look at the different types of insurance.

If you are planning on camping, caravanning or motorcaravanning abroad, this is what you will need.

Road traffic insurance

As previously stated, your ordinary car or motorcaravan road insurance will cover you anywhere in the EU. *However* many policies only provide minimum cover. So if you have an accident your insurance may only cover the cost of damage to the other person's property.

To maintain the same level of cover abroad as you enjoy at home you need to tell your vehicle insurer. Some will automatically cover you abroad with no extra cost and no extra paperwork. Some will say you need a Green Card (which is neither green or on card) but won't charge for it. Some will charge extra for the green card. Ideally you should contact your vehicle insurer 3-4 weeks before you set off, and confirm your conversation with them in writing.

A good insurance company will provide a European recognised accident report form. On this you mark details of damage to yours and the other party's property and draw a little diagram showing where the vehicles were in relation to each other. You give a copy of your form to the other motorist; he gives you a copy of his. It prevents all the shouting which often accompanies accidents in this country.

Holiday insurance

This is a multi-part insurance. One part covers your vehicles. If they breakdown or are involved in an accident they can be repaired or returned to this country. The best will even arrange to bring your vehicle home if the driver is unable to proceed.

Many new vehicles come with a free breakdown and recovery insurance which extends into Europe. Some professional motoring journalists have reported that the actual service this provides can be patchy and may not cover the recovery of a caravan or trailer. Our advice is to buy the motoring section of your holiday insurance.

The second section of holiday insurance covers people. It will include the cost of doctor, ambulance and hospital treatment if needed. If needed the better companies will even pay for English language speaking doctors and nurses and will bring a sick or injured holidaymaker home by air ambulance.

The third part of a good holiday insurance policy covers things. If someone breaks in to your motorhome and steals your passports and money, one phone call to the insurance company will have everything sorted out. If you manage to drive over your camera, it's covered.

An important part of the insurance that is often ignored is the cancellation section. Few things are as heartbreaking as having to cancel a holiday because a member of the family falls ill. Cancellation insurance can't take away the disappointment, but it makes sure you don't suffer financially as well.

There are a number of good insurance policies available including those provided for their members by the two major clubs and those offered by the leading camping holiday agents already mentioned in this guide.

Which ever insurance you choose we would advise not picking any of the policies sold by the High Street travel trade. Whilst they may be good, they don't cover the specific needs of campers, caravanners and motorcaravanners. And ideally you should arrange your holiday insurance at least four weeks before you set off.

Form E111

By arrangement between the British Government and rest of the European Community Governments, British holidaymakers can enjoy the same health care as that Government offers its own citizens. The form which shows you are entitled to take advantage of this arrangement is called E111.

E111 doesn't replace holiday insurance, but is in addition to. The form is available from all main UK Post Offices. Fill out one for every member of your family. Get it stamped by the counter staff and take it on holiday with you.

In theory one Form E111 lasts you for ever. But we've had reports that in some rural areas in Europe they may not understand that, so our advice is to get a new E111 every year. It is free.

And that is all you need to know about insurance. You know what they say about insurance, don't you? You'll only need it if you haven't got it.

www.insure④europe.com

Taking your own tent, caravan or motorhome abroad?

Looking for the best cover at the best rates?

Our prices considerably undercut most high street prices and the 'in-house insurance' of many tour operators whilst offering equivalent (or higher) levels of cover.

Our annual multi-trip policies offer superb value, covering you not only for your european camping holiday but also subsequent trips abroad for the next 12 months.

Total Peace of Mind

To give you total peace of mind during your holiday our insurance policies have been specifically tailored to cover most potential eventualities on a self-drive camping holiday. Each is organised through Voyager Insurance Services Ltd who specialize in travel insurance for Europe and for camping in particular. All policies are underwritten by UK Underwriting Ltd, on behalf of a consortium of insurance companies that are members of the Association of British Insurers and the Financial Ombudsman services.

24 Hour Assistance

Our personal insurance provides access to the services of Inter Group Assistant Services (IGAS), one of the UK's largest assistance companies. European vehicle assistance cover is provided by Green Flag who provide assistance to over 3 million people each year. With a Europe-wide network of over 7,500 garages and agents you know you're in very safe hands.

Both IGAS and Green Flag are very used to looking after the needs of campsite-based holidaymakers and are very familiar with the location of most European campsites, with contacts at garages, doctors and hospitals nearby.

Save with an Annual policy

If you are likely to make more than one trip to Europe over the next 12 months then our annual multi-trip policies could save you a fortune. Personal cover for a couple starts at just £95 and the whole family can be covered for just £115.
Cover for up to 17 days wintersports participation is included.

Low Cost Annual multi-trip insurance

Premier Annual Europe self-drive
including 17 days wintersports

£95.00 per couple

Premier Annual Europe self-drive
including 17 days wintersports

£115.00 per family

Low Cost Combined Personal and Vehicle Assistance Insurance

Premier Family Package
10 days cover for vehicle, 2 adults plus dependent children under 16.

£75.00*

Premier Couples Package
10 days cover for vehicle and 2 adults

£61.00*

* Motorhomes, cars towing trailers and caravans, all vehicles over 4 years old and holidays longer than 10 days attract supplements – ask us for details. See leaflet for full terms and conditions.

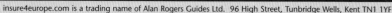

TRY AN ISSUE FOR 1p

No risk, no commitment

Practical Motorhome is an essential read packed with exclusive features and stories, competitions and a comprehensive buyers guide. It brings unrivalled practical advice and inspirational ideas for touring at home and abroad. We continue to preview and review the very latest motorhome models on the market and offer substantial buying advice for those looking to buy new and second hand. It is little surprise that we are the fastest-growing motorhome magazine in the market.So, try the first issue for 1p.

It beats paying £2.99 for an issue in the shops! And if for some reason you don't enjoy your issue, simply write to us within the first month and no further payment will be taken! But we are sure you'll love it - and you don't have to do anything - your subscription will automatically continue at the low rate of £8.00 every 3 issues - saving you 10% off the shop price!

PLUS
- **GET EVERY ISSUE DELIVERED TO YOUR DOOR**
- **NEVER MISS AN ISSUE**
- **PAY IN HANDY INSTALMENTS**

call our hotline number now

CALL 08456 777 812

PLEASE HAVE YOUR BANK DETAILS READY AND QUOTE ARFW3

Reports by Readers

We always welcome reports from readers concerning sites which they have visited. Generally reports provide us with invaluable feedback on sites already included in the guides or, in the case of those not yet featured, they provide information which we can follow up with a view to adding them in future editions. However, if you have a complaint about a site, this should be addressed to the campsite owner, preferably in person before you leave.

Please make your comments either on this form or on plain paper. It would be appreciated if you would indicate the approximate dates when you visited the site and, in the case of potential new ones, provide the correct name and address and, if possible, include a site brochure. Send your reports to:

Alan Rogers Guides, Manor Garden, Burton Bradstock, Bridport DT6 4QA

Name of Site and Ref. No. (or address for new recommendations):

....

....

Dates of visit: ....

Comments:

Reader's Name and Address: ....

....

....

....

Open all year

The following sites are understood to accept caravanners and campers all year round, although the list also includes some that are open for at least ten months. These sites are marked with a star (*) – please refer to the site's individual entry for details. It is always wise to contact them directly to check as the facilities available, for example, may be reduced.

Piedmont & Valle d'Aosta

IT6220   Mombarone

Lombardy

IT6250   Lac de Como

Trentino-Alto Adige

IT6200   Olympia
IT6201   Antholz
IT6202   Toblacher See
IT6212   Latsch an der Etsch *
IT6214   Lago-Molveno

Veneto

IT6053   Fusina

Liguria

IT6401   Dei Fiori
IT6403   Baciccia
IT6404   Dei Fiori
IT6414   Arenella *
IT6412   Valdeiva

Emilia-Romagna

IT6060   Estense
IT6602   Bologna *
IT6603   Ecochiocciola *
IT6623   San Marino

Tuscany

IT6605   Mugello Verde
IT6610   Panoramico
IT6614   Michelangelo
IT6665   Le Soline
IT6667   La Finoria

Lázio

IT6810   Seven Hills
IT6815   Holiday Village
IT6814   Flaminio

Abruzzo & Molise

IT6808   La Genziana

Campania

IT6830   Zeus

Puglia & Basilicata

IT6850   Sea World

Calabria

IT6875   Vascellero
IT6858   Il Salice
IT6890   Dolomiti sul Mare

Sicily

IT6880   Biscione
IT6920   Due Rocche

Sardinia

IT6969   La Cernie

Dogs

For the benefit of those who want to take their dogs with them or for people who do not like dogs at the sites they visit, we list here the sites that have indicated to us that they do not accept dogs. If you are, however, planning to take your dog we do advise you to contact them first to check – there my be limits on numbers, breeds, etc. or times of the year when they are excluded.

Never – these sites do not accept dogs at any time:

Lake Garda

IT6256	Del Garda
IT6263	Bella Italia
IT6265	Ideal Molino

Veneto

IT6003	Pra' Delle Torri
IT6021	Italy
IT6022	Portofelice
IT6010	Capalonga
IT6025	Residence
IT6015	Il Tridente
IT6020	Union Lido
IT6032	Cavallino
IT6035	Mediterraneo
IT6040	Garden Paradiso
IT6055	Isamar
IT6030	Dei Fiori

Friuli-Venezia Giulia

IT6000	Mare Pineta

Liguria

IT6401	Dei Fiori
IT6414	Arenella
IT6418	Framura

Emília-Romagna

IT6065	Tahiti
IT6624	Rubicone

Tuscany

IT6630	Montescudaio
IT6645	Delle Piscine
IT6671	Argentario

Marche

IT6618	Stella Maris

Lázio

IT6815	Holiday Village

Abruzzo & Molise

IT6800	Europe Garden
IT6801	Holiday

Campania

IT6820	Baia Domizia
IT6853	Athena
IT6820	Baia Domizia
IT6853	Athena

Puglia & Basilicata

IT6848	Punta Lunga

Sardinia

IT6963	Isuledda

Maybe – accepted at any time but with certain restrictions:

Trentino-Alto Adige

IT6210	Steiner	not July/Aug

Tuscany

IT6660	Maremma	not 16/6-31/8

Abruzzo & Molise

IT6800	Europe Garden	not in high season

Campania

IT6842	Sant' Antonio	not in August

Puglia & Basilicata

IT6845	San Nicola	not in high season

Fishing

We are pleased to include details of sites which provide facilities for fishing on the site. Where we have been given details, we have included this information in the individual site reports. It is always best to contact them directly to check that they provide for your individual requirements.

Piedmont & Valle d'Aosta

IT6220	Mombarone
IT6240	Valle Romantica
IT6245	Riviera
IT6246	Isolino
IT6249	Continental

Lombardy

IT6250	Lac de Como
IT6258	Rio Vantone
IT6259	Punta d'Oro

Trentino-Alto Adige

IT6200	Olympia
IT6202	Toblacher See
IT6214	Lago-Molveno
IT6232	Al Sole

Lake Garda

IT6264	San Benedetto
IT6266	Gasparina
IT6265	Ideal Molino
IT6277	Fontanelle

IT6270	La Gardiola
IT6285	Zocco
IT6275	Fornella

Veneto

IT6003	Pra' Delle Torri
IT6022	Portofelice
IT6010	Capalonga
IT6015	Il Tridente
IT6028	Vela Blu
IT6035	Mediterraneo
IT6050	Serenissima
IT6045	Marina Venezia

Friuli-Venézia Giúlia

IT6005	Europa
IT6007	Belvedere Pineta

Ligúria

IT6401	Dei Fiori

Emília-Romagna

IT6624	Rubicone

Tuscany

IT6640	Pappasole

Umbria

IT6652	Italgest
IT6653	Listro
IT6654	Badiaccia

Lázio

IT6813	Porticciolo
IT6815	Holiday Village

Puglia & Basilicata

IT6848	Punta Lunga

Calabria

IT6852	Marina Rossano

Sardinia

IT6955	La Tortuga

Boat Launching

We understand that the following sites have boat slipways on site. Where facilities are within easy reach and we have been given details, we have included this information in the individual reports. However, we recommend that you contact them directly to check that they meet your requirements.

Piedmont & Valle d'Aosta

IT6245	Riviera
IT6246	Isolino
IT6249	Continental

Lombardy

IT6250	Lac de Como
IT6259	Punta d'Oro
IT6258	Rio Vantone

Trentino-Alto Adige

IT6214	Lago-Molveno
IT6227	Al Pescatore

Lake Garda

IT6252	San Francesco
IT6254	Lido
IT6287	San Biagio

IT6264	San Benedetto
IT6266	Gasparina
IT6265	Ideal Molino
IT6277	Fontanelle
IT6275	Fornella
IT6285	Zocco

Veneto

IT6003	Pra' Delle Torri
IT6010	Capalonga
IT6028	Vela Blu
IT6032	Cavallino
IT6050	Serenissima
IT6045	Marina Venezia

Friuli-Venézia Giúlia

IT6005	Europa
IT6007	Belvedere Pineta

Emília-Romagna

IT6063N	Classe

Tuscany

IT6665	Le Soline

Lázio

IT6813	Porticciolo

Campania

IT6820	Baia Domizia

Sardinia

IT6955	La Tortuga

Bicycle Hire

We understand that the following sites have bicycles to hire on site or can arrange for bicycles to be delivered. However, we would recommend that you contact them directly to check as the situation can change.

Piedmont & Valle d'Aosta
IT6246 Isolino
IT6249 Continental

Lombardy
T6250 Lac de Como
IT6258 Rio Vantone
IT6261 Del Sole

Trentino-Alto Adige
IT6202 Toblacher See
IT6225 Due Laghi
IT6230 San Cristoforo
IT6232 Al Sole

Lake Garda
IT6235 Monte Brione
IT6252 San Francesco
IT6253 Piani di Clodia
IT6256 Del Garda
IT6265 Ideal Molino
IT6280 Week-End

Veneto
IT6003 Pra' Delle Torri
IT6021 Italy
IT6022 Portofelice
IT6025 Residence
IT6020 Union Lido

IT6028 Vela Blu
IT6035 Mediterraneo
IT6050 Serenissima
IT6040 Garden Paradiso
IT6055 Isamar
IT6045 Marina Venezia

Friuli-Venézia Giúlia
IT6007 Belvedere Pineta
IT6005 EuropaLiguria

Ligúria
IT6401 Dei Fiori
IT6403 Baciccia
IT6412 Valdeiva

Emília-Romagna
IT6060 Estense
IT6065 Tahiti
IT6603 Ecochiocciola
IT6623 San Marino

Tuscany
IT6600 Barco Reale
IT6608 Torre Pendente
IT6611 Il Poggetto
IT6632 Valle Gaia
IT6641 Blucamp
IT6635 Le Pianacce
IT6637 Il Gineprino

IT6640 Pappasole
IT6662 Le Marze
IT6665 Le Soline
IT6664 Colliverdi

Umbria
IT6652 Italgest
IT6653 Listro
IT6654 Badiaccia
IT6656 Il Collaccio
IT6655 Assisi

Lázio
IT6813 Porticciolo
IT6811 Ipini

Abruzzo & Molise
IT6805 Heliopolis

Campania
IT6820 Baia Domizia

Puglia & Basilicata
IT6848 Punta Lunga

Calabria
IT6852 Marina Rossano

Sardinia
IT6955 La Tortuga

Horse Riding

We understand that the following sites have horse riding stables on site. Where facilities are within easy reach and we have been given details, we have included this information in the individual site reports. However, we recommned that you contact them directly to check that they meet your requirements.

Lake Garda
IT6255 La Quercia

Veneto
IT6020 Union Lido
IT6055 Isamar

Tuscany
IT6612 Norcenni

Trentino-Alto Adige, Friuli-Venézia Giúlia, Veneto, Lombardy, Lake Garda

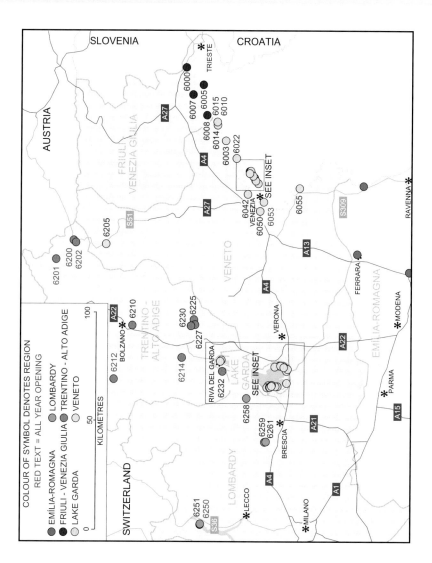

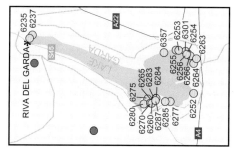

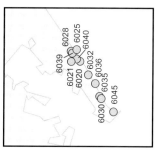

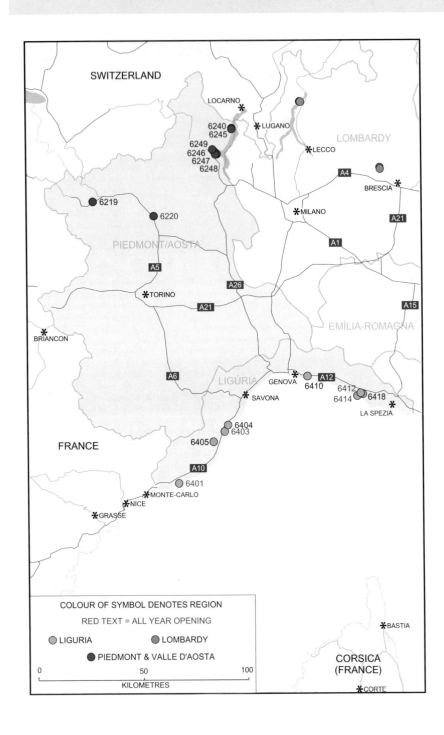

SWITZERLAND

LOCARNO

6240
6245

LUGANO

LOMBARDY

6249
6246
6247
6248

LECCO

A4

BRESCIA

6219

6220

MILANO

A21

PIEDMONT/AOSTA

A1

A5

A26

TORINO

A21

A15

BRIANCON

EMÍLIA-ROMAGNA

A6

LIGÚRIA

GENOVA

A12

6410

6412
6414

6418

SAVONA

LA SPEZIA

6404
6403

FRANCE

6405

A10

6401

MONTE-CARLO

NICE

GRASSE

COLOUR OF SYMBOL DENOTES REGION

RED TEXT = ALL YEAR OPENING

BASTIA

○ LIGURIA   ● LOMBARDY

● PIEDMONT & VALLE D'AOSTA

0   50   100

CORSICA
(FRANCE)

KILOMETRES

CORTE

Emilia-Romagna, Tuscany, Umbria, Marche

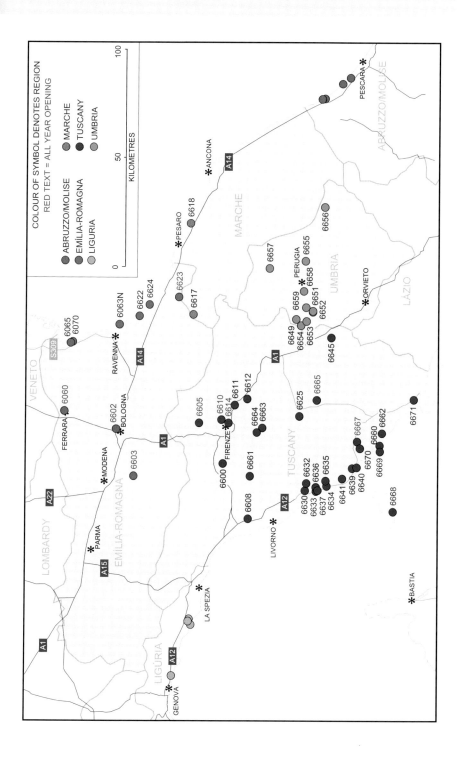

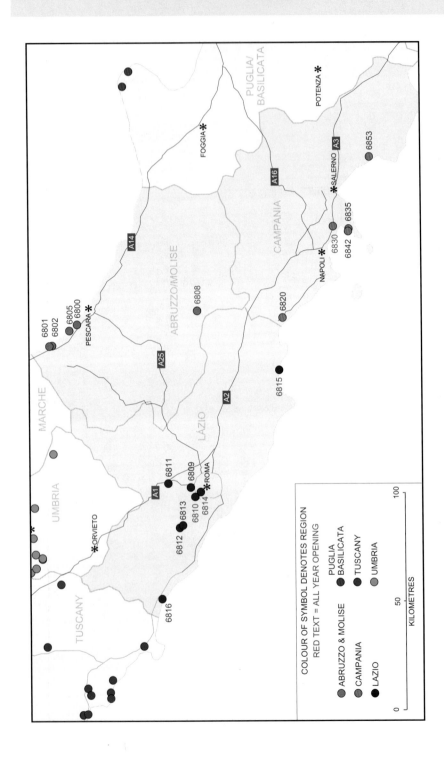

COLOUR OF SYMBOL DENOTES REGION
RED TEXT = ALL YEAR OPENING

ABRUZZO & MOLISE
CAMPANIA
LAZIO
PUGLIA/
BASILICATA
TUSCANY
UMBRIA

KILOMETRES

0   50   100

Calabria, Puglia & Basilicata

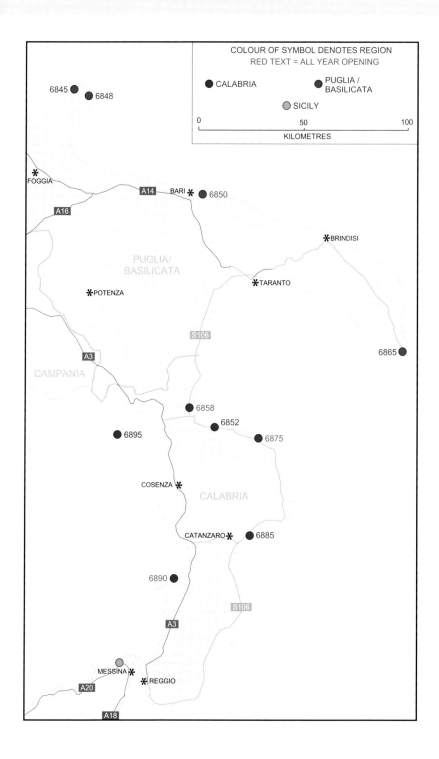

COLOUR OF SYMBOL DENOTES REGION
RED TEXT = ALL YEAR OPENING

● CALABRIA   ● PUGLIA /
              BASILICATA

○ SICILY

0   50   100
KILOMETRES

6845 ● ● 6848

✳FOGGIA

A14 BARI ✳ ● 6850

A16

✳BRINDISI

PUGLIA/
BASILICATA

✳TARANTO

✳POTENZA

S106

A3

6865 ●

CAMPANIA

● 6858
      ● 6852
● 6895 ● 6875

COSENZA ✳

CALABRIA

CATANZARO ✳ ● 6885

6890 ●

S106

A3

MESSINA ○ ✳
A20 ✳ REGGIO

A18

Sicily

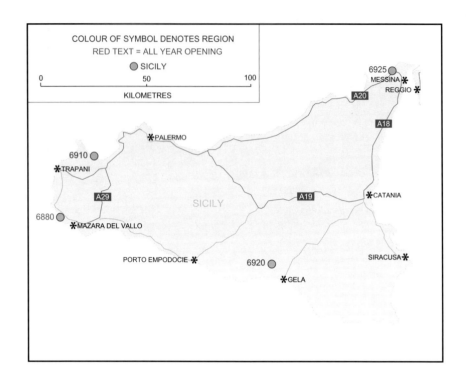

COLOUR OF SYMBOL DENOTES REGION
RED TEXT = ALL YEAR OPENING

⬤ SICILY

0   50   100

KILOMETRES

6925 ⬤
MESSINA ✳
A20
REGGIO ✳

A18

✳PALERMO

6910 ⬤
✳TRAPANI

A29

SICILY

A19

✳CATANIA

6880 ⬤
✳MAZARA DEL VALLO

PORTO EMPODOCIE ✳

6920 ⬤

SIRACUSA ✳

✳GELA

Sardinia

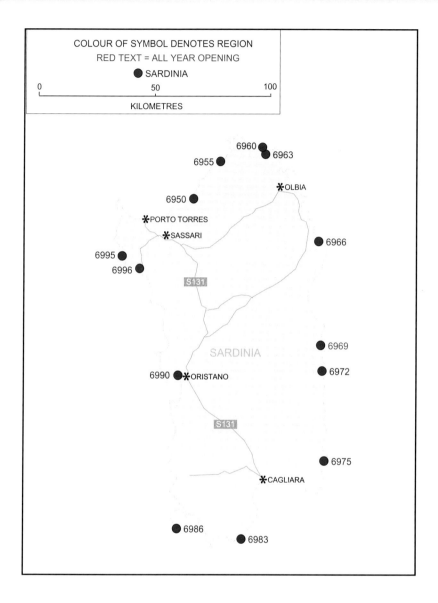

COLOUR OF SYMBOL DENOTES REGION
RED TEXT = ALL YEAR OPENING
● SARDINIA

0   50   100

KILOMETRES

6960 ●
6963
6955 ●

＊OLBIA

6950 ●

＊PORTO TORRES
＊SASSARI

6995 ●
6996 ●

S131

6966 ●

SARDINIA

6969 ●

6990 ●＊ORISTANO
6972 ●

S131

6975 ●

＊CAGLIARA

6986 ●
6983 ●

Town and Village Index

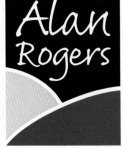

Campsite Index by Number

Campsite Index by Number

Campsite Index by Region

Campsite Index by Region